ACCA Certificate in Taxation
(RQF Level 4)

FTX (FA2025)

Foundations in Taxation

EXAM KIT

KAPLAN
PUBLISHING

British Library Cataloguing-in-Publication Data

A catalogue record for this book is available from the British Library.

Published by:

Kaplan Publishing UK

Unit 2 The Business Centre

Molly Millar's Lane

Wokingham

Berkshire

RG41 2QZ

ISBN: 978-1-83996-618-7

Printed and bound in Great Britain

Acknowledgements

The CBE specimen exam and past ACCA exam questions are the copyright of the Association of Chartered Certified Accountants. The original answers to the questions were produced by the examining team and have been updated by Kaplan Publishing.

We are grateful to HM Revenue and Customs for the provision of tax forms, which are Crown Copyright and are reproduced here with kind permission from the Office of Public Sector Information.

INTRODUCTION

This new edition of the ACCA Foundation Exam Kit is packed with exam-type questions, to help you to prepare for your exam successfully.

- Questions are grouped by syllabus topics and provide extensive coverage of all syllabus areas.
- All questions are of exam standard and format – this enables you to master the exam techniques.

Past exam questions have been incorporated into the main body of questions within the kit and are grouped by syllabus area.

Key features in this edition

In addition to providing a wide ranging bank of examination style questions, we have also included in this edition:

- Exam specific information and advice on exam technique.
- Our recommended approach to make your revision for this particular subject as effective as possible. This includes step by step guidance on how best to use our Kaplan material (study text, pocket notes and exam kit) at this stage in your studies.
- An increased number of enhanced tutorial answers packed with specific key answer tips, technical tutorial notes and examination technique tips from our experienced tutors.

You will find a wealth of other resources to help you with your studies on the following sites:

www.MyKaplan.co.uk

www.accaglobal.com/student

ANSWER ENHANCEMENTS

We have added the following enhancements to the answers in this exam kit:

Key answer tips

All long form answers include key answer tips to help your understanding of each question.

Tutorial note

All long form and many multiple choice answers include tutorial notes to explain some of the technical points in more detail.

CONTENTS

Quality and accuracy are of the utmost importance to us so if you spot an error in any of our products, please send an email to mykaplanreporting@kaplan.com with full details, or follow the link to the feedback form in MyKaplan.

Our Quality Coordinator will work with our technical team to verify the error and take action to ensure it is corrected in future editions.

INDEX TO QUESTIONS AND ANSWERS

EXAM TECHNIQUE

- We recommend that you always read the questions and examination requirements carefully.
- **Divide the time** you spend on questions in proportion to the marks on offer:
  - there are 1.2 minutes available per mark in the examination
  - within that, try to allow time at the end of each question to review your answer for errors.

  Whatever happens, always keep an eye on the clock and **do not over run on any part of any question!**
- Always start by carefully reading the question.
- Spend the last **five minutes** of the examination:
  - reading through your answers, and
  - **making any additions or corrections**.
- If you **get completely stuck** with a question, flag it in the CBE software and **return to it later.**

Multiple choice questions

- No credit for workings will be given in these questions; the answers will either be correct (2 marks) or incorrect (0 marks).
- Read the question thoroughly and try to figure out the answer without referring to the options available. Take note of words such as never/always or least/most which can change the meaning of the question.
- Work steadily. Rushing leads to careless mistakes and questions are designed to include answers that result from common mistakes.
- It is still important to carry out full workings for numerical questions, not just in your head or on your calculator as you are less likely to skip steps in the calculation this way. Then compare your answer to the choices given and (hopefully) pick the correct one. If your answer does not match any of the choices given, try to rework your answer.

  Remember, that the wrong answers (or 'distractors') have been deliberately calculated to provide answers students will calculate if they make simple mistakes such as forgetting to apply an exemption.

  For centre based exams these workings can be done on scrap paper or using the on-screen scratchpad. For remote invigilated exams you will not be able to use scrap paper but will have to use the scratchpad. It is therefore essential to practice using this functionality prior to your exam. The ACCA practice platform can be used to familiarise yourself with using this function.
- Make sure you answer all the multiple-choice questions. There is no negative marking, meaning that you will not be penalised for an incorrect answer.

  If you are unsure of the answer to a particular question, try to eliminate the options you are sure are incorrect and see if the correct answer becomes more obvious. If you are still unsure, remember that one of the choices must be correct, so guess!

Long form questions

- It is not necessary to copy out the question or to repeat the requirement in your answer.
- Unless you know exactly how to answer the question, spend some time **planning your answer**.
- Stick to the question and **tailor your answer** to what you are asked.
  - pay particular attention to the verbs in the question, e.g. 'Calculate', 'State', 'Explain'.
- If you do not understand what a question is asking, **state your assumptions**.

  Even if you do not answer in precisely the way the examining team hoped, you should be given some credit if your assumptions are reasonable.
- You should do everything you can to make things easy for the marker.

  The marker will find it easier to identify the points you have made if your **answers are laid out logically.** Set out all workings clearly.

  Adopt a logical approach and cross reference workings to the main computation to enable the marker to find them easily. Do not leave a large gap between your answer and the workings.
- If you leave something out of a calculation, perhaps because it is exempt from tax, state why you have left it out.
- **Written questions**:

  Your answer should have:
  - a clear structure
  - a brief introduction, a main section and a conclusion.

  Fully explain all your points but be as concise as possible. It is better to write a little about a lot of different points than a great deal about one or two points.
- **Computations:**

  It is essential to include all your workings in your answers.

  Many computational questions require the use of a standard format. For example, income tax, corporation tax and capital gains tax computations.

  Be sure you know these formats thoroughly before the examination and use the layouts that you see in the answers given in this book and in model answers.

  A number of standard spreadsheet functions are available via the menu and tool bar for you to use when responding to the question.

  If you are asked to comment or make recommendations on a computation, you must do so. There are important marks to be gained here. Even if your computation contains mistakes, you may still gain marks if your reasoning is correct.
- **Reports, memos and other documents:**

  Some questions ask you to present your answer in the form of a report, a memo, a letter or other document.

  Make sure that you use the correct format – there could be easy marks to gain here.

- **Additional tips**

  On the ACCA website there is a CBE specimen exam. It is ESSENTIAL that you look at this before your real CBE. You can use it to familiarise yourself with the question types and features, the functionality contained within the live CBE exam and how to move around the CBE screens, increasing your confidence and speed in the actual examination. However, you should note that the specimen on the ACCA website is based on legislation applicable at the time it was published and has not been updated to FA2025. The specimen CBE exam at the end of this kit has been updated to FA2025.

  Be sure you understand how to use the software before you start the examination. If in doubt, ask the assessment centre staff to explain it to you.

  Questions are displayed on the screen and answers are entered using keyboard and mouse.

EXAM SPECIFIC INFORMATION

THE EXAM

FORMAT OF THE EXAM

The examination is a two-hour computer-based exam.

	Number of marks
Section A	
15 Multiple choice questions worth 2 marks each	30
Section B	
Eight compulsory questions	
Two questions (15 marks each)	30
Two questions (10 marks each)	20
Four questions (5 marks each)	20
	100

One of the 15-mark questions will focus on income tax.

The other 15-mark question will focus on corporation tax.

The remaining questions will examine topics from any area of the syllabus, and this means there will be a wide coverage of the syllabus in every examination. It is therefore vital to study the entire syllabus and not just the basic principles.

Total time allowed: 2 hours

PASS MARK

The pass mark is 50%.

Remote invigilated exams

In certain geographical areas it may be possible for you to take your exam remotely. This option, which is subject to strict conditions, can offer increased flexibility and convenience under certain circumstances. Further guidance, including the detailed requirements and conditions for taking the exam by this method, is contained on ACCA's website at:

https://www.accaglobal.com/an/en/student/exam-entry-and-administration/about-our-exams/remote-exams/remote-session-exams.html

EXAMINER'S REPORT COMMENTS

GENERAL COMMENTS FROM RECENT EXAMS

The following general comments have been made by the examining team in response to the examinations under the syllabus and examination format introduced from the (delayed) September 2020 sitting. We have also included some older comments which are still relevant to the current exam format.

In the June 2024 examiner's report, it said "It was pleasing to note that most candidates presented their answers in the required format; however markers did experience some issues in terms of following through the computations and the logic of candidates' answers."

Section A

The June 2024 examiner's report stated that "It was pleasing to note that most candidates attempted all 15 of the questions in this section. However, candidates appeared to struggle with some questions which impacted on the overall performance in this part of the exam."

The June 2024 examiner's report highlighted that questions in this section can test any topic from the syllabus. It reminded candidates "of the need to equip themselves with adequate knowledge in all the various topics of the syllabus in order to improve their chances of scoring well. Studying only selected topics in detail or studying superficially over a broader range of topics is likely to result in poorer overall results".

The importance of reading the question carefully is often emphasised.

Previous examiner's reports have also warned candidates that they must be better prepared for this section and advise them to **revise sample questions**, as well as **reading the examining team's article on answering multiple choice questions**.

This section allows the examining team to test the understanding of a candidate's technical knowledge. Questions range from basic facts, such as tax payment dates, to the calculation of benefits and the rules for the use of losses. The answers are either right or wrong – there are no part marks and therefore candidates must be aware of basic rules to score any marks.

Section B

The June 2024 examiner's report stated that:

"Most candidates attempted all questions in Section B.

Candidates are reminded of the need to answer the requirements of a question in full. For example, if a Section B requirement states that candidates need to indicate by the use of "0" any items referred to in the question for which no adjustments need to be made, then this must be done in order to earn the mark. Simply leaving something out of the computation will not earn a mark.

Some common issues noted in candidates' answers were as follows:

- Lack of workings – if an answer is wrong, credit cannot be awarded if the marker cannot see the workings the candidate has performed in arriving at their answer.
- Tax administration is an area where candidates appear to be poorly prepared. Going forward, it is an aspect of the syllabus to which it is recommended candidates should pay greater attention.

Candidates are reminded of the helpful articles on our FTX technical page [link below], including a very helpful article about how to succeed when tackling the 15-mark corporation tax question and further articles regarding how to improve exam technique."

https://www.accaglobal.com/ca/en/student/exam-support-resources/foundation-level-study-resources/ftx/ftx-technical-articles.html

The June 2024 examiner's report stated that:

"The questions which produced the best answers were the 15-mark income tax question and the 15-mark corporation tax question.

Answers to a 10-mark capital gains tax question were not very good, in large part because candidates struggled with how to deal with the capital gains tax chargeable on the disposals of a business asset and on a residential property.

One of the weakest responses related to a 5-mark question concerning the payments on account and balancing payment payable by a sole trader.

Overall, questions which required knowledge of tax administration were poorly answered; future candidates should not neglect this part of the syllabus."

The September 2020 examiner's report stated that:

"Most candidates attempted all questions in section B. Candidates seemed to be poorly prepared for theory type questions and therefore provided [some] weak answers. This appears to demonstrate that candidates are learning to reproduce numerical answers without really understanding what they are calculating and, when it comes to describing the tax rules, their lack of knowledge shows through.

Candidates must also remember to answer the requirements of a question in full. If the requirement states, for instance, that a reason must be given for why an item has been left out of a calculation, then this must be done, otherwise full marks cannot be allocated.

A number of common issues arose in candidates' answers:

- Lack of workings
- Poor layouts – candidates should learn and adopt layouts shown in the recommended text books
- Not checking their answers."

Section B examines numerical and theoretical elements of the syllabus. Overall, the standard of answers tends to be better than Section A, although theory questions are poorly answered, which must be addressed by candidates who wish to succeed in the paper.

Previous examiner's reports have also warned candidates that it is important to follow the instructions given in the question requirements as this will help achieve higher marks." The instructions ignored were stating why an item was not included in the computation, and starting with the net profit figure in the accounts and noting with a zero any item that did not require adjustment.

It has also been noted that many candidates miss out on an easy mark for the date of payment, required by the question and equally, they missed a mark for stating the carried forward loss, as required by the question.

Reading the question carefully, answering the question asked and **considering what each piece of information in the question relates to is imperative**. "If a question requires you to identify and state why any items are not included in your answer you MUST do so."

In the past the standard on the questions which always test the same areas has generally been much better than that on the remaining questions. The examination format allows a large area of the syllabus to be examined at each sitting. The examiner's reports remind candidates that they **need to study the entire syllabus** and not just the basic principles that are always examined. In December 2015 the report commented that "it is not an advisable strategy for candidates wishing to pass to rely on good knowledge in the areas of income tax, corporation tax and capital allowances only."

Many areas, which candidates previously gambled on as being fringe topics and thus not often examined, will now be examined more frequently and therefore the entire syllabus should be considered as possibly being examined at every sitting.

Candidates must also **be prepared to answer different styles of questions**. The December 2016 examiner's report concluded that "candidates should **not rely on numerical questions** to pass this [exam]. MCQs and theoretical questions will enable the broad spectrum of this syllabus to be examined and, therefore, it is essential that candidates practise these types of questions."

Other common and important issues are:

- Candidates should study past exam papers as many areas are examined time and time again. The recent CBE questions released by the ACCA have been included in this kit.
- All requirements should be completed.
- Requirements should be read carefully and answered in the way requested. No marks can be scored for writing about something irrelevant to what was asked.
- There is no need to copy out the requirement before doing the answer.
- Candidates should think about their answer and reconsider the results of calculations where it appears to be unlikely, for example £25,000 for the personal allowance.
- Do not use the wrong rates and allowances – the correct rates are provided in the examination, so be sure to use the information given.
- Try not to confuse the rules for different taxes – make sure you are clear as to which tax the question you are answering relates to and the appropriate rules to apply.
- Practice answering theoretical questions – it is important to be able to express an answer in writing as well as answering numerical questions.
- Candidates should check their answers.

On the plus side candidates have been congratulated on the following points:

- Showing all workings in full.
- Presenting answers in a way that is clear and easy to follow.

SPECIFIC COMMENTS

Specific comments in the examiner's reports relating to specific topics have been built into the tutorial notes within the answers to questions in this kit where appropriate.

ACCA SUPPORT

For additional support with your studies please also refer to the ACCA Global website.

KAPLAN'S RECOMMENDED REVISION APPROACH

QUESTION PRACTICE IS THE KEY TO SUCCESS

Success in professional examinations relies upon you acquiring a firm grasp of the required knowledge at the tuition phase. In order to be able to do the questions, knowledge is essential.

However, the difference between success and failure often hinges on your examination technique on the day and making the most of the revision phase of your studies.

The **Kaplan study text** is the starting point, designed to provide the underpinning knowledge to tackle all questions. However, in the revision phase, poring over text books is not the answer.

Kaplan pocket notes are designed to help you quickly revise a topic area; however, you then need to practise questions. There is a need to progress to full examination standard questions as soon as possible, and to tie your examination technique and technical knowledge together.

The importance of question practice cannot be over-emphasised.

The recommended approach below is designed by expert tutors in the field, in conjunction with their knowledge of the examining team and recent real examinations.

You need to practise as many questions as possible in the time you have left.

OUR AIM

Our aim is to get you to the stage where you can attempt examination standard questions confidently, to time, in a closed book environment, with no supplementary help (i.e. to simulate the real examination experience).

Practising your examination technique on real past examination questions, in timed conditions, is also vitally important for you to assess your progress and identify areas of weakness that may need more attention in the final run up to the examination.

In order to achieve this, we recognise that initially you may feel the need to practice some questions with open book help and exceed the required time.

The approach below shows you which questions you should use to build up to coping with examination standard question practice, and references to the sources of information available should you need to revisit a topic area in more detail.

Remember that in the real examination, all you must do is:

- attempt all questions required by the examination
- only spend the allotted time on each question, and
- get them at least 50% right!

Try and practice this approach on every question you attempt from now to the real examination.

Good examination technique is vital.

KAPLAN'S FTX EXAM REVISION PLAN

Stage 1: Assess areas of strengths and weaknesses

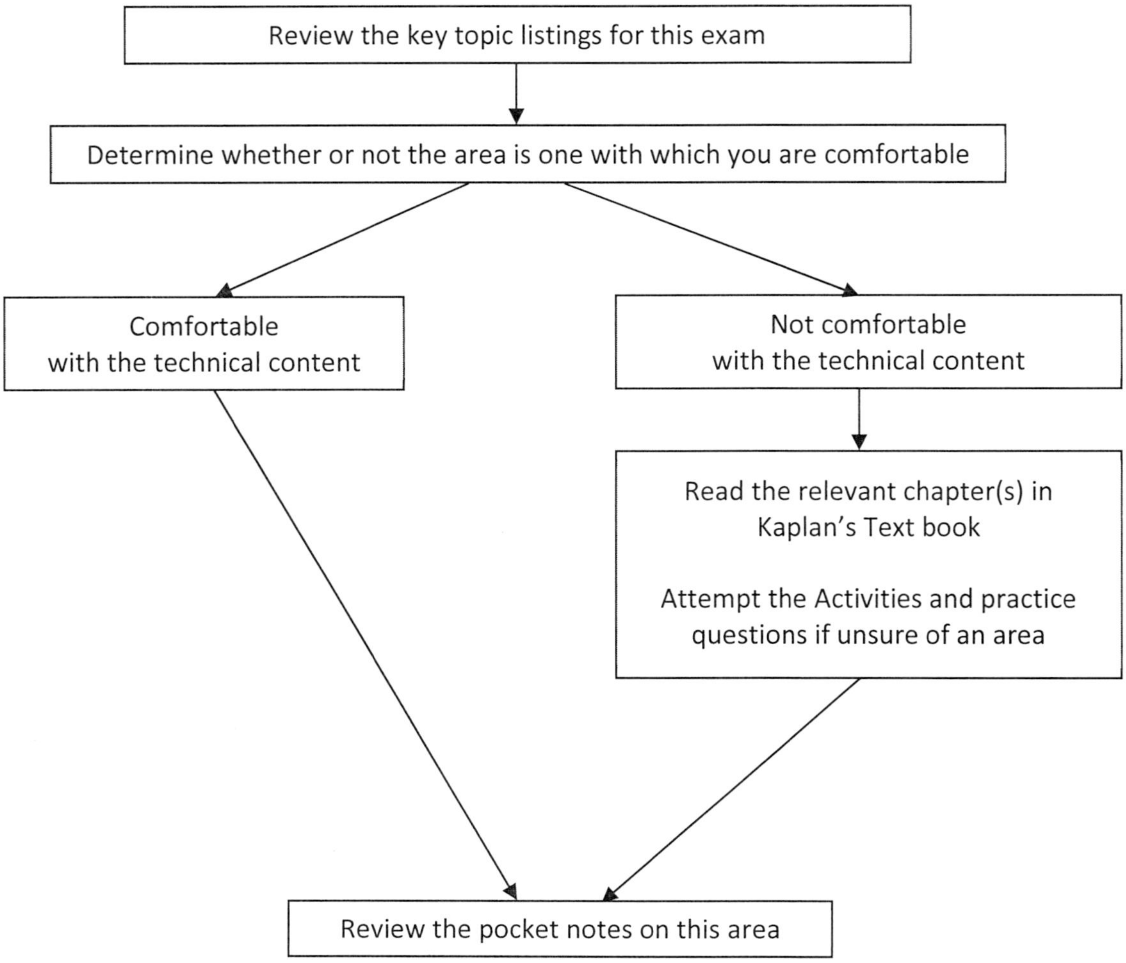

Stage 2: Practise questions

Follow the order of revision of topics as presented in this kit and attempt the questions in the order suggested.

Try to avoid referring to textbooks and notes and the model answer until you have completed your attempt.

Try to answer the question in the allotted time.

Review your attempt with the model answer and assess how much of the answer you achieved in the allocated examination time.

Fill in the self-assessment box below and decide on your best course of action.

Comfortable with question attempt

Only revisit when comfortable with questions on all topic areas

Not comfortable with question attempts

Focus on these areas by:

- Reworking Activities and practice questions from the Kaplan study text
- Revisiting the technical content from Kaplan's pocket notes
- Working any remaining questions on that area in the exam kit
- Reattempting an examination standard question in that area, on a timed, closed book basis

Stage 3: Final pre-examination revision

We recommend that you **attempt at least one two hour mock examination** containing a set of previously unseen examination standard questions.

It is important that you get a feel for the breadth of coverage of a real examination without advance knowledge of the topic areas covered – just as you will expect to see on the real examination day.

Ideally this mock should be sat in timed, closed book, real examination conditions and could be:

- a mock examination offered by your tuition provider, and/or
- the specimen CBE exam at the end of this kit.

TAX RATES AND ALLOWANCES

Throughout this exam kit:

1 **Calculations and workings need only be made to the nearest £.**

2 **All apportionments should be made to the nearest month.**

3 **All workings should be shown when answering section B.**

Income tax

		Normal rates	Dividend rates
Basic rate	£1 – £37,700	20%	8.75%
Higher rate	£37,701 – £125,140	40%	33.75%
Additional rate	£125,141 and over	45%	39.35%

Savings income nil rate band	– Basic rate taxpayers	£1,000
	– Higher rate taxpayers	£500
Dividend nil rate band		£500

A starting rate of 0% applies to savings income where it falls within the first £5,000 of taxable income.

Personal allowance

Personal allowance	£12,570
Income limit	£100,000

Where adjusted net income is £125,140 or more, the personal allowance is reduced to zero.

Car benefit percentage

The relevant base level of CO_2 emissions is 55 grams per kilometre.

The percentage rates applying to petrol cars (and diesel cars meeting the RDE2 standard) with CO_2 emissions up to this level are:

51 grams to 54 grams per kilometre	16%
55 grams per kilometre	17%

The percentage for electric cars with zero CO_2 emissions is 3%.

For hybrid-electric cars with CO_2 emissions between 1 and 50 grams per kilometre, the electric range of the car is relevant:

Electric range

130 miles or more	3%
70 – 129 miles	6%
40 – 69 miles	9%
30 – 39 miles	13%
Less than 30 miles	15%

Car fuel benefit

The base figure for calculating the car fuel benefit is £28,200.

Company van benefits

The company van benefit scale charge is £4,020, and the van fuel benefit is £769.

Rent-a-room relief

The rent-a-room relief limit is £7,500.

Pension scheme limits

Annual allowance	£60,000

The maximum contribution that can qualify for tax relief without any earnings is £3,600.

Approved mileage allowances: cars

Up to 10,000 miles	45p
Over 10,000 miles	25p

Capital allowances: rates of allowance

Plant and machinery	
Main pool	18%
Special rate pool	6%
Cars	
New cars with zero CO_2 emissions	100%
Second-hand cars with zero CO_2 emissions	18%
CO_2 emissions between 1 and 50 grams per kilometre	18%
CO_2 emissions over 50 grams per kilometre	6%
Annual investment allowance	
Rate of allowance	100%
Expenditure limit	£1,000,000
Enhanced Capital allowances for companies	
Main pool first year allowance	100%
Special rate pool first year allowance	50%
Structures and buildings allowance	
Straight line allowance	3%

Corporation tax

Financial year	2023	2024	2025
Small profits rate	19%	19%	19%
Main rate	25%	25%	25%
Lower limit	£50,000	£50,000	£50,000
Upper limit	£250,000	£250,000	£250,000
Standard fraction	3/200	3/200	3/200

Marginal relief

$$(\text{Upper limit} - \text{Augmented profits}) \times \text{Standard fraction} \times \frac{\text{Taxable total profits}}{\text{Augmented profits}}$$

Quarterly instalments

Profit threshold	£1,500,000

Value added tax

Standard rate	20%
Registration limit	£90,000
Deregistration limit	£88,000

Capital gains tax

Lower rate	18%
Higher rate	24%
Annual exempt amount	£3,000

Business asset disposal relief

Lifetime limit	£1,000,000
Rate of tax	14%

National insurance contributions

Class 1	Employee	£1 – £12,570 per year	Nil
		£12,571 – £50,270 per year	8%
		£50,271 and above per year	2%
Class 1	Employer	£1 – £5,000 per year	Nil
		£5,001 and above per year	15%
		Employment allowance	£10,500
Class 1A			15%
Class 4		£1 – £12,570 per year	Nil
		£12,571 – £50,270 per year	6%
		£50,271 and above per year	2%

Where weekly or monthly calculations are required the class 1 limits shown above should be divided by 52 (weekly) or 12 (monthly) as applicable.

Official rate of interest (assumed)

3.75%

Standard penalties for errors

Taxpayer behaviour	Maximum penalty	Minimum penalty – unprompted disclosure	Minimum penalty – prompted disclosure
Deliberate and concealed	100%	30%	50%
Deliberate but not concealed	70%	20%	35%
Careless	30%	0%	15%

TIME LIMITS AND ELECTION DATES

Note that this information is NOT supplied in your examination but is included here to help you with your revision.

Income tax

Election/claim	**Time limit**	**For 2025/26**
Agree the amount of trading losses to carry forward	4 years from the end of the tax year in which the loss arose	5 April 2030
Current and prior year set-off of trading losses against total income	12 months from 31 January following the end of the tax year in which the loss arose	31 January 2028

National Insurance Contributions

Election/claim	**Time limit**	**For 2025/26**
Class 1 employee and employer's – pay days	17 days after the end of each tax month under PAYE system (14 days if not paid electronically)	22nd of each month (19th if not paid electronically)
Class 1A NICs – pay day	22 July following end of tax year (19 July if not paid electronically)	22 July 2026 (19 July 2026 if not paid electronically)
Class 4 NICs – pay days	Paid under self-assessment with income tax	See self-assessment

Capital gains tax

Election/claim	**Time limit**	**For 2025/26**
Replacement of business asset relief for individuals (Rollover relief)	4 years from the end of the tax year: – in which the disposal occurred or – the replacement asset was acquired whichever is later New asset to be purchased within the period one year before and three years after the disposal of old asset	5 April 2030 for 2025/26 sale and acquisition
Gift holdover relief of gain on the gift of a business asset (Gift relief)	4 years from the end of the tax year in which the disposal occurred	5 April 2030
Business asset disposal relief	12 months from 31 January following the end of the tax year in which the disposal occurred	31 January 2028

Self-assessment – individuals

Election/claim	Time limit	For 2025/26
Pay days for income tax and class 4 NIC	1st instalment: 31 January in the tax year 2nd instalment: 31 July following the end of tax year Balancing payment: 31 January following the end of tax year	31 January 2026 31 July 2026 31 January 2027
Pay day for CGT on residential property disposals	60 days after the disposal	
Pay day for CGT (balance)	31 January following the end of tax year	31 January 2027
Filing dates If notice issued by 31 July following end of tax year If notice issued by 31 October following end of tax year If notice not issued by the above dates	Paper return: 31 October following end of tax year Electronic return: 31 January following end of tax year 3 months from the date of issue of the notice to file a return	31 October 2026 31 January 2027
Retention of records Business records Personal records	5 years from 31 January following end of the tax year 12 months from 31 January following end of the tax year	31 January 2032 31 January 2028
HMRC right to correct errors	9 months from date the return was filed	
Taxpayer's right to amend a return	12 months from 31 January following end of the tax year	31 January 2028
Taxpayer's overpayment relief claim	4 years from the end of the tax year	5 April 2030
Taxpayer's right of appeal against an assessment	30 days from the assessment – appeal in writing	

Corporation tax

Election/claim	**Time limit**
Replacement of business asset relief for companies (Rollover relief)	4 years from the end of the accounting period: – in which the disposal occurred or – the replacement asset was acquired whichever is later
Offset of trading losses brought forward against total profits	2 years from the end of the accounting period in which the loss is **relieved**
Current year set-off of trading losses against total profits (income and gains), and 12 month carry back of trading losses against total profits (income and gains)	2 years from the end of the accounting period in which the loss **arose**

Self-assessment – companies

Self-assessment matters	**Due date**
Pay day	9 months and one day after the end of the accounting period
Pay day with instalments	Instalments due on 14th day of: – Seventh, tenth, thirteenth, and sixteenth month **after the start** of the accounting period
Filing dates	Later of: – 12 months from the end of the accounting period – 3 months from the issue of a notice to deliver a corporation tax return

Election/claim	**Time limit**
HMRC right of repair (i.e. to correct mistakes)	9 months from the date the return was filed
Companies right to amend a return	12 months from the filing date
Companies claim for overpayment relief for errors or mistakes	4 years from the end of the accounting period
HMRC can open an enquiry	12 months from the actual submission of the return
Retention of records	6 years from the end of the accounting period

Value added tax

Election/claim	**Time limit**
Compulsory registration Historic test: – Notify HMRC – Charge VAT Future test: – Notify HMRC – Charge VAT	 30 days from end of the month in which the threshold was exceeded First day of second month after the month when taxable supplies exceeded the threshold 30 days from the date it is anticipated that the threshold will be exceeded The date it is anticipated that the threshold will be exceeded (i.e. the beginning of the 30 day period)
Compulsory deregistration	Notify HMRC 30 days from cessation
Filing of VAT return and payment of VAT	One month and seven days after the end of the return period

Section 1

MULTIPLE CHOICE QUESTIONS

INTRODUCTION TO THE UK TAX SYSTEM

1 *December 2020 Section A question*

Which of the following are direct taxes?

1 Corporation tax

2 Capital gains tax

3 Income tax

4 Value added tax

A 1, 2, 3 and 4

B 1, 2 and 3 only

C 2 and 3 only

D 1 and 4 only **(2 marks)**

2 Which of the following statements are correct?

1 Companies pay corporation tax on their chargeable gains.

2 HMRC statements of practice have legal force.

3 National insurance contributions are a revenue tax.

A 1 and 2 only

B 1 and 3 only

C 2 and 3 only

D All of them **(2 marks)**

3 Which of the following is not a duty of HMRC?

A Issue notices to file tax returns

B Collect taxes

C Examine returns and accounts of individuals, businesses and companies

D Pass the annual Finance Act **(2 marks)**

4 Which of the following statements are not correct?

1 If a taxpayer disagrees with a decision made by HMRC the taxpayer must appeal it within 30 days.

2 If a taxpayer chooses to have his, her or their case reviewed by another HMRC officer the taxpayer can never take the case to the Tax tribunal.

3 The Tax tribunal holds a hearing in public for all cases it receives.

A 1 and 2 only

B 1 and 3 only

C 2 and 3 only

D All of them **(2 marks)**

5 Paddy is an employee.

Which of the following taxes does Paddy not suffer?

A Income tax

B National insurance contributions

C VAT

D Corporation tax **(2 marks)**

6 Gamila wishes to appeal against an amendment to her income tax self-assessment return for the tax year 2025/26.

How long, from the date of the amendment, has Gamila got to lodge the appeal with HMRC?

A 14 days

B 30 days

C 1 month

D 9 months **(2 marks)**

7 Which one of the following is not statutory legislation?

A Capital Allowances Act 2001

B Extra Statutory Concession A16

C Income Tax (Trading and Other Income) Act 2005

D Statutory Instrument 2008/2682 **(2 marks)**

8 Which of the following is not correct?

A Treasury appointed civil servants are responsible for the collection of UK taxation

B The Tax tribunal is administered by the Tribunals service of the Ministry of Justice

C A taxpayer has no right of appeal against the interpretation of legislation contained in HMRC guidance notes

D The Chancellor of the Exchequer is responsible for the imposition of taxation

(2 marks)

9 **Taxes can apply to capital or revenue. Which of the following is not a revenue tax?**

A Income tax

B Corporation tax

C National insurance contributions

D Capital gains tax **(2 marks)**

TAX ADMINISTRATION

10 ***September 2020 Section A question***

Which form must an employer use to inform HM Revenue and Customs (HMRC) of taxable benefits provided to an employee and by which date must it be filed?

A P60 by 31 May following the relevant tax year

B P60 by 6 July following the relevant tax year

C P11D by 31 May following the relevant tax year

D P11D by 6 July following the relevant tax year **(2 marks)**

11 Samkelo is a sole trader.

On which dates were/are Samkelo's payments on account due in respect of the tax year 2025/26?

A 31 January 2025 and 31 July 2025

B 31 July 2025 and 31 January 2026

C 31 January 2026 and 31 July 2026

D 31 July 2026 and 31 January 2027 **(2 marks)**

12 Bertha submitted a paper tax return for the tax year 2025/26 on 21 October 2026.

What is the latest date by which she can amend her return?

A 21 October 2027

B 31 January 2028

C 31 October 2027

D 31 January 2027 **(2 marks)**

13 Jean's income tax and capital gains tax liabilities for the tax year 2024/25 were £15,000 and £4,000 respectively. Tax of £6,100 was paid through PAYE for the tax year 2024/25.

What payment on account of her tax liability for the tax year 2025/26 should Jean pay on 31 July 2026? Ignore national insurance.

A £8,900

B £6,450

C £7,500

D £4,450 **(2 marks)**

14 ***June 2023 Section A question***

Marlon has been trading as a sole trader for many years and is required to make payments on account of his income tax liability. His income tax liability for 2024/25 was £15,600 and he estimates that his income tax liability for 2025/26 will be £17,800.

What amount should Marlon pay as his first payment on account on 31 January 2026 in respect of his income tax liability for 2025/26? Ignore national insurance.

A £7,800

B £8,900

C £2,200

D £15,600 **(2 marks)**

15 **Which of the following statements is incorrect?**

A Business records for the tax year 2025/26 must be kept until 31 January 2027

B A taxpayer who submits a tax return 2 months late may receive a penalty of £100

C An electronic tax return for the tax year 2025/26 should normally be filed by 31 January 2027

D HMRC has until 12 October 2027 to correct an obvious error in a tax return for the tax year 2025/26 which was submitted electronically on 13 January 2027 **(2 marks)**

16 Fran submitted their tax return for the tax year 2025/26, which is later discovered to contain some errors.

Which of the following statements about possible penalties is correct?

A Fran will be given an automatic penalty of £100

B Fran may receive a penalty ranging from 0% to 100% of their total tax liability for the year

C Fran may receive a penalty ranging from 0% to 100% of the tax underpaid as a result of the errors

D Penalties are not levied for incorrect returns **(2 marks)**

17 **In which one of the following circumstances can an accountant divulge confidential information about a client?**

A If the information is over 6 years old

B If a member of the public asks for it

C If the accountant has written authority to disclose

D If the client's spouse requests the information **(2 marks)**

18 Belinda paid her balance of tax due for the tax year 2025/26 of £7,400 on 10 March 2027.

Which of the following statements are correct?

1 Belinda will have to pay interest on late paid tax from 31 January 2027 to 10 March 2027.

2 Belinda will have to pay an immediate £100 penalty because the payment is late.

3 Belinda will have to pay a 5% penalty because the payment is more than 30 days late.

A 1 and 2

B 1 and 3

C 1 only

D 2 only **(2 marks)**

19 How long must a sole trader keep and retain all records required to make and deliver correct tax returns?

A Five years after the 31 January following the tax year

B To the end of the next tax year (i.e. 5 April)

C To the 31 January following the filing date

D For 6 years after the actual filing date **(2 marks)**

20 An individual taxpayer who does not normally receive a notice to file a tax return must notify HMRC of any chargeability for the tax year 2025/26 by which date?

A 30 September 2026

B 5 October 2026

C 31 October 2026

D 31 December 2026 **(2 marks)**

21 Which one of the following statements is not correct?

A As a student member of ACCA you are bound by the duty of confidentiality to a client

B The duty of confidentiality does not apply when a husband asks for information about his wife's tax affairs

C The duty of confidentiality continues even after a client relationship has ended

D Confidentiality means not disclosing information which you acquire due to your job **(2 marks)**

22 Which of the following is not one of the fundamental principles set out in the ACCA Professional code of ethics?

A Objectivity

B Integrity

C Professional behaviour

D Punctuality **(2 marks)**

23 Which one of the following is not the correct action when an accountant becomes aware that a client has not declared all his, her or their taxable income?

A Advise the client in writing to disclose the income

B Cease to act for the client even if the client agrees to disclose the income

C Consider whether a report should be made under the Money Laundering Regulations

D Consider whether the non-disclosure was an error or deliberate act **(2 marks)**

24 Which of the following correctly explains why a taxpayer who has only ever received income from self-employment would NOT have to make payments on account of income tax and class 4 NIC liabilities for the tax year 2025/26?

A Tax deducted via PAYE during the tax year 2024/25 amounted to more than 80% of the tax liability for that tax year

B Tax liability for the tax year 2025/26 is expected to be less than £1,000

C Tax deducted via PAYE during the tax year 2025/26 is expected to be more than 80% of the tax liability for that tax year

D Tax payable (i.e. tax liability net of PAYE) for the tax year 2024/25 was less than £1,000 **(2 marks)**

25 What is the normal payment date for capital gains tax for the tax year 2025/26?

A 31 July 2025

B 31 January 2026

C 31 July 2026

D 31 January 2027 **(2 marks)**

26 ***September 2020 Section A question***

Timothy is a sole trader. He paid his first payment on account, of £4,000, for the tax year 2025/26 on 14 March 2026.

What penalty, if any, will be imposed on Timothy in respect of this late payment?

A £100

B £200

C £400

D £0 **(2 marks)**

TRADING PROFIT, CAPITAL ALLOWANCES AND LOSSES

27 Fred started to trade on 1 January 2026. He paid the following expenditure in the 12 months before he started to trade:

Rent for his business property	£5,000
A new suit so he could impress prospective customers	£600
Payments to an advertising agency for an advertising campaign to run through January 2026	£1,000

How much of this expenditure can Fred deduct for tax purposes when preparing his first set of accounts for the year ended 31 December 2026?

A £0

B £5,000

C £6,000

D £6,600 **(2 marks)**

28 X Ltd has included a deduction of £3,200 from its accounting profit in respect of the annual leasing cost for a car, which has CO_2 emissions of 55g/km.

The car has been used for the whole of the 12-month period ended 31 March 2026.

When calculating the adjusted profit for tax purposes, what adjustment must be made to the accounting profit in the statement of profit or loss in respect of the leasing cost in the year ended 31 March 2026?

A £480 deduction

B £480 add back

C £0

D £2,720 add back **(2 marks)**

29 Mabel runs a small business which she started on 1 September 2025. She prepares her first accounts to 31 March 2026.

On 1 October 2025 she bought a car for £18,000 which has CO_2 emissions of 47g/km and which she uses 40% for business use.

What capital allowances can Mabel claim, for the period ended 31 March 2026?

A £252

B £1,296

C £756

D £1,890 **(2 marks)**

30 Paul runs a small business as a hairdresser. He started trading on 1 July 2025 and prepared his first set of accounts to 31 March 2026. He uses the accruals basis.

During this first period of account he purchased the following items:

Car	£8,000 (100% business use, CO_2 emissions 77g/km)
Plant and machinery	£15,000

What is Paul's maximum capital allowance claim for the period ended 31 March 2026?

A £15,480

B £15,360

C £16,080

D £23,000 **(2 marks)**

31 Kelly runs a small business which she started 1 May 2025. She prepared her first set of accounts for the nine months to 31 January 2026. On 1 June 2025, she purchased a car for £31,500 which she uses 30% for business purposes. The car has zero CO_2 emissions.

What are the capital allowances available to her for the nine-month period ended 31 January 2026?

A £4,253

B £31,500

C £1,276

D £9,450 **(2 marks)**

32 Norman is a sole trader who uses the accruals basis. He has accounting profits for the year ended 31 December 2025 of £160,000.

Included within this figure are:

1 Legal fees for acquiring a new 15-year lease of his business premises of £3,000.

2 Car parking fines incurred by Norman whilst on business trips of £180.

3 Interest for late payment of his previous year's income tax of £40.

How much must be added back to the accounting profit when calculating the tax adjusted trading profit figure for the year ended 31 December 2025?

A £3,180

B £3,220

C £220

D £3,040 **(2 marks)**

33 Rowan is a sole trader who uses the accruals basis. They have deducted the following items of expenditure in the statement of profit or loss for their most recent accounting period:

Loss on sale of non-current asset		£1,000
Entertainment of	: staff	£2,800
	: clients	£6,300

How much should be added back to Rowan's net profit to arrive at their tax adjusted trading profit?

A £10,100

B £3,800

C £7,300

D £6,300 **(2 marks)**

34 A company has the following expenses in its statement of profit or loss:

Legal fees for the purchase of a new building	£800
Legal fees for defending an action for faulty goods	£1,500
Staff Christmas party (the company has 20 employees)	£3,200
Bank fee for arranging a trade related long term loan	£1,000

How much must be added back to the company's accounting profit when computing the tax adjusted trading profit?

A £2,300

B £800

C £4,700

D £3,300 **(2 marks)**

35 Del is a sole trader who paid for the following expenditure during the year ended 31 March 2026:

Goods for resale	£5,000
Computer with 40% private use by Del	£3,000
Redecoration of office completed in March 2025	£1,000

How much can Del deduct when calculating his trading profits for the year ended 31 March 2026?

A £6,000

B £6,800

C £7,200

D £7,800 **(2 marks)**

36 Sui is a sole trader. During the year ended 31 March 2026, Sui bought a zero-emission car for £20,000. They used the car to travel 6,000 miles, all of which were for business purposes. The total running costs for the car during the year were £3,000.

How much can Sui deduct when calculating their trading profits for the year ended 31 March 2026, assuming they claim flat rate expenses?

A £2,700

B £3,000

C £5,700

D £23,000 **(2 marks)**

37 Laureen started business as a sole trader on 1 June 2025 and prepared her first accounts to 31 July 2026. She uses the accruals basis.

On 1 July 2026 she bought several large items of plant and machinery costing £1,100,000 in total.

What is the maximum capital allowances claim that Laureen can make for her first period of trading to 31 July 2026?

A £1,018,000

B £194,667

C £166,667

D £1,100,000 **(2 marks)**

38 Aziz leases a car used by an employee, which has CO_2 emissions of 73g/km. The car has been used for the whole of the year ended 31 March 2026. Aziz made lease payments totalling £4,800 during the year.

What amount can Aziz deduct when calculating his trading profit for the year ended 31 March 2026?

A £0

B £720

C £4,080

D £4,800 **(2 marks)**

39 Ramona is a sole trader who operates a business as a wine merchant. She uses the accruals basis. Her accounts for the year ended 31 March 2026 include the following items:

Impaired trade debts written off	£1,200
Subscription to World Wines magazine	£500
Late payment interest in respect of the tax on the business profits for the year ended 31 March 2025	£275
Legal fees in respect of the acquisition of a new shop	£2,500

What amount is added back to the accounting profit in respect of the above items when calculating the adjusted trading profits for the year ended 31 March 2026?

A £2,500

B £2,775

C £3,000

D £4,475 **(2 marks)**

40 Ralph is a sole trader who operates a bed and breakfast. He lives in the premises with his sister. The total business expenses in the year were £12,300 for the year ended 31 March 2026. The private use adjustment for two occupants is £6,000. Ralph uses the accruals basis.

What amount of Ralph's expenses is allowable for the year ended 31 March 2026?

A £12,300

B £18,300

C £6,300

D £6,000 **(2 marks)**

41 Yuval prepares accounts to 30 June each year. On 5 August 2026 he sold a car for £17,560 which had originally been purchased on 1 September 2025 for £18,000. This car has CO_2 emissions of 120g/km.

On 1 July 2025 there was no balance on either the main or special rate pool.

Assume 2025/26 rates apply throughout.

For the year ended 30 June 2027, the sale of the car results in capital allowances of:

A £640 balancing charge

B £640 balancing allowance

C £2,800 balancing charge

D £2,800 balancing allowance **(2 marks)**

42 Noor ceased trading on 31 March 2026, having been self-employed since 1 April 2008. She used the accruals basis. On 1 April 2025, the tax written down value of her plant and machinery main pool was £9,300. On 20 February 2026, Noor purchased a desk for £2,400. All of the items included in the main pool were sold for £14,700 on 31 March 2026, no items were sold for more than their original cost.

What is the balancing charge that will arise on the disposal of the main pool items upon the cessation of Noor's trade?

A £7,074

B £5,106

C £3,000

D £5,400 **(2 marks)**

43 Cora has always prepared her accounts to 31 October. On 1 May 2025 she purchased a newly constructed building which she brought into use on 1 June 2025. Cora spent £550,000 on the purchase of the building and £30,000 renovating the building. Cora used the accruals basis.

What is the maximum structures and buildings allowance (SBA) Cora may claim for the year ended 31 October 2025?

A £17,400

B £8,700

C £7,250

D £6,875 **(2 marks)**

44 ***June 2023 Section A question***

Georgia is a sole trader who for many years has prepared her accounts annually to 31 March each year on the accruals basis. Georgia bought a new commercial building for use in her business on 1 January 2026, paying £180,000, which included £20,000 for the land, and immediately started using the building for her trade.

What is the maximum structures and buildings allowance which Georgia could claim for the year ended 31 March 2026?

A £4,800

B £1,350

C £1,200

D £5,400 **(2 marks)**

45 ***June 2024 Section A question***

Danny is a sole trader who for many years has prepared his accounts annually to 31 December each year on the accruals basis.

Danny bought a newly constructed commercial building for use in his business on 1 March 2025, paying £250,000. During March 2025, Danny spent £20,000 renovating the building for business purposes.

The building was brought into business use on 1 April 2025.

What is the maximum structures and buildings allowance in respect of the new commercial building, which Danny could claim for the year ended 31 December 2025?

A £5,625

B £6,750

C £6,075

D £7,500 **(2 marks)**

46 ***September 2020 Section A question***

Bali is a sole trader preparing financial statements to 31 March annually. He uses the accruals basis. On 1 December 2025 Bali hired an asset under a hire purchase agreement for use in his business. Bali paid a deposit of £8,000 and contracted to pay 24 monthly payments of £1,000 each commencing on 1 January 2026. The cash price of the asset was £28,000.

What cost must Bali include in his capital allowances calculation for his accounting period ended 31 March 2026?

A £8,000

B £28,000

C £11,000

D £32,000 **(2 marks)**

47 ***December 2020 Section A question***

Which of the following statements is TRUE in respect of losses made by an individual?

A A loss on a UK property business can be offset against general income in future tax years

B A trading loss can be offset against general income in future tax years

C A loss on a UK property business is carried forward and offset against the taxable property income in the following tax year

D A trading loss can be offset against general income of the previous two tax years

(2 marks)

48 Himanshe has been trading for many years preparing accounts to 31 August each year. His recent and forecast trading profits are:

Year ended 31 August 2025	£95,000
Year ended 31 August 2026 (forecast)	£105,000

What are Himanshe's taxable trading profits for the tax year 2025/26?

A £95,000

B £99,167

C £100,833

D £105,000 **(2 marks)**

49 Karishma started trading on 1 November 2025 and prepared her first set of accounts to 30 June 2026. Her recent and forecast trading profits are:

Eight-month period ended 30 June 2026	£16,000
Year ended 30 June 2027 (forecast)	£19,000

What are Karishma's taxable trading profits for the tax year 2025/26?

A £6,667

B £10,000

C £18,250

D £20,250 **(2 marks)**

50 Mindy traded for many years preparing accounts to 31 December each year. She ceased trading on 30 June 2025. Her trading profits for the last two accounting periods were:

Year ended 31 December 2024	£5,000
Six-month period ended 30 June 2025	£2,000

What are Mindy's taxable trading profits for the tax year 2025/26?

A £500

B £1,000

C £2,000

D £4,750 **(2 marks)**

PARTNERSHIPS

51 Derek and Eric have been in partnership for a number of years preparing accounts to 31 December.

Layla joined the partnership on 1 January 2026 and Derek, Eric and Layla agreed to share profits in the ratio 3:2:1.

The partnership made a trading profit for the year ended 31 December 2026 of £60,000.

What are Layla's trading profits for the tax year 2025/26?

A £2,500

B £5,000

C £10,000

D £15,000 **(2 marks)**

52 Elizabeth and Henry have been in partnership for many years, preparing accounts to 31 December each year.

Until 31 July 2025 profits were shared in the ratio 70:30 to Elizabeth and Henry respectively, with no salary allocated to either partner. From 1 August 2025 the profit sharing ratio was adjusted to 80:20 to Elizabeth and Henry respectively, after allocating a salary of £24,000 per annum to Henry.

The trading profits for the accounting year ended 31 December 2025 are £120,000.

How much of the profit for the year ended 31 December 2025 is allocated to Henry?

A £41,000

B £31,000

C £43,200

D £39,000 **(2 marks)**

EMPLOYMENT INCOME

53 Which of the following gifts given to an employee is an exempt benefit?

A Jewellery costing £60 as a birthday present

B A £20 voucher to spend at the local sandwich shop

C Champagne costing £40 as a reward for winning a new contract

D Flowers costing £30 following the birth of a baby **(2 marks)**

54 Shu was provided with a computer for private use on 1 November 2025. The market value of the computer on that date was £3,600.

What is the value of the benefit for the tax year 2025/26?

A £0

B £720

C £300

D £360 **(2 marks)**

55 Sarah earns £37,000 per annum as a marketing executive for Ad Ltd, which prepares accounts to 31 March each year. In addition to her annual salary, Sarah also earned bonuses, paid as follows:

Year end	**Paid**	£
31 March 2025	31 May 2025	3,500
31 March 2026	31 May 2026	5,500

In addition, her employer pays £3,000 per annum for a parking space for Sarah at a car park near her place of work.

What is Sarah's taxable employment income for the tax year 2025/26?

A £40,500

B £37,000

C £42,500

D £43,500 **(2 marks)**

56 Lee was provided with accommodation by his employer on 1 June 2025. The employer bought the house in 2020 for £135,000 and the annual value of the property is £2,950.

Assuming the accommodation is not job related, what is the taxable benefit for Lee for the tax year 2025/26?

A £5,200

B £4,333

C £2,458

D £6,677 **(2 marks)**

57 ***September 2020 Section A question***

Fai is an employee and his employer has given him the use of a petrol driven car for both business and private purposes throughout the tax year 2025/26. The list price of the car is £32,000 but the employer had purchased it for £25,000. Fai paid £6,000 towards the cost of the car. The car has a CO_2 emissions rate of 55g/km.

What is Fai's annual taxable benefit in respect of the use of the car for the tax year 2025/26?

A £4,420

B £4,590

C £3,230

D £3,400 **(2 marks)**

58 During the tax year 2025/26 Jana received £12 per night incidental expenses allowance from her employer in respect of 14 nights working overseas.

How much of this expense allowance is taxable?

A £0

B £168

C £98

D £28 **(2 marks)**

59 Ernest works for Adama plc and is provided with a hybrid-electric diesel company car which does meet the RDE2 standard for the whole of the tax year 2025/26. He uses the car 40% privately and 60% for business. The car has a list price of £10,000, CO_2 emissions of 40g/km and an electric range of 45 miles.

What is Ernest's car benefit for the tax year 2025/26?

A £1,300

B £900

C £360

D £600 **(2 marks)**

60 **Which one of the following is not business travel for the purpose of an income tax employment expense claim?**

A Travel to visit a client

B Travel from home to a temporary place of work

C Travel to and from a permanent place of work

D Travel to visit a trade fair relevant to the employer's business **(2 marks)**

61 Dizzy was provided with a company car by his employer on 1 June 2025. The petrol car has a list price of £18,750 and CO_2 emissions of 172g/km. Dizzy uses the car for private purposes but is not provided with private fuel.

What is the taxable benefit on Dizzy for the tax year 2025/26 for the provision of the car?

A £6,250

B £5,781

C £7,500

D £6,938 **(2 marks)**

62 Protector Ltd is an insurance company and provided the following benefits to a number of its employees during the tax year 2025/26.

Which one of the following is NOT taxable as employment income for the tax year 2025/26?

A Medical insurance provided to a key member of staff

B Free membership to the gym situated next door to the company headquarters

C A second mobile phone provided to the chief executive of the company

D An interest free loan of £6,000 made on 6 April 2025 **(2 marks)**

63 Adin was provided with a house to live in by his employer. The employer rented the house from a local landlord and paid rent of £32,000 p.a. Adin paid rent of £12,000 pa to his employer. The property has an annual value of £9,750 p.a.

What is the taxable benefit, assuming the accommodation is not job-related?

A £9,750

B £12,000

C £20,000

D £0 **(2 marks)**

64 ***September 2020 Section A question***

Jules' employer gave her a television to keep on 6 October 2025. The television had been purchased by her employer in 2024 for £1,800 and the market value on 6 October 2025 was £700. Neither Jules, nor any other employees have previously used the television for private purposes.

What is Jules' taxable benefit in respect of the gift for the tax year 2025/26?

A £1,800

B £900

C £700

D £350 **(2 marks)**

65 ***December 2020 Section A question***

On 1 October 2025 Samantha received a loan of £8,000 from her employer to help purchase her residential house. She was charged interest of 1% per annum. The full amount of the loan is still outstanding.

What is Samantha's taxable benefit in respect of the loan for the tax year 2025/26?

A £220

B £150

C £110

D £0 **(2 marks)**

66 ***December 2020 Section A question***

Jon is a director of a UK company which prepares accounts annually to 31 May each year. Jon becomes entitled to a bonus on 31 December 2025 in relation to the accounting period ended 31 May 2025. The bonus is paid to him on 30 June 2026 and is credited in the company accounts on 15 July 2026.

On which date is the bonus treated as being received by Jon for tax purposes?

A 31 December 2025

B 31 May 2025

C 15 July 2026

D 30 June 2026 **(2 marks)**

INVESTMENT INCOME

67 Peter rents out a home fully furnished. For the tax year 2025/26 he paid the following in relation to furnishing the property:

New desk	£800
Replacement bed	£1,200
Repair to broken washing machine	£150

How much can Peter claim against his property income in respect of the above expenses in the tax year 2025/26?

A £150

B £1,350

C £1,200

D £2,150 **(2 marks)**

68 Paul rents out a home fully furnished. He paid the following expenses in relation to the property:

1 July 2024	House insurance (in respect of the year ended 30 June 2025)	£800
1 July 2025	House insurance (in respect of the year ended 30 June 2026)	£1,000
15 April 2026	Decoration costs (work carried out in March 2026)	£500

How much can Paul claim against his property income in respect of the above expenses in the tax year 2025/26?

A £1,000

B £950

C £1,500

D £1,450 **(2 marks)**

69 For the tax year 2025/26, Ashok has taxable income of £133,640 comprising non-savings income of £116,140 and dividend income of £17,500.

What is the tax liability on Ashok's dividends for the tax year 2025/26?

A £6,690

B £6,186

C £6,214

D £6,383 **(2 marks)**

70 ***December 2020 Section A question***

Isamu receives a pension of £12,000 and savings interest of £4,000 in the tax year 2025/26.

How much income tax must Isamu pay for the tax year 2025/26?

A £486

B £686

C £0

D £586 **(2 marks)**

71 Sammi had taxable income (after the personal allowance) of £13,100 comprising trading income of £4,100 and dividends of £9,000 in the tax year 2025/26.

What is Sammi's income tax liability for the tax year 2025/26?

A £1,608

B £1,564

C £2,520

D £2,620 **(2 marks)**

72 Alma received the following income during the tax year 2025/26.

1 Interest on an NS&I investment account

2 Interest on company loan stock

3 Proceeds from NS&I savings certificates

4 Profit on the sale of shares

Which are taxable for income tax purposes?

A 1, 2 and 3

B 1, 2 and 4

C 1 and 2 only

D 3 and 4 only **(2 marks)**

73 Manon's income for the tax year 2025/26 comprises a salary of £120,000 and dividends of £20,000. She is not entitled to a personal allowance.

How will her dividends be taxed?

A All at 39.35%

B £500 at 0% and £5,140 at 33.75% and £14,360 at 39.35%

C £500 at 0% and £4,640 at 33.75% and £14,860 at 39.35%

D £5,140 at 33.75% and £14,860 at 39.35% **(2 marks)**

74 Alexandru granted a 45-year lease on a warehouse on 5 July 2025, charging a premium of £50,000 and an annual rent of £10,000 payable in advance.

What is his property income for the tax year 2025/26?

A £6,000

B £10,000

C £16,000

D £13,500 **(2 marks)**

75 Daria rents out a furnished room in her house at an annual rent of £8,050. Her household expenses in relation to the room are £450 (none of which are capital).

Assuming she elects the most beneficial treatment, what is her property income for the tax year 2025/26?

A £100

B £550

C £7,600

D £7,500 **(2 marks)**

PENSIONS AND NIC

76 ***September 2020 Section A question***

Rod earned a salary of £24,000 and received non-cash taxable benefits of £4,000 in the tax year 2025/26.

What are Rod's total national insurance contributions (NICs) in respect of the above amounts?

A £914

B £1,234

C £1,920

D £2,240 **(2 marks)**

77 Isa is self-employed. Their relevant earnings for the tax year 2025/26 were £90,000. They made net personal pension contributions of £32,000 in the tax year 2025/26.

By how much is Isa's basic rate band extended for the tax year 2025/26?

A £3,600

B £90,000

C £32,000

D £40,000 **(2 marks)**

78 Hari earns £115,000 a year from employment and has no other income. He pays personal pension contributions of £5,600 each year.

What is his personal allowance for the tax year 2025/26?

A £5,070

B £4,000

C £7,870

D £8,570 **(2 marks)**

79 Jasper has a personal pension scheme.

Which of the following correctly describes who can contribute to his pension scheme in the tax year 2025/26?

A Jasper only

B Jasper and his employer only

C Jasper, his employer and Jasper's self-employed wife

D Jasper and his self-employed wife only **(2 marks)**

80 Nuray is employed by Deller Ltd at a monthly salary of £2,700. In December 2025 she received a bonus of £1,700.

What are the employee class 1 national insurance contributions due for December 2025?

A £339

B £352

C £132

D £255 **(2 marks)**

81 Sally is employed by A Ltd. She earns a salary of £52,000 per year. In addition, Sally receives taxable non-cash benefits of £3,000 every year.

What are A Ltd's employer's class 1 national insurance contributions (NICs) for the tax year 2025/26? Ignore the employment allowance.

A £7,500

B £7,800

C £3,051

D £7,050 **(2 marks)**

82 Jimmy is an employee earning £36,000 a year, payable in equal monthly amounts. In addition, in December 2025 he received a bonus of £8,000.

What were Jimmy's national insurance contributions (NIC) for December 2025?

A £796

B £387

C £471

D £880 **(2 marks)**

83 ***September 2020 Section A question***

Haya received a salary of £7,000, taxable benefits of £2,000 and bank deposit interest of £3,000 in the tax year 2025/26. Haya was a member of a registered pension scheme throughout the tax year 2025/26.

What is the maximum amount of pension contributions Haya can make on which tax relief is available in respect of the tax year 2025/26?

A £3,600

B £12,000

C £7,000

D £9,000 **(2 marks)**

84 ***December 2020 Section A question***

Aneel is a sole trader. She has trading profits of £54,000 and property income of £6,000 in the tax year 2025/26.

What are Aneel's class 4 national insurance contributions (NICs) in respect of the above amounts for the tax year 2025/26?

A £3,091

B £2,486

C £2,337

D £2,457 **(2 marks)**

85 ***June 2024 Section A question***

Chiva Ltd makes employer contributions into an occupational pension scheme for all its employees.

In respect of Chiva Ltd's employer contributions into the occupational pension scheme, which of the following statements is NOT true?

A Chiva Ltd's employer contributions to the pension scheme can be deducted from the employee's earnings when calculating the income tax to deduct under PAYE.

B Chiva Ltd's employer contributions to the pension scheme are tax deductible in calculating Chiva Ltd's taxable total profits.

C Chiva Ltd's employer contributions to the pension scheme are an exempt benefit for the employee.

D Chiva Ltd's employer contributions to the pension scheme count towards the annual allowance available to the employee. **(2 marks)**

CORPORATION TAX

86 Cardwell Ltd has tax adjusted trading profits of £20,000, chargeable gains of £15,000, property business profit of £8,000 and dividends received of £3,000 from a non-group company.

What is the corporation tax liability of Cardwell Ltd for the year ended 31 March 2026?

A £8,740

B £8,170

C £5,320

D £10,750 **(2 marks)**

87 A Ltd has one 100% owned subsidiary, B Ltd. In addition, A Ltd holds 40% of the shares in another company, C Ltd. For the year ended 31 March 2026, A Ltd has taxable total profits of £67,000 and receives dividends of £9,000 from B Ltd and £4,500 from C Ltd.

What are A Ltd's augmented profits for year ended 31 March 2026?

A £68,800

B £80,500

C £76,000

D £71,500 **(2 marks)**

88 Sargent Ltd made a trading loss of £920,000 in the year ended 31 March 2026. The company did not have any other income that year and has elected to carry back the loss.

The results for the year ended 31 March 2025 were as follows:

Tax adjusted trading profit	£662,200
Property income	£80,000
Qualifying charitable donation	£2,000

How much corporation tax will be refunded to Sargent Ltd as a result of the loss carry back to the year ended 31 March 2025?

A £165,550

B £185,050

C £185,550

D £140,638 **(2 marks)**

89 Davies Ltd has the following results:

	Year ended 31 March 2025	Year ended 31 March 2026
	£	£
Tax adjusted trading profit/(loss)	25,000	(60,000)
Bank interest receivable	6,000	3,000
Qualifying charitable donations paid	3,000	1,000

Assuming that Davies Ltd uses its losses as early as possible, what is the trading loss available to carry forward to the year ended 31 March 2027?

A £26,000

B £57,000

C £35,000

D £30,000 **(2 marks)**

90 Orange plc made a trading loss of £80,000 in its year ended 31 December 2025. Orange plc wishes to make a claim to use this loss against total profits in the year ended 31 December 2025.

By when must Orange plc submit its loss relief claim to HM Revenue and Customs?

A 1 October 2026

B 31 December 2026

C 31 December 2027

D 31 December 2029 **(2 marks)**

91 Grape plc is a large UK company and has always had taxable total profits in excess of £1,500,000.

During its year ended 31 March 2026 Grape plc had taxable total profits of £1,600,000.

By which date must Grape plc make its final payment of corporation tax?

A 1 January 2027

B 31 March 2027

C 14 July 2026

D 14 October 2026 **(2 marks)**

92 ABC Ltd has taxable total profits below £1,500,000. It prepares accounts to 31 December every year.

By which dates must ABC Ltd file its tax return and pay its corporation tax liability for the accounting period ended 31 December 2025?

	Return date	**Tax payable date**
A	31 January 2027	31 January 2027
B	31 December 2026	1 October 2026
C	31 January 2027	1 October 2026
D	31 December 2026	31 January 2027

(2 marks)

93 P Ltd is a UK resident company and has trading profits of £255,000 for the year ended 31 March 2026. During the same period P Ltd received dividends of £27,000 from non-group companies and paid a donation to a national charity of £11,000.

What is P Ltd's corporation tax liability for the year ended 31 March 2026?

A £61,000

B £60,313

C £60,910

D £67,750 **(2 marks)**

94 Laugh Ltd is a UK resident company and has trading profits of £119,000 for the year ended 31 March 2026. During the year Laugh Ltd received dividends of £12,000.

What is Laugh Ltd's corporation tax liability for the year ended 31 March 2026?

A £22,610

B £29,750

C £28,129

D £27,785 **(2 marks)**

95 Mirth Ltd is a UK resident company and has taxable total profits of £34,000 for the six-month period ended 31 March 2026. The company has three associated companies during the period.

What is Mirth Ltd's corporation tax liability for the six-month period ended 31 March 2026?

A £6,460

B £7,135

C £8,072

D £8,500 **(2 marks)**

96 Smile Ltd is a UK resident company and has trading profits of £195,000 for the year ended 31 March 2026. During the year Smile Ltd received dividends of £25,000 from non-group companies and £45,000 from group companies.

What is Smile Ltd's augmented profits for the purpose of calculating the corporation tax liability for the year ended 31 March 2026?

A £195,000

B £220,000

C £240,000

D £265,000 **(2 marks)**

97 **Which of the following statements is/are true?**

1 Only companies with revenue of £100,000 or more are required to file returns and pay corporation tax electronically.

2 All companies must file their accounts using iXBRL.

3 iXBRL stands for inline eXtended Blank Reports Limits.

A 1 and 2

B 1 and 3

C 2 only

D None of them **(2 marks)**

98 Johnson Ltd had the following results for the year ended 31 March 2026:

Tax adjusted trading profit	£150,000
Property loss	(£50,000)
Chargeable gains	£70,000

Johnson Ltd also had a brought forward trading loss at 1 April 2025 of £160,000.

What are Johnson Ltd's taxable total profits for the year ended 31 March 2026 assuming that all losses are offset in the year to 31 March 2026 so far as is possible?

A £20,000

B £60,000

C £70,000

D £10,000 **(2 marks)**

99 Farsight Ltd had a TWDV brought forward on the main pool of £25,000 as at 1 April 2025, and purchased new plant and machinery during the year costing £1,650,000.

What are Farsight Ltd's capital allowances for the year ended 31 March 2026?

A £1,654,500

B £301,500

C £1,675,000

D £1,121,500 **(2 marks)**

100 ***June 2024 Section A question***

Drumba Ltd prepares accounts for the year ended 31 March 2026.

The tax written down value of the special rate pool was £64,000 on 1 April 2025. On 1 October 2025 Drumba Ltd purchased a second-hand van for £19,500.

What are the maximum capital allowances which Drumba Ltd may claim for the year ended 31 March 2026?

A £5,010

B £7,350

C £23,340

D £31,020 **(2 marks)**

101 ***September 2020 Section A question***

A company made a trading loss in its final 12 months of trading.

Which of the following statements is TRUE in respect of the loss?

A It may be carried back a maximum of two years on a first in first out (FIFO) basis

B It may be carried back a maximum of two years on a last in first out (LIFO) basis

C It may be carried back a maximum of three years on a last in first out (LIFO) basis

D It may be carried back a maximum of three years on a first in first out (FIFO) basis

(2 marks)

102 ***September 2020 Section A question***

CHD Ltd's trading profit for the period of account ended 31 March 2026 has been arrived at after deducting the following items:

A loss on the sale of a van used in the business	£2,000
Legal fees relating to trading transactions	£1,500
A donation to a national charity	£4,000

What amount should be added back to the trading profit when calculating the tax adjusted profit?

A £7,500

B £6,000

C £2,000

D £5,500 **(2 marks)**

103 ***December 2020 Section A question***

PKL Ltd is four months late filing its corporation tax return for the third consecutive time.

What penalty will be imposed on PKL Ltd in respect of the late filing of its corporation tax return?

A £100

B £500

C £200

D £1,000 **(2 marks)**

104 ***December 2020 Section A question***

MNC Ltd rented out a furnished property at £2,000 a month throughout its 12-month period of account ended 31 March 2026. The rent was always paid on time until February 2026. In March 2026 the tenants left and did not pay that month's rent until June 2026. For the 12-month period of account ended 31 March 2026 the expenses of letting amounted to £9,000 in total, of which £3,000 related to mortgage interest.

How much property business income will MNC Ltd be taxed on for the 12-month period of account ended 31 March 2026?

A £15,000

B £18,000

C £13,000

D £16,000 **(2 marks)**

105 ***December 2020 Section A question***

JHF Ltd prepares financial statements annually to 31 December. The tax payable for the years ended 31 December 2024 and 31 December 2025 was £1,800,000 and £2,400,000 respectively.

In respect of the year ended 31 December 2025, when is JHF Ltd's second instalment of corporation tax due and what is the amount to be paid?

A 14 October 2025 – £450,000

B 31 July 2025 – £450,000

C 14 October 2025 – £600,000

D 31 July 2025 – £600,000 **(2 marks)**

106 ***June 2023 Section A question***

The accountant for Wowder Ltd has accidentally thrown away all the receipts, invoices and accounting records for its accounting period ended 31 December 2025.

Which of the following amounts is the maximum penalty which HM Revenue and Customs (HMRC) can impose?

A £0

B £100

C £3,000

D £500 **(2 marks)**

CAPITAL GAINS TAX

107 Mustafa had taxable gains (after the annual exempt amount) in the tax year 2025/26 as follows:

Gains on non-wasting chattels	£21,000
Gains on residential property	£11,300

Mustafa's taxable income (after deducting the personal allowance) was £21,700 for the tax year 2025/26.

What is his capital gains tax liability for the tax year 2025/26?

A £6,450

B £7,752

C £6,792

D £5,814 **(2 marks)**

108 Kel purchased a freehold office building in September 2010 and sold it for £450,000 in May 2025, generating a gain of £190,000.

They purchased a new office building in February 2026 for £415,000. Both buildings are used for trade purposes.

Assuming a claim for rollover relief is made, what is the chargeable gain arising in May 2025 on the sale of the building?

A £190,000

B £155,000

C £35,000

D £14,778 **(2 marks)**

109 Gaynor sold an antique vase for gross proceeds of £7,800 in July 2025, incurring an auctioneer's fee of 1% of the gross sales value. She bought the vase in December 2011 for £2,300.

What is Gaynor's chargeable gain?

A Nothing, the transaction is exempt from capital gains tax

B £5,422

C £5,500

D £3,000 **(2 marks)**

110 Linda sold her private residence on 1 December 2025 for £275,000, which she purchased on 1 August 2016 for £120,000. During her period of ownership, the following has occurred:

1 Aug 2016 – 31 Dec 2017	Linda lived in the house
1 Jan 2018 – 30 Jun 2018	Linda lived with her mother, while the house was repaired after a storm
1 Jul 2018 – 30 Apr 2025	Linda lived in the house
1 May 2025 – 1 Dec 2025	Linda left the house because it was haunted and lived in rented accommodation until she sold her house

For how many months does the private residence relief exemption NOT apply?

A 0

B 6

C 7

D 13 **(2 marks)**

111 Taha sold his business, which he has run for many years, in November 2025. The only chargeable asset was a freehold warehouse, which he sold and realised a chargeable gain of £800,000. Taha has no other chargeable gains during the tax year 2025/26 and has taxable income of £35,700.

What is Taha's capital gains tax liability for the tax year 2025/26 assuming all available reliefs are claimed?

A £191,280

B £111,580

C £191,160

D £112,000 **(2 marks)**

112 In August 2025, Greengrass plc sold a property for £750,000 which it purchased in April 1999 for £125,000. In February 2024 the property was extended at a cost of £30,000. Structures and buildings allowances were not available.

What is the chargeable gain arising on the disposal?

The indexation factor is:

April 1999 – December 2017 0.683

A £595,000

B £539,625

C £509,625

D £489,135 **(2 marks)**

113 ***September 2020 Section A question***

Don gifted 1,000 shares in a quoted trading company to his daughter on 4 November 2025. The shares had cost £3,000 in May 2021. The closing prices of the shares on the stock exchange daily official list on 4 November 2025 were £4.10 and £4.50.

What is the value of the shares, for capital gains purposes, on the date of the gift?

A £3,000

B £4,500

C £4,300

D £4,100 **(2 marks)**

114 XYZ Ltd sold a factory for £634,000 on 15 March 2026. The company had paid £120,000 for the factory on 2 January 2011. XYZ Ltd had incurred expenses of £8,000 in buying the factory. Structures and buildings allowances were not available.

Indexation factors are:

January 2011 to December 2017 0.214

What is XYZ Ltd's chargeable gain arising on the above disposal?

A £480,320

B £478,608

C £488,320

D £506,000 **(2 marks)**

115 ***December 2020 Section A question***

Which of the following disposals are exempt from capital gains tax (CGT)?

1 A disposal of a war medal which had been awarded to the seller

2 The sale of gilt-edged securities

3 The destruction of an asset

4 A gift to a friend

A 1, 2 and 3

B 3 and 4 only

C 2, 3 and 4

D 1 and 2 only **(2 marks)**

116 ***September 2020 Section A question***

In November 2025 Margaret sold a factory that she had used in her business. The full proceeds were used to purchase fixed plant and machinery on 5 May 2026. Margaret plans to use the fixed plant and machinery in her business and sell it in 2032. Margaret always claims any reliefs available.

Which of the following statements is TRUE?

A The gain on the factory reduces the cost of the fixed plant and machinery

B The gain on the factory is chargeable in the tax year 2025/26

C The gain on the factory could be held over until the disposal of the fixed plant and machinery in 2032

D The gain on the factory becomes chargeable ten years from the date of the disposal of the factory **(2 marks)**

117 Alexander has taxable income of £17,500 for the tax year 2025/26. He also has chargeable gains of £19,900 not qualifying for business asset disposal relief (BADR) and £40,000 of gains qualifying for BADR.

What is his capital gains tax liability for the tax year 2025/26?

A £8,642

B £9,656

C £9,956

D £10,376 **(2 marks)**

118 Assil sells some unquoted trading company shares. She does not work for the company.

The shares are sold for their full market value. Three months later, Assil reinvests all the proceeds in some more unquoted trading company shares.

Which of the following reliefs are available, if any?

A Rollover relief

B Business asset disposal relief

C Gift holdover relief

D None of the above **(2 marks)**

119 Antonella gives an antique vase to her son for his birthday. It has a market value of £7,000.

Which of the following reliefs are available, if any?

A Rollover relief

B Business asset disposal relief

C Gift holdover relief

D None of the above **(2 marks)**

120 Mikaela sells her 1% interest in unquoted trading company shares to her friend Stuart for £3,000 when their market value is £5,000.

Which of the following reliefs are available, if any?

A Rollover relief

B Business asset disposal relief

C Gift holdover relief

D None of the above **(2 marks)**

121 ***December 2020 Section A question***

Matilda carried out the following transactions in relation to her shareholding in DFT Ltd:

14 May 2012	purchased 1,000 shares
16 June 2025	purchased 500 shares
16 October 2025	purchased 2,000 shares
16 October 2025	sold 500 shares
8 November 2025	purchased 3,000 shares

The purchase on 16 June 2025 was part of a rights issue made by DFT Ltd.

Which purchase of shares must be matched to the disposal made by Matilda on 16 October 2025 for capital gains tax (CGT) purposes?

A The shares purchased on 14 May 2012

B The shares purchased on 16 June 2025

C The shares purchased on 16 October 2025

D The shares purchased on 8 November 2025 **(2 marks)**

122 ***June 2023 Section A question***

Gray Ltd sold 700 shares in Azra plc on 29 October 2025.

Gray Ltd had acquired the shares in Azra plc as follows:

Date of purchase	**Number of shares**
25 October 2025	500
29 October 2025	400
31 October 2025	600

For the purposes of calculating a chargeable gain on the disposal of Azra plc shares on 29 October 2025, which of the acquired shares are matched with the 700 sold shares?

A 400 of the shares acquired on 29 October 2025 and 300 of the shares acquired on 25 October 2025.

B 400 of the shares acquired on 29 October 2025 and 300 of the shares acquired on 31 October 2025.

C 500 of the shares acquired on 25 October 2025 and 200 of the shares acquired on 29 October 2025.

D 600 of the shares acquired on 31 October 2025 and 100 of the shares acquired on 29 October 2025. **(2 marks)**

123 ***September 2020 Section A question***

On 18 November 2025 Herman sold a painting for £5,000 incurring expenses of sale of £400. The painting had cost £7,000 in 2018.

What is Herman's allowable capital loss on the sale of the painting?

A £2,400

B £1,400

C £2,000

D £1,000 **(2 marks)**

124 ***December 2020 Section A question***

Which of the following is TRUE in respect of business asset disposal relief?

1 The minimum period of ownership of a qualifying asset is two years.

2 There is an annual limit of £1 million of gains on which relief can be claimed.

3 A personal company is one where an individual owns at least 10% of the ordinary share capital.

4 An individual must claim the relief on or before 31 January following the tax year in which the disposal is made.

A 1 and 2 only

B 2, 3 and 4

C 3 and 4 only

D 1 only **(2 marks)**

VALUE ADDED TAX

125 Y Ltd is registered for value added tax (VAT) and uses the flat rate scheme.

In the VAT quarter ended 31 March 2026, the company had a VAT-inclusive turnover of £40,000. This comprises standard-rated sales of £30,000, zero-rated sales of £8,000 and exempt sales of £2,000.

The flat rate scheme percentage for the company's trading sector is 9%.

What is the VAT payable by Y Ltd for the quarter ended 31 March 2026?

A £3,600

B £2,700

C £3,420

D £2,880 **(2 marks)**

126 Bennett Ltd has the following purchases in the quarter to 31 December 2025 (all exclusive of VAT unless stated otherwise)

Purchases:

Standard-rated	£95,000
Capital purchases:	
Car (used by sales director partly for private purposes)	£15,000
Van (inclusive of VAT)	£14,400

What is Bennett Ltd's recoverable input VAT for the quarter ended 31 December 2025?

A £21,880

B £24,400

C £19,000

D £21,400 **(2 marks)**

127 Banana plc is registered for value added tax (VAT). In the quarter ended 31 March 2026 it made sales of £172,000, exclusive of VAT. The sales were mainly standard-rated but also included £52,000 of zero-rated sales.

Banana plc is now checking the VAT return which has been automatically produced from its digital VAT records.

What is the amount that should be included in the box on the VAT return labelled 'Total value of sales and all other outputs excluding any VAT' for the quarter ended 31 March 2026?

A £144,000

B £120,000

C £196,000

D £172,000 **(2 marks)**

128 Apple plc prepared a value added tax (VAT) return for the quarter ended 31 May 2025.

By which date should this return have been received by HM Revenue and Customs?

A 31 July 2025

B 7 July 2025

C 30 June 2025

D 7 June 2025 **(2 marks)**

129 J Ltd received an order for 18,000 widgets on 14 December 2025. J Ltd despatched them to the customer on 18 December 2025. An invoice was sent on 31 December 2025 and full payment was received on 15 January 2026.

What is the tax point (i.e. the deemed date of sale for VAT purposes) for the sale of the widgets?

A 14 December 2025

B 18 December 2025

C 31 December 2025

D 15 January 2026 **(2 marks)**

130 On 17 March 2026, Z Ltd wrote off impairment losses of £1,710 and £3,660 in respect of invoices which were due for payment on 21 June 2025 and 12 November 2025 respectively. The figures are inclusive of VAT.

How much VAT can Z Ltd claim in respect of these losses in its VAT return for the quarter ended 31 March 2026?

A £895

B £1,074

C £285

D £342 **(2 marks)**

131 Which of the following is a requirement for a business to be allowed to join the value added tax (VAT) flat rate scheme?

A A VAT-exclusive annual taxable turnover of up to £150,000

B A VAT-exclusive standard-rated turnover of up to £150,000

C A VAT-inclusive annual taxable turnover of up to £150,000

D A VAT-inclusive standard-rated turnover of up to £150,000 **(2 marks)**

132 X Ltd is a VAT registered trader that prepares quarterly VAT returns.

When should the VAT for the quarter ending 30 April 2026 be paid to HM Revenue and Customs?

A 31 May 2026

B 7 June 2026

C 7 July 2026

D 7 August 2026 **(2 marks)**

133 Which of the following statements, if any, about VAT registration are true?

1 A business making wholly zero-rated supplies cannot register for VAT.

2 A business which has a taxable turnover of £60,000 in its first year of trading cannot register for VAT.

3 A business making only exempt supplies can register for VAT.

A 1 and 2 only

B 2 and 3 only

C None of them

D All of them **(2 marks)**

134 Trouper Ltd issued an invoice on 1 December 2025 for the sale of standard-rated goods worth £2,000 (VAT-exclusive) to Alson Ltd. Trouper Ltd offers a 5% discount for payment within 14 days. Alson Ltd paid the invoice on 20 December 2025.

How much output VAT should Trouper Ltd account for in respect of the sale to Alson Ltd?

A £400

B £333

C £317

D £380 **(2 marks)**

135 ***September 2020 Section A question***

Dhyana had the following expenses in her financial statements for the accounting period ended 31 March 2026:

1 Entertainment of overseas customers

2 Entertainment of UK customers

3 Entertainment of UK employees

4 A car used 100% for business purposes

On which of the above items can input value added tax (VAT) be recovered?

A 1, 2, 3 and 4

B 1, 2 and 3 only

C 2 and 4 only

D 1, 3 and 4 only **(2 marks)**

136 ***September 2020 Section A question***

UHN Ltd reported a turnover of £2,500,000 in its value added tax (VAT) return for the quarter ended 31 March 2026. In June 2026 UHN Ltd discovered an error in its VAT return for that period.

What is the de minimis limit that UHN Ltd must use to decide whether to disclose the error separately or on its next VAT return?

A £50,000

B £10,000

C £75,000

D £25,000 **(2 marks)**

137 ***December 2020 Section A question***

Dev made a business gift to a client. The cost of the gift was £80 and it would normally sell for £100. Both of these figures are exclusive of value added tax (VAT).

How much output VAT should Dev include in the VAT return in respect of the gift?

A £16

B £6

C £20

D £10 **(2 marks)**

138 ***December 2020 Section A question***

What is the turnover limit for a taxpayer wishing to join the cash accounting scheme for value added tax (VAT) purposes?

A £1,600,000 inclusive of VAT

B £1,350,000 exclusive of VAT

C £1,350,000 inclusive of VAT

D £1,600,000 exclusive of VAT **(2 marks)**

139 ***June 2024 Section A question***

APL Ltd is registered for value added tax (VAT) and uses the flat rate scheme.

In the VAT quarter ended 30 September 2025, the company had a VAT-inclusive turnover of £74,000. This comprised standard-rated sales of £60,000, zero-rated sales of £9,000 and exempt sales of £5,000.

The flat rate scheme for APL Ltd's trading sector is 10%.

How much VAT is payable by APL Ltd for the quarter ended 30 September 2025?

A £6,900

B £5,000

C £6,000

D £7,400 **(2 marks)**

Section 2

LONG FORM QUESTIONS

INTRODUCTION TO THE UK TAX SYSTEM

1 APPEALS

Eduarda has received a tax assessment from HMRC demanding £3,500 tax. Eduarda disagrees with the amount and has asked you what action she can take.

Required:

Write brief notes for a meeting with Eduarda explaining the actions she can take. You are not required to describe the working of the Tax Tribunal. (10 marks)

2 DIFFERENT TYPES OF TAXES

Amelie is a new trainee in the accountancy practice where you work. She is confused about the differences between the various taxes paid by individuals and companies.

She also does not know which ones are direct or indirect and which are capital and which revenue.

She has asked you to prepare a simple summary to help her learn these.

Required:

Complete the following table. Income tax has been completed for you. (10 marks)

Tax	**paid to HMRC by**	**On**	**Direct/ indirect**	**Capital/ revenue**
Income tax	Individuals	Employment income Self-employed income Investment income	Direct	Revenue
Corporation tax				
Capital gains tax				
VAT				
National insurance contributions				

EMPLOYMENT INCOME

3 MARY

Mary works for AB (UK) Ltd, a large UK resident company, and during the tax year 2025/26 she received the following benefits:

1. A loan to help her purchase a yacht. AB (UK) Ltd advanced her £40,000 on 6 April 2025 and charged her interest at the rate of 1% per annum. Mary repaid £8,000 of the loan on 6 July 2025, but the remaining £32,000 remains outstanding.
2. Use of a diesel Vauxhall car with a CO_2 emission rate of 106 grams per kilometre and a recommended list price of £15,000. The car does not meet the RDE2 standard. The car was first provided to Mary on 6 September 2025 for both her private and business use. The private usage is 40% and the business usage 60%. The company pays for all the running costs of the vehicle, which amounted to £1,800 (of which £500 related to fuel for private use) for the period to 5 April 2026. Mary was required to contribute £20 per month towards the private use of the car and £10 per month towards the cost of private fuel.
3. Use of a home cinema system. This was first provided to Mary to use at home on 6 April 2022, the date it was purchased by AB (UK) Ltd at a cost of £4,000. The system was gifted to Mary outright on 5 April 2026, when it was worth £900.
4. Occupational pension contributions amounting to £4,000 during the tax year 2025/26. These were paid by AB (UK) Ltd, on Mary's behalf.
5. AB (UK) Ltd paid £350 for medical treatment to enable Mary to return to work following an accident.

Required:

Calculate the total value of benefits provided to Mary for the purposes of income tax, for the tax year 2025/26. (15 marks)

4 JANA

Jana is employed by Aardvark Ltd. The company has provided her with the use of a petrol engine Jaguar car costing £26,000 from 6 April 2025. The distributor's list price for the car was £26,700. The CO_2 emissions of the car are 117 grams per kilometre. Whilst she had use of the Jaguar, Jana contributed a total of £120 being 50% of the cost of her private fuel.

Jana is also provided with a second car throughout the tax year 2025/26. This is a hybrid-electric car, with CO_2 emissions of 48g/km and an electric range of 20 miles. It cost £15,000, which was the list price. The company meets all running costs and fuel bills. The car is mainly driven by her husband and so has no business use.

Required:

Compute the total amount of benefits taxable on Jana for the two cars for the income tax year 2025/26. (5 marks)

5 MACKENZIE

Mackenzie is employed by Albatross Ltd and during the income tax year 2025/26 he is provided with the following benefit:

He occupies a house which had cost the company £80,000 when purchased in 2000. Expenditure of £40,000 had been incurred on improvements to the house prior to being occupied by Mackenzie. The house had a market value of £140,000, in 2011, when it was first occupied by Mackenzie.

Its annual value is agreed at £3,600. Mackenzie pays no rent but does meet all running costs.

Required:

(a) **Compute the total amount of accommodation benefit taxable on Mackenzie for the income tax year 2025/26. (4 marks)**

(b) **Compute any additional cost which will be borne by the company as a result of providing the above benefit. (1 mark)**

(Total: 5 marks)

6 BENEFITS PLC

You have been asked to assist in the completion of forms P11D in respect of the directors of a client company for the tax year 2025/26.

The following benefits are provided to various directors:

1 The use of a private house, owned by the company, and bought for £110,000 in 2022. The annual value of the house is £2,000 and the director concerned pays rent to the company of £1,500 per year plus all running costs.

2 A TV, which had been provided since 6 April 2022 for the private use of a director and which had cost the company £1,500, was given to the director on 6 April 2025 for a payment of £600. The market value of the TV at 6 April 2025 was £800.

3 A director has a loan of £4,000 at a 1.25% interest rate per year to help pay for a holiday. The director does not have any other loans from the company.

4 A dishwasher was purchased by the company for £280 and given to a director. The retail price was £350.

5 Medical health insurance premiums were paid for a director and his family under a group scheme at a cost to the company of £1,200. Had the director paid for this as an individual the cost would have been £1,600.

Required:

Show how each of the above benefits would be quantified for inclusion in the forms P11D. (15 marks)

7 RAVI

Ravi is a computer expert working for a UK resident company.

He is provided with a company car. The details for the tax year 2025/26 are as follows:

The car is a hybrid-electric car with a CO_2 emission rate of 34 grams per kilometre, an electric range of 60 miles, and a list price of £12,400. This was provided for Ravi's use on 6 April 2025.

Accessories amounting to £800 were added when the car was first provided.

Ravi contributed £1,000 towards the capital cost of the car. The car is used 20% for business purposes and 80% for private purposes.

The company pays for all the petrol but Ravi contributes £40 per month towards this cost. The cost to the company of providing the fuel for private use is £60 per month.

Required:

Compute the total amount of car benefit taxable on Ravi for the income tax year 2025/26. (5 marks)

8 SAMI

Sami, an employee of Newco Ltd, has asked for help in calculating the value of the benefits they are receiving from Newco Ltd. They have provided the following information regarding the benefits received during the tax year 2025/26:

1 A loan to help them purchase a new home. Newco Ltd advanced £25,000 on 6 June 2025 at an interest rate of 1% per year. Sami repaid £10,000 on 6 December 2025. The remaining £15,000 was still outstanding on 5 April 2026.

2 During the year Newco Ltd paid £3,500 into Sami's personal pension plan.

3 Assistance with relocation costs from the Newco Ltd office in Manchester to the Newco Ltd office in Winchester (a distance of 210 miles), totalling £9,500.

4 Private medical insurance cover, which had an annual cost to the company of £560. If Sami had arranged this cover personally, it would have cost them £750.

5 Workplace parking which cost the company £400.

6 Newco Ltd paid Sami's golf club subscription of £1,450. Sami occasionally takes customers of the company for a round of golf at the club.

Required:

Calculate the total value of Sami's benefits to be charged to income tax for the tax year 2025/26.

Clearly identify any benefits which are exempt from tax and, where applicable, include any alternative calculations in full as part of your workings. (10 marks)

9 AMAIA

Amaia is employed by Camel Ltd and during the tax year 2025/26 she received the following benefits:

1 A commercial van, used privately for 40% of the time. This was made available for Amaia's use for the whole of the tax year 2025/26. Camel Ltd paid for all of the running costs including petrol, which amounted to £600 for the year.

2 A home entertainment system. This was first provided for Amaia to use at home on 6 April 2023, the date it was purchased by her employer at a cost of £1,200. The system was given to Amaia to keep on 6 October 2025 when it was worth £300.

3 An allowance of £14 per night to cover miscellaneous expenses for overseas business trips totalling 80 nights.

4 A mileage allowance of 55p per mile for the 6,000 business miles travelled by Amaia in her own car.

5 Gift of a new iPad purchased on 6 August 2025 for £510.

Required:

Calculate the total value of Amaia's taxable benefits for the tax year 2025/26. (10 marks)

10 PEPPY

Peppy has worked in the London office of Pepster Ltd for the last ten years. On 1 August 2025 he was transferred to Pepster Ltd's Newcastle office, which is nearly 300 miles away.

During the tax year 2025/26 Peppy received the following benefits from Pepster Ltd:

1 A BMW car, which has a list price of £28,000. The car has a CO_2 emission rate of 178 grams per kilometre and is petrol driven. The car was first made available to Peppy on 1 July 2025 and is used for both business and private purposes. Pepster Ltd paid for all the running costs of the car, including private petrol, which amounted to £2,400 in the tax year 2025/26. Peppy paid £6,000 towards the cost of the car and £40 per month for the private use of the car.

2 A computer was provided on 6 November 2025. The computer is used at home by Peppy, exclusively for private use. Pepster Ltd paid £4,000 for the computer when it was first provided.

3 To help with Peppy's move to Newcastle, Pepster Ltd paid Peppy £10,000 in July 2025 towards his relocation costs.

4 A free place in Pepster Ltd's after-school childcare centre for Peppy's two children. The centre costs Pepster Ltd £2,600 per year, per child to run the facility.

Required:

Calculate, for the purposes of income tax, the total value of the benefits provided to Peppy in the tax year 2025/26. (10 marks)

11 JUANA

Juana is an employee of a UK resident company and received the following benefits during the tax year 2025/26:

1 Use of a house. The house was purchased by the company in 2022 for £195,000 and first occupied by Juana in 2023 when the market value was £240,000. The annual value for the tax year 2025/26 was £1,400. Juana paid £100 a month for the use of the house for the whole of the tax year 2025/26. Juana also paid all of the household expenses.

2 Loan of furniture. Juana used this furniture for the whole of the tax year 2025/26. It had a market value of £8,000 when first provided in 2023.

3 Use of the company subsidised canteen. Juana used the onsite canteen facilities for four days each week for 47 weeks. Her lunch cost her £2.50 a day but cost the company £3.50 a day to provide and would cost Juana £5.50 for the same food in a commercial restaurant.

4 Mileage allowance. Juana used her own car for both business and private purposes. She drove a total of 15,000 miles during the tax year 2025/26 of which 10,000 miles were for visits to business clients, 2,000 miles were for journeys to and from work and the remaining 3,000 miles were for private journeys. Juana's employer paid her 50p a mile for every business mile.

Required:

Calculate, for the purposes of income tax, the total value of the benefits provided to Juana in the tax year 2025/26. (10 marks)

12 DAVID

David, an employee, received the following benefits during the tax year 2025/26:

1 The use of a diesel powered company car that meets the RDE2 standard, with a list price of £100,000. The car was first provided on 6 April 2025 and was used throughout the tax year 2025/26 for both business and private purposes. The car has CO_2 emissions of 107 grams per kilometre. David paid £100 a month towards the cost of the fuel. The fuel cost the company a total of £2,900 during the tax year 2025/26 of which £2,000 was in respect of private motoring.

2 A loan of £15,000 was advanced in January 2025 to help David purchase a yacht. David repaid £3,000 of the loan on 6 January 2026 and £12,000 was outstanding on 5 April 2026. The company charged David an interest rate of 1.5% per year throughout the tax year 2025/26.

3 Course fees amounting to £3,000 were paid by the company in respect of training courses relevant to David's employment.

4 A computer, with a value of £800 when first provided in January 2025, was made available to David for his private use throughout the tax year 2025/26. The computer was not used for business purposes.

5 His employer paid David's incidental expenses amounting to £12 per night for 60 days overseas business travel, and £4 per night for 40 days UK business travel, during the tax year 2025/26.

6 David is required to work at home and receives a home working allowance of £4 per week.

Required:

Calculate, for the purposes of income tax, the value of each of the benefits provided to David for the tax year 2025/26. **(15 marks)**

13 BERNARD

On 1 October 2025 Bernard's employer provided him with a petrol driven car for his private use for the remainder of the tax year 2025/26.

The car has a CO_2 emission rate of 115 grams per kilometre and a list price of £32,000.

Bernard made a contribution of £6,000 towards the cost of the car.

Bernard's employer did not provide any fuel for private purposes.

Required:

Calculate the taxable benefit for Bernard in respect of the car for the tax year 2025/26.
(5 marks)

PERSONAL TAX

14 YUSIF

Yusif has worked for AB (UK) Ltd since 2012 and he has provided you with the following information regarding his income and outgoings for the tax year 2025/26:

Income

1 A gross salary of £92,000.

2 A bonus of £8,000, received in May 2025, in respect of the company's accounting year ended 31 December 2024. A bonus of £10,000 was received in May 2026 in respect of AB (UK) Ltd's accounting year ended 31 December 2025.

3 Taxable benefits with a value for tax purposes of £4,350.

4 Dividends received from UK companies of £2,000.

5 Interest credited to his bank account of £3,000.

6 Interest received from NS&I savings certificates of £400.

7 Premium bond prizes received of £1,500.

Expenditure

1 Pension contributions paid to AB (UK) Ltd's HMRC registered occupational pension scheme of £400 per month.

2 A donation of £800 (net) paid to a UK registered charity in August 2025 under the gift aid scheme.

For the tax year 2025/26, £27,987 was deducted from Yusif's employment income under PAYE.

Required:

Calculate the income tax payable by Yusif for the tax year 2025/26. **(15 marks)**

15 ANITA AND GREGORY

Anita's only income in the tax year 2025/26 was £18,125 interest received from savings invested in a building society account.

Gregory's only income for the tax year 2025/26 was dividends from shares held in a UK company. His taxable income (after the personal allowance) was £6,400.

Required:

Calculate the income tax liability (if any) of Anita and Gregory respectively for the tax year 2025/26. (5 marks)

16 CARLOTA

Carlota is a client of Nuttal & Co, Chartered Certified Accountants. She has sent in the papers for completing her tax return for the year ended 5 April 2026 and, as the tax assistant, you have been asked to prepare her tax computation.

The envelope contains the following:

1 P60s – extracted details:

	Gross	Tax	Net
	£	£	£
ABC plc	1,927	292	1,635

2 Self-employment

Carlota has operated a small business from home, realising trading profits of £4,000 during the tax year 2025/26. She also has a transition profit of £796 for the tax year 2025/26.

3 Statements of bank and building society interest – extracted details:

Account	Type of account	Income
		£
NS&I	Investment	70
Walton Bank	Deposit	5,806
Walton Bank	ISA	328
Guilding Building Society	Deposit	6,813

4 Dividend vouchers received from various companies totalling £17,000.

5 A photocopy of a gift aid declaration in respect of a gift of £100 to Oxfam on 1 June 2025.

Required:

(a) Prepare Carlota's income tax computation for the tax year 2025/26 showing tax payable. (12 marks)

(b) State the dates on which income tax is payable under self-assessment and describe how the payments on account are calculated. (3 marks)

(Total: 15 marks)

17 ZARA

Zara is employed as an advertising manager for Ads4U Ltd, a UK resident company.

It is now 14 June 2026 and Zara is preparing her tax return for the tax year 2025/26. She has gathered together the following documents and other information for that year:

1 Form P60 showing taxable employment income of £99,110 and income tax deducted under PAYE of £28,746

2 Form P11D showing total taxable benefits received of £2,290

3 A bank statement from County Bank plc showing interest credited of £350

4 An interest statement from Town Building Society showing interest credited of £450

5 A statement from City Building Society showing interest credited of £120 from an individual savings account (ISA)

6 Dividend vouchers showing cash dividends received totalling £300

7 A letting agent's statement showing taxable property income of £820

8 An amount of £320 was paid to a registered charity under the gift aid scheme.

Required:

Calculate Zara's income tax payable for the tax year 2025/26. **(15 marks)**

18 CORAL

Coral is employed by Pepster Ltd and has provided you with the following information regarding her income and outgoings for the tax year 2025/26:

Income

1 A gross salary of £45,050.

2 A bonus of £6,000 received in May 2025.

3 Benefits with a taxable value for income tax purposes of £2,500.

4 Dividends of £500 received from UK companies in August 2025.

5 Bank interest of £500 credited to her UK bank account in December 2025.

6 Building society interest of £360 credited to her individual savings account (ISA) in March 2026.

7 A prize of £2,400 from gambling on the national lottery.

8 Rental income of £4,800. This is the total taxable amount for the tax year 2025/26 from a house owned jointly with her husband.

Expenditure

1 A total amount of £120 paid to a UK charity under an approved payroll giving scheme, administered by Pepster Ltd.

2 Personal pension contributions amounting to £3,728 (net) paid to an HM Revenue and Customs (HMRC) registered pension provider.

3 Professional subscriptions of £180 to an HMRC approved professional body relevant to Coral's employment.

£7,305 was deducted from Coral's employment income under PAYE for the tax year 2025/26.

Required:

Calculate the income tax payable by Coral for the tax year 2025/26. **(15 marks)**

19 FREDA

Freda works as a senior manager receiving an annual salary of £45,650.

Freda received a bonus of £8,000 in February 2026.

For the tax year 2025/26 Freda's employer deducted £7,546 income tax (under PAYE) from Freda's income.

Freda also received the following income during the tax year 2025/26:

Dividends from UK companies	£1,000
Bank interest	£2,000
NS&I savings certificate interest	£600
NS&I investment account interest	£400

All the above sums were the amounts received or credited to the accounts.

Freda paid professional subscriptions of £240 to an HM Revenue and Customs (HMRC) approved professional body relevant to her employment.

Freda is a member of the company's occupational pension scheme. In the tax year 2025/26 the company paid £2,400 into the scheme on Freda's behalf. Freda, herself, contributed £1,800.

Required:

Calculate the income tax payable by Freda for the tax year 2025/26. (15 marks)

20 DIEGO

Diego has been in partnership with Fahrid for many years. During the accounting years ending 30 April 2025 and 30 April 2026 the partnership had taxable trading profits of £200,300 and £211,500 respectively. The profits are always split 60% to Diego and 40% to Fahrid.

Diego borrowed £10,000 from a local bank in January 2025 to help purchase plant and machinery for use in the partnership. Interest is charged at a rate of 8% per year. The full amount of the loan is still outstanding.

Diego paid £1,600 net to a personal pension plan during the tax year 2025/26.

Diego received the following investment income during the tax year 2025/26:

Interest from a NS&I savings certificate	£1,800
Interest from a NS&I investment account	£2,100
Premium bond prizes	£250
UK dividends	£8,000

The above amounts are the actual amounts received or credited to the account.

Required:

Calculate Diego's income tax liability for the tax year 2025/26. (15 marks)

21 GEMING

Geming ceased to trade on 30 September 2025. His trading profits for the year ended 30 September 2025 were £24,000. On 1 October 2025 Geming started part time employment earning a gross salary of £38,850 for the six-month period ended 31 March 2026. His employer deducted £5,270 income tax (under PAYE) in the tax year 2025/26.

Geming purchased a house in July 2025 and let the house to students from 1 August 2025 at a total monthly rent of £1,100. The students paid the monthly rent in advance for every month until February 2026. However, in March 2026 they left without paying the amount due for that month.

Geming paid £300 house insurance for the year commencing 1 August 2025. He also purchased furniture for £800 to replace older furniture which was sold for £200. A new shed was purchased for £1,600 in November 2025.

In addition to the above Geming received the following amounts for the tax year 2025/26:

	£
Dividends from UK companies	3,500
Interest from UK building societies	1,800
Interest from National Savings & Investments (NS & I) certificates	900

Geming made a gift aid payment of £800 in June 2025 and contributed £3,000 to a registered occupational pension scheme during the tax year 2025/26.

Required:

Calculate the income tax payable by Geming for the tax year 2025/26. Your answer should identify any item which is not taxable, tax exempt or not deductible and state why the amount is not included in your computation. (15 marks)

22 STEPHEN

Stephen is one of three partners in SP & Sons. Recently, he also started part-time employment.

SP & Sons had a trading profit of £38,500 for the year ended 31 March 2026. Profits were shared as follows: 3 parts to partner A and 2 parts each to partner B and to Stephen. There were no salaries nor interest paid on capital.

On 1 August 2025 Stephen started earning a gross salary of £108,000 a year from his employment. For the period 1 August 2025 to 31 March 2026, Stephen's employer deducted £15,100 income tax (under PAYE) and also paid £12,000 towards his occupational pension scheme.

In addition to the above Stephen received the following amounts for the tax year 2025/26:

	£
Interest from an individual savings account (ISA)	3,500
Dividends from UK companies	4,000
Interest from a UK building society	3,000

During the tax year 2025/26 Stephen paid the following amounts:

	£
Interest on a loan to purchase equipment to be used in his new employment	2,000
Fees to a professional body approved by HM Revenue and Customs (HMRC)	400
Golf club membership fee where he entertains clients for SP & Sons	500
Contributions to a registered occupational pension scheme	3,000
Contributions to a HMRC approved private pension scheme	6,000

Required:

Calculate the income tax payable by Stephen for the tax year 2025/26. Your answer should identify any item that is not taxable, tax exempt or not deductible. (15 marks)

23 MORGAN

Morgan has just started business as a sole trader.

Required:

Write brief notes, explaining the following matters to Morgan:

(i) The dates on which payments on account (POA) are due.

(ii) How POA are calculated.

(iii) The circumstances in which POA would not be required. (5 marks)

PROPERTY INCOME

24 BERNICE

Bernice works as a systems analyst for a large UK resident company. During the tax year 2025/26 she received a salary of £82,000 from her employer.

In addition to the above the company paid, on behalf of Bernice, £200 a month into the company's occupational pension scheme. Bernice does not make any contributions to the pension scheme herself.

Bernice also received £160 a week throughout the tax year 2025/26 from her lodger, who occupies a furnished room in her home. It is estimated that 10% of Bernice's household expenses, which amount to £1,800 in total for the year, relate to letting the room to the lodger. The lodger has lived with Bernice for many years.

Required:

(a) Calculate Bernice's taxable property income for the tax year 2025/26. (3 marks)

(b) State the tax implications for both Bernice and the company of the pension contributions made by the company on behalf of Bernice. (2 marks)

(Total: 5 marks)

25 ADRIANA

Adriana owns a house, which is not her main residence and which is let furnished to tenants.

The annual rent payable in advance by equal monthly instalments on the 6th of each month was £7,200 until December 2025 but was increased to £7,800 with effect from 6 January 2026. All amounts were received on time with the exception of that due for 6 March 2026, which was not received until 2 May 2026.

Expenditure relating to the property for the tax year 2025/26 was as follows:

	£
Water rates	300
Insurance	250
Decoration costs	2,250
Free-standing kitchen units	3,200
New TV cabinet	400

All these amounts were paid in the tax year 2025/26 by Adriana with the exception of £500 of the decoration costs. The total cost of decoration work which was carried out in May 2025 was £2,250 however, Adriana had to pay a deposit of £500 to the trader in March 2025. The balance of £1,750 was paid in June 2025.

The kitchen units were purchased to replace the existing out-dated units in an attempt to modernise the property. They are the modern equivalent of the previous units. The property did not previously have a TV cabinet.

Required:

Calculate the amount of property income taxable for the tax year 2025/26. You are not required to calculate the amount of tax payable. (10 marks)

26 HASNAA

Hasnaa owns a house, which she rents out fully furnished.

The house had been rented for £800 a month for the two years up to 31 December 2025. The same family had been occupying the house during this period and all the rent had been paid on time at the end of each month, with the exception of the last amount due for December 2025. Despite all possible attempts to recover this month's rent it still remains unpaid and it is doubtful that it will ever be collected.

From 1 January 2026 a new tenant occupied the property and the rent was increased to £880 per month. The rent due for January 2026 and February 2026 was paid on time but the rent for March 2026 was not paid until 24 April 2026.

Hasnaa's expenditure in respect of the house was:

1 House contents insurance: £600 paid in January 2025 and £800 paid in January 2026. Both amounts were paid in advance for the year to come.

2 Letting agent's commission: 10% of the gross rents received in the year to 31 March 2026 was paid on 31 March 2026.

3 Minor repairs: £250 paid in August 2025.

4 Water rates: £300 for the period 1 April 2025 to 31 March 2026 paid on 10 April 2025.

5 A new garage building: £15,000 paid in June 2025.

6 A new fridge-freezer costing £2,500. This was purchased in May 2025 to replace the existing fridge, which was sold for £100. The modern equivalent of the old fridge would have cost £1,200.

Required:

Calculate the amount taxable on Hasnaa in respect of property income for the tax year 2025/26. (10 marks)

27 ROBERTA

Roberta rents a property from Paula. She paid a premium of £20,000 for a 26-year lease, which started on 1 May 2025. Roberta also paid annual rent of £800 in advance on 1 May 2025.

The property is used in Roberta's business, which has an accounting year end of 31 December 2025. Roberta uses the accruals basis to calculate her trading profits.

Required:

Calculate:

(a) the amount of property income taxable on Paula for the tax year 2025/26, and

(b) the amount that Roberta may deduct from her taxable trading profit for the accounting period ending 31 December 2025. (5 marks)

28 JOHANN

(a) Johann decided to lease new business premises. He paid a premium of £18,000 for the grant of a ten-year lease. Johann uses the accruals basis to calculate his trading profits.

Required:

Calculate the annual amount Johann is able to deduct from his taxable trading profits in respect of the premium paid. (3 marks)

(b) Gilbert received £75 a week from his lodger throughout the tax year 2025/26. The extra household expenses that Gilbert incurred as a result of letting out the furnished room were £15 per week. In addition Gilbert incurred £3,390 on replacing carpets and curtains in the lodger's bedroom in the tax year 2025/26.

Required:

Calculate Gilbert's taxable profit or allowable loss on his letting assuming he makes any beneficial elections. (2 marks)

(Total: 5 marks)

29 AYANA

Ayana rents out a fully furnished house. In the tax year 2025/26 she had the following income and expenditure.

Rental income	£1,200 received each month when let
Insurance	£200 per year paid 1 April 2025, £240 paid 1 April 2026
Agents fees	12% of gross income received – paid 5 April 2026

The house was let throughout the whole of the tax year 2025/26 apart from one month when Ayana lived in the property herself.

Ayana also drove 800 miles on property business during the year. She claims the approved mileage allowance payment in respect of this mileage.

Required:

Calculate Ayana's taxable property income for the tax year 2025/26. (5 marks)

TRADING PROFIT

30 OLGA

Olga is a sole trader. She has provided the following information about her business for the year ended 31 March 2026:

1 During the year, Olga received £45,000 from sales. This included £3,000 which Olga was owed at 31 March 2025 and which the customer paid in April 2025. At 31 March 2026, Olga was owed a further £7,000 from sales made in March 2026.

2 Olga paid office insurance costs of £2,000 on 1 July 2025 for the year ended 30 June 2026. She had paid £1,800 on 1 July 2024 for insurance costs for the year ended 30 June 2025.

3 Olga paid £18,000 to buy land near her office for clients to use to park in December 2025. She paid £4,000 for office equipment in January 2026.

4 She paid £500 to entertain clients at a restaurant in February 2026.

5 Other allowable business costs incurred during the year were £15,000, including £1,000 owed to suppliers at the year end. No amounts were owing at 1 April 2025.

Required:

Calculate the trading profit for the year ended 31 March 2026. Ignore VAT.

Any item that is not deductible or taxable should be shown with the number zero (i.e. 0). (10 marks)

31 TANYA

Tanya runs a small retail business selling Do-It-Yourself (DIY) items. She has been in business for many years preparing accounts annually to 31 October. Tanya uses the accruals basis.

The following is her statement of profit or loss for the year ending 31 October 2025.

	£	£
Gross profit		25,000
Bank interest received		280
Profit on sale of cash register		100
		25,380
Less Expenses:		
Electricity	380	
Car expenses (Tanya's car)	600	
Lease rental for Tanya's car	1,000	
Depreciation of equipment/car	450	
Repairs and renewals	800	
Administration expenses	10,351	
Rent	4,800	
Donations	350	
		(18,731)
Net profit per accounts		6,649

Notes:

1 The car is used 75% for business purposes and 25% for private purposes, and has CO_2 emissions of 68g/km.

2 The depreciation is in respect of:

Shop equipment	£300
Car	£150

3 The repairs and renewals comprise:

General shop repairs	£200
New shop counters	£600

4 The administration expenses are all tax deductible business expenses.

5 The donations were:

To the local Conservative Party	£200
To the local Chamber of Commerce	£150

6 Tanya lives in the flat above the shop and the rent and electricity are to be split 60% to the shop and 40% to the flat.

7 Capital allowances for the year amounted to £600 (this has been calculated taking into account any relevant detail from the above notes).

Required:

Calculate the tax adjusted trading profit for the year ended 31 October 2025.

Any item that does not require adjustment should be shown as the number zero (i.e. 0).
(10 marks)

32 DUNCAN

Duncan is a sole trader who elects for the accruals basis. He had the following transactions relating to plant and machinery during his nine-month accounting period ended 31 March 2026:

Purchases:

14 January 2026	A machine was purchased for £180,000.
17 March 2026	A car, with a CO_2 emission rate of 90 grams per kilometre, was purchased for £27,000.

Disposals:

6 July 2025	A machine, which had cost £95,000, was sold for £38,000.
12 December 2025	A car, with a CO_2 emission rate of 70 grams per kilometre, was sold for £13,000. This car had cost Duncan £17,000.

The car sold in December 2025 was used by Duncan 40% for private purposes and 60% for business purposes. The car purchased in March 2026 is used by him 50% for each of private and business purposes.

For capital allowances purposes Duncan brought forward the following tax written down values as at 1 July 2025:

Main pool	£52,000
Private use asset	£12,000

Required:

Calculate the maximum capital allowances Duncan can claim for the nine-month accounting period ended 31 March 2026. **(10 marks)**

33 SUSAN

Susan has been a sole trader for the last ten years, selling bathroom accessories. She elects to use the accruals basis.

Susan's most recent trading results for the year ended 31 December 2025 are as follows:

	Note	£	£
Gross profit			84,000
Expenses:			
Wages	1	38,000	
Shop rent		3,000	
Electricity	2	4,400	
Business rates		2,200	
Depreciation		1,000	
Car expenses	3	1,800	
Irrecoverable trade debt written off		200	
Parking fine	4	400	
Legal fees	5	300	
Donations to local trade association		100	
			(51,400)
Net profit			32,600

Notes:

1 Included in the wages figure of £38,000 is an amount of £24,000 in respect of Susan's drawings and £2,000 in wages for her son, Mike, who works part time in the shop. All other employees receive the same hourly rate of pay as Susan's son.

2 The electricity cost relates to the whole building. Susan lives in the flat above the shop and 40% of the electricity relates to the shop and 60% to the flat above.

3 Susan's car is used 30% for business purposes and 70% for private purposes.

4 The parking fine was issued to Susan whilst she was on a business trip.

5 The legal fees comprise:

Expenses relating to the renewal of the ten-year lease of the shop	£250
Personal capital gains tax advice	£50

6 Capital allowances of £800 have been claimed by Susan for the year ended 31 December 2025.

7 Susan takes inventory from the shop for her own use. During the year ended 31 December 2025 the inventory taken had a cost of £800 and a normal selling price of £1,250. No adjustment for the withdrawal of this inventory has been made in the books of account.

Required:

Calculate Susan's tax adjusted trading profit for the year ended 31 December 2025.

Any item that does not require adjustment should be shown as the number zero (i.e. 0).

List any items that do not require adjustment and give reasons why no adjustment has been made. (10 marks)

34 JI-HO

Ji-ho started a new business on 1 November 2024 and his first set of accounts was prepared to 31 December 2025. He registered for VAT from the first day of business. He elects to use the accruals basis.

On 14 January 2025, Ji-ho purchased plant and machinery for £85,920 (inclusive of VAT) and on 16 May 2025 he purchased a car for £14,000 (inclusive of VAT). The car was used 60% for business and 40% for private purposes by Ji-ho and has CO_2 emissions of 50g/km. On 1 July 2025, Ji-ho purchased a computer for £6,144 (inclusive of VAT) which he uses 100% for business purposes.

Required:

Calculate the maximum capital allowances for plant and machinery available to Ji-ho in his first period of account. **(10 marks)**

LOSSES

35 KEVIN

Kevin started trading as a builder in May 2015. His trading profit for the year ended 31 March 2026 was £15,000. In the year ended 31 March 2027 Kevin expects to make a trading loss of £20,000 for income tax purposes.

Kevin's only other source of income is an account with a UK bank. The interest credited on 31 March 2026 was £1,237.

His wife, Susan, is a teacher at a girls' boarding school. The following information is provided:

1 Susan's remuneration for the year ended 5 April 2026 was £25,000.

2 She was also provided with a house throughout the tax year 2025/26, where she is required to live by her employer for the better performance of her duties. The gross annual value of the house, which is owned by the school, is £1,000. The house cost £170,000 in 2022.

3 In the tax year ended 5 April 2026, the school paid £1,500 for gas, electricity and decorating in respect of the house.

Required:

(a) **Calculate the income tax liability of Kevin for the tax year 2025/26 assuming that Kevin claims relief for his trading loss against his total income for the tax year 2025/26.**

Explain the effect (if any) on the savings income nil rate band of making a claim against total income.

(b) **State the amount of trading loss remaining and the options available for this remaining loss.**

(c) **Calculate the income tax liability of Susan for the tax year 2025/26.** **(15 marks)**

36 BI

Bi runs a small business from home which she commenced in 2004.

Her recent trading profits/(losses) are:

	£
Tax year 2024/25	13,500
Tax year 2025/26	(15,000)
Tax year 2026/27	3,400

Bi has other non-savings income of £16,000 in the tax year 2024/25, £4,000 in the tax year 2025/26 and £26,000 in the tax year 2026/27.

She has written to you asking for advice on the use of the trading loss arising in the tax year 2025/26.

Required:

Write brief notes for a meeting with Bi, covering the following:

- **the tax years in which the loss can be used**
- **the income it can be used against, and**
- **three planning points to consider when deciding which loss relief claim to make.**

Note: You are not required to make a final decision or to show any calculations.

(10 marks)

37 NICOLE

Nicole has been trading as a sole trader for several years preparing accounts to 31 December.

Her trading profit for the tax year 2024/25 has already been calculated as £21,850.

Further details of her trading profits/(losses) for accounting periods are:

Year ended 31 December 2025	£(40,000)
Year ended 31 December 2026 (estimated)	£6,600

Nicole expects to make trading profits in all future years.

In addition to her income as a sole trader, Nicole receives savings income of approximately £3,000 every tax year.

Required:

(a) **Calculate Nicole's trading loss for the tax year 2025/26.**

(b) **Show how the loss can be used as early as possible. Nicole is keen not to waste her personal allowance if this can be avoided.**

(c) **State the date by which Nicole must make her loss relief claim.**

Assume that the tax rules for the tax year 2025/26 apply throughout. **(10 marks)**

38 MICHELLE

Michelle has been trading as a sole trader for many years. Michelle's trading profits/(losses) for recent tax years are:

	£
2023/24	22,000 profit
2024/25	(44,000) loss
2025/26	16,000 profit

Michelle's only other income was the following amounts of property income for the tax years shown:

	£
2023/24	4,000
2024/25	3,000
2025/26	6,000

Required:

On the assumption that Michelle claims loss relief in the most beneficial manner, calculate her taxable income for each of the three tax years concerned and show the amount of trade loss carried forward to 2026/27.

Notes:

1 Your answer should consider all possible loss relief claims, clearly stating if a claim is not beneficial and why.

2 You should assume that the personal allowance for 2025/26 applies to all tax years.

(10 marks)

PARTNERSHIPS

39 SEAN AND LAUREN

Sean and Lauren had been in partnership for several years preparing accounts to 31 December every year.

On 1 January 2026 Helena was admitted as a partner.

Prior to 1 January 2026 profits and losses had always been shared equally but from 1 January 2026 the profit sharing ratio was changed to 2:2:1 between Sean, Lauren and Helena respectively.

No salaries or interest on capital are paid.

Trading profits for the partnership are:

Year to 31 December 2025	£18,000
Year to 31 December 2026 (estimated)	£25,000

Required:

For each partner calculate the taxable trading profits for the tax year 2025/26. (5 marks)

40 MCBETH, MCDUFF AND MCBRIDE

Gary McBeth was a partner in McBeth, McDuff and McBride, a firm of carpenters based in Scotland. The partnership had been in existence since October 2007.

On 31 October 2025 Gary decided to leave the partnership and start his own business.

The partnership has always made up accounts to 31 December annually and had agreed that profits should be shared 50% to McBeth and 25% to each of the other partners. Each partner was paid an annual salary of £9,600 and interest on capital of 2%. McBeth, McDuff and McBride had contributed capital of £24,000, £18,000 and £12,000 respectively to the business.

After Gary's departure the remaining two partners carried on the partnership with the same salaries, however they no longer received interest on capital and shared the remaining profit equally.

The partnership's trading profit for the year ended 31 December 2025 was £54,000.

Required:

Calculate each partner's share of the trading profit for the year ended 31 December 2025. (10 marks)

41 CHARLES, MEG AND RODNEY

Charles, Meg and Rodney have been in partnership for several years making up their accounts to 31 December annually. Profits have always been shared equally after allocation of salaries of £10,000 and £8,000 to Charles and Meg respectively and interest on capital of 5% to each of the three partners.

The partners have capital invested amounting to:

Charles	£20,000
Meg	£16,000
Rodney	£12,000

On 30 June 2025 Rodney left the partnership and withdrew his capital to start his own business. The remaining two partners carried on the partnership, no longer paying salaries but continuing to pay interest on capital and sharing any balance of profits equally between them.

The trading profit for the year ended 31 December 2025 was £120,000.

Required:

Calculate the profit share attributable to each partner for the accounting period ending 31 December 2025. (10 marks)

42 CAROL, WENDY AND BOB

Carol, Wendy and Bob have been in partnership for several years. Carol receives an annual salary of £10,000 and each partner receives 4% interest on the capital they have contributed. The balance of profits is shared in the ratio of 3:1:1 to Carol, Wendy and Bob respectively.

The capital amounts contributed are:

Carol	£40,000
Wendy	£20,000
Bob	£10,000

For the accounting year ended 31 January 2026 the partnership's trading loss was £80,000.

Required:

Calculate each partner's share of the trading loss from the partnership for the accounting year ended 31 January 2026. (5 marks)

43 PETER, SAM AND MARTHA

Peter, Sam and Martha have been in partnership since early 2010. Due to a fall in demand for their services Martha decided to leave the partnership on 30 September 2025.

Taxable trading profits for the partnership for the two most recent periods of account have been:

Year to 31 December 2024	£60,000
Year to 31 December 2025	£45,000

Up to 30 September 2025 each partner received a salary of £10,000 per year and shared the remaining profits as follows: Peter 40%, Sam 40% and Martha 20%.

Following Martha's departure, the salaries for Peter and Sam remained the same and the remaining profits were shared equally.

Required:

Compute each partner's share of the trading profit for the years ended 31 December 2024 and 2025, and Martha's trading profits for the tax year 2025/26. (10 marks)

PENSIONS AND NIC

44 AVERY

Avery, who is aged 36, is the only employee of Modern Fashions Ltd and received a salary of £48,000 for the tax year 2025/26. In addition she had a car benefit calculated as £2,400 for that year. She is not a director and did not receive any bonuses.

Required:

Calculate for both Avery and Modern Fashions Ltd, the total national insurance contributions due for the tax year 2025/26. (5 marks)

45 KARLA

Karla is 41 years old. She has never previously been a member of a pension plan, but feels it is now time to think about her retirement.

Her only income for the tax year 2025/26 is trading income, estimated to be £37,000.

It is now 1 March 2026.

Required:

Advise Karla of:

(a) **the maximum gross amount that she may contribute into a private personal pension plan on which she will obtain tax relief for the tax year 2025/26** **(3 marks)**

(b) **the implications of the annual allowance** **(2 marks)**

(c) **how tax relief will be given for the contributions paid** **(3 marks)**

(d) **how your answer to (a) would differ if her only income was dividend income of the same amount.** **(2 marks)**

(Total: 10 marks)

46 PETER

Peter, aged 45, works for Sports (UK) Ltd. During the tax year 2025/26 he was paid a basic salary of £2,210 per month. In addition he received a cash bonus of £7,500 in February 2026.

Peter contributed 5% of his basic salary to the company's occupational pension scheme. Sports (UK) Ltd provided Peter with private medical insurance which cost the company £200 per year and a free place for his daughter in its childcare facilities. Each place costs the company £2,000 per year.

Required:

Calculate the amount of national insurance contributions (NICs) payable by Peter and Sports (UK) Ltd for the tax year 2025/26, clearly show your treatment of each element of Peter's employment package. You should ignore the NIC employment allowance in your answer. **(10 marks)**

47 PAUL

Paul wants to start making contributions to a pension plan. His employer has advised him that it has an HMRC registered occupational pension scheme that he can join. However, a friend has told him that both he and his employer can contribute to a personal pension plan instead.

He has asked you, as his tax advisor, for information on the two forms of pension scheme. You have arranged a meeting with Paul to discuss the information he requires.

Required:

Write brief notes, to be used at a meeting with Paul, explaining the following points:

- **The maximum contributions allowed per year on which tax relief is available.**
- **The method(s) of him obtaining tax relief.**
- **The tax effects, if any, of the company making contributions to the plans on his behalf.**

Your answer should only cover the above points.

You are not required to mention the rules on receiving benefits from the pension fund.
(10 marks)

48 NORMAN

Norman was self-employed throughout the tax year 2025/26 and had trading profits of £52,000. He made a gross personal pension contribution of £1,000 in the tax year 2025/26.

Required:

Calculate the national insurance contributions (NICs) payable by Norman for the tax year 2025/26 and state the due dates of payment of these contributions. (5 marks)

49 LEON

Leon is a sole trader. His understanding of national insurance contributions (NIC) is very poor. He knows he must account for and pay NICs in respect of himself and his staff but does not know how to do this.

All of his employees are paid monthly and none receive any benefits.

Required:

List the classes of national insurance contributions (NIC) that Leon must account for, for both himself and his employees.

In each case state on what income they are calculated and by when they should be paid to HMRC.

You are not required to calculate the actual amounts of NICs due. (10 marks)

50 JAVIER

Javier is a sole trader. His trading profits are:

	£
Year ended 31 December 2025	51,000
Year ended 31 December 2026 (estimated)	59,000

Required:

Calculate the national insurance contributions (NIC) payable by Javier for the tax year 2025/26 and state by when each of the amounts calculated should be paid. (5 marks)

INCOME TAX ADMINISTRATION

51 MATILDA

Matilda has run a small tea shop for several years.

Matilda is thinking of employing a friend, part-time, paying her £11 per hour. This will take place sometime in May 2026.

She has come to you as her accountant for advice on this.

Required:

State what action, in respect of tax and national insurance, is required by Matilda if she does employ her friend in her business.

Brief notes only are required. (5 marks)

52 KARTER

Karter is about to complete their tax return for the tax year 2025/26. They intend to submit a paper return but also wish to know the deadline to submit the return online.

Required:

(a) **State which form gives details of Karter's total taxable earnings and tax deducted for the tax year 2025/26, and by which date they must receive a copy of this form from their employer. (2 marks)**

(b) **State which form gives details of the cash equivalents of Karter's benefits received for the tax year 2025/26, and by which date they must receive a copy of this form from their employer. (2 marks)**

(c) **State the latest date by which Karter must submit their tax return for the tax year 2025/26 to HMRC if they wish to submit an electronic return. (1 mark)**

(Total: 5 marks)

53 NOAM

Noam is a sole trader and has made trading profits every year for the last six years.

His income tax payable for the tax year 2024/25 was £5,800 and has been paid in full.

Noam's final tax bill for the tax year 2025/26 has been calculated as £6,400.

Required:

State how the liability of £6,400 for the tax year 2025/26 will be settled and prepare a schedule showing the date and amount of each payment. (5 marks)

54 ALTHEA

In the tax year 2024/25 Althea's income tax liability was £8,600 of which £7,000 was paid through PAYE. In the tax year 2025/26 her income tax liability is expected to be £10,400 of which £4,800 will be deducted through PAYE.

Required:

State, with supporting explanations, the amount of income tax that Althea is required to pay on 31 January 2027. (5 marks)

55 RICHARD

Richard has just left his employment with Auckland plc. He is planning to start his own business in which he will have three full time employees paid monthly.

Required:

(a) State which form Auckland plc must give to Richard when he leaves. (1 mark)

(b) Explain what information Richard must supply each month to HMRC under the Real Time information (RTI) scheme in respect of his employees. (4 marks)

(Total: 5 marks)

56 ESTHER

Esther has been a sole trader for several years and her tax payable for the tax year 2024/25 was as follows:

	£
Income tax payable	7,490
Class 4 national insurance contributions (NIC)	3,370
Capital gains tax payable	5,400
Total tax payable	16,260

Required:

(a) Calculate the amounts of payments on account payable by Esther for the tax year 2025/26. (2 marks)

(b) State the dates on which payments on account payable by Esther for the tax year 2025/26 are due. (2 marks)

(c) State the date on which the balancing payment payable by Esther for the tax year 2025/26 will be due. (1 mark)

(Total: 5 marks)

57 LIN

Lin, a sole trader, paid the following amounts of tax for the tax year 2024/25:

Income tax	£16,000
Class 4 national insurance contributions (NIC)	£3,000
Capital gains tax	£1,700

For the tax year 2025/26 Lin's tax liabilities are expected to be as follows:

Income tax	£19,300
Class 4 NIC	£3,500
Capital gains tax	£2,300

Lin had no income tax deducted from his income via PAYE.

Required:

In respect of Lin's tax liabilities for the tax year 2025/26, state the due dates of payment of tax, together with the amounts payable on each date.

You should ignore any payments on account for the tax year 2026/27. (10 marks)

CAPITAL GAINS: INDIVIDUALS

58 YE-JUN

Ye-jun disposed of several capital assets in the tax year 2025/26 as follows:

14 July 2025:

Four hectares of land were sold for £240,000. They had been part of a larger plot of 12 hectares, which had been purchased on 2 May 2010 for £360,000. Auctioneer's fees of 5% were payable on the sale proceeds. The market value of the remaining eight hectares in July 2025 was £400,000.

14 December 2025:

An antique desk that had cost £3,916 in September 2002 was sold for £9,009 net of 10% auctioneers' fees.

6 February 2026:

A painting, which had cost £42,000 in May 2009, was sold for £9,500 after it was discovered it was not an original.

None of the assets had been used in a business.

Required:

Calculate the total net chargeable gains (before deducting the annual exempt amount) for Ye-jun for the tax year 2025/26. (10 marks)

59 JOHN AND IMRAN

(a) John made the following chargeable gains, none of which qualify for business asset disposal relief (BADR), in the tax year 2025/26:

£92,000 in respect of an investment residential property

£14,000 in respect of shares in X plc

£3,000 in respect of an antique table

John also made an allowable capital loss of £5,000 on the sale of a fourth asset in the tax year 2025/26.

John's taxable income for the tax year 2025/26 was £29,500.

Required:

Calculate the capital gains tax payable by John for the tax year 2025/26. (6 marks)

(b) In the tax year 2025/26 Imran has gains of £15,000, allowable capital losses of £2,000 and capital losses brought forward of £13,000.

Required:

Calculate how much capital loss (if any) Imran has to carry forward to the tax year 2026/27. (4 marks)

(Total: 10 marks)

60 LETHABO

Lethabo is a UK resident with an annual taxable income of £50,000.

During the tax year 2025/26 he made the following capital disposals:

12 July 2025:

10 hectares of farmland, sold for £90,000. The farmland was part of a 25-hectare field that Paul had purchased in November 2008 for £54,000 plus purchase expenses of £3,000. The market value of the remaining 15 hectares on 12 July 2025 was £180,000.

14 November 2025:

A vintage car, sold for £36,000. The car had been purchased in October 2008 for £21,000.

2 February 2026:

A painting, sold for £5,000. The painting had been inherited in May 2010. The market (probate) value at the date of the inheritance was £8,200.

Required:

Calculate the total net chargeable gains (before deducting the annual exempt amount) for Lethabo for the tax year 2025/26. (10 marks)

61 AMEER

Ameer made the following disposals of capital items in the tax year 2025/26:

15 July 2025:

A bronze statuette was sold for £7,200. It had originally cost £4,100 in May 2015.

14 August 2025:

His entire holding of 12,000 shares in ABC plc, a UK trading company quoted on the stock exchange, was given to his friend Adele. The shares had cost Ameer £5,300 in May 2009. ABC plc has 1 million shares in issue.

On 14 August 2025 ABC plc shares were quoted at 140p – 146p.

Ameer had unused capital losses of £800 which were brought forward from the tax year 2024/25. His taxable income for the tax year 2025/26 was £200,000.

Required:

Calculate Ameer's capital gains tax payable for the tax year 2025/26. (10 marks)

62 DONALD

On 14 July 2025 Donald sold 4,000 shares in XYZ plc for £18,000.

Donald's record of purchases of XYZ plc's shares is as follows:

1. 14 October 2011: 4,000 shares for £6,000.
2. 18 May 2015: a 1 for 2 rights issue at £2.50 per share was taken up in full.
3. 10 December 2017: a 1 for 5 bonus issue. The shares were valued at £3 each at the time of the bonus issue.
4. 30 July 2025: 500 shares for £2,100.

Required:

Calculate the total chargeable gain arising on the disposal of the shares in the tax year 2025/26. (10 marks)

63 ALBERTO

Alberto, a UK resident, made the following disposals during the tax year 2025/26:

14 August 2025:

A statuette was sold for £48,000. The statuette had been part of a set of three, which had been purchased on 10 January 2013 for a total cost of £32,000. Alberto incurred selling expenses of £1,000. The market value of the remaining two statuettes on 14 August 2025 was £85,000.

19 August 2025:

A painting was sold for £3,000. The painting had been purchased in June 2013, when it was mistakenly thought to be a rare portrait, for £8,700.

Alberto also had unused capital losses of £1,000 brought forward from the tax year 2024/25. He had taxable income for the tax year 2025/26 of £32,430.

Required:

(a) **Calculate the chargeable gains/allowable losses arising in the tax year 2025/26.** **(5 marks)**

(b) **Calculate the capital gains tax payable by Alberto for the tax year 2025/26 and state the due date of payment.** **(5 marks)**

(Total: 10 marks)

64 KATRIN

Katrin made the following disposals of capital assets during the tax year 2025/26:

2 July 2025:

Six hectares of land were sold for £30,000 with expenses of sale amounting to £2,000. The six hectares had been part of a much larger field, which had been purchased in May 2009 for £80,000. The market value of the remaining part of the field on 2 July 2025 was £190,000.

3 August 2025:

A vase was sold for £5,800. It had cost £3,000 on 2 September 2013.

17 November 2025:

A vintage car was sold for £48,000. It had cost £25,000 in May 2001.

14 January 2026:

A painting, which had cost £10,000 in June 2014, was destroyed in a fire. Katrin received £18,000 from an insurance company and immediately reinvested £15,000 in a replacement painting. Katrin made a no gain/no loss election in respect of this disposal.

None of these assets had been used in a business.

Required:

Calculate the chargeable gain (if any) arising in the tax year 2025/26 on each of the above disposals. **(10 marks)**

65 JUAN

Juan, a UK resident, made the following disposals of capital assets in the tax year 2025/26:

14 July 2025:

10,000 shares in a UK trading company were sold for £28,000.

These had been purchased as follows:

4,000 shares for £8,180 on 16 May 2009

3,000 shares for £9,600 on 14 August 2011

3,500 shares as a result of a 1 for 2 rights issue for £2.00 each in June 2016

18 August 2025:

A painting was sold for £7,500. It had been purchased for £3,500 in November 2011.

2 February 2026:

A vintage car was sold for £42,000. It had cost £13,000 in September 1990.

Required:

Calculate Juan's chargeable gains for the tax year 2025/26. **(10 marks)**

66 BANDILE

Bandile, a UK resident, made the following disposals of capital assets in the tax year 2025/26:

15 July 2025:

An antique table was sold for £3,000. The table had originally been purchased in June 2010 for £8,000. Bandile incurred selling expenses of £300.

17 August 2025:

A 20% share of a painting was sold for £28,000. The original painting had been purchased for £60,000 and the remaining 80% share had a current market value of £140,000. Bandile incurred selling expenses of £200.

12 February 2026:

A Victoria Cross medal was sold for £50,000. The medal had been awarded to Bandile's father and had a value of £22,000 when inherited by Bandile in May 2015.

Bandile had unused capital losses of £2,000 brought forward from the tax year 2024/25 and he is a higher rate taxpayer.

Required:

Calculate the capital gains tax payable by Bandile for the tax year 2025/26 and state the due date of payment. **(10 marks)**

67 BARTHOLOMEW

In the tax year 2025/26 Bartholomew realised the following chargeable gains/allowable losses:

Residential property	£27,000
Chattels	£16,000
Allowable loss	(£2,000)

Bartholomew's taxable income for 2025/26 is £16,000.

Required:

Calculate Bartholomew's capital gains tax liability for the tax year 2025/26. **(5 marks)**

68 HANS

Hans disposed of the following capital assets during the tax year 2025/26:

12 August 2025	A painting was sold for £7,600 incurring expenses of sale of £400. The painting had cost £4,500 in November 2012.
7 September 2025	A set of armour, which had cost £74,000 in June 2016, was damaged. Hans received £42,000 from an insurance company and £14,000 from a scrap dealer. Hans did not replace the asset.
4 February 2026	An antique was sold for £140,000. The antique had cost £60,000 in September 2014.

Hans' taxable income (after the deduction of his personal allowance) for income tax purposes in the tax year 2025/26 was £72,000.

Required:

Calculate Hans' capital gains tax (CGT) payable for the tax year 2025/26 and state the due date of payment. (10 marks)

69 SYED

Syed disposed of the following capital assets during the tax year 2025/26:

17 June 2025	Qualifying corporate bonds were sold for £27,000. The qualifying corporate bonds had cost £14,000 in October 2010.
1 November 2025	A residential investment property was sold for £316,000. Syed inherited the property from his grandmother. His grandmother bought the property for £90,000 in 2000 and it was worth £105,000 at the date of his grandmother's death. The property has never been used as Syed's main residence.
15 March 2026	An antique was sold for £15,000. Expenses of sale amounted to £1,000. The antique had cost £23,000 in 2017.

Syed has a capital loss brought forward from 2024/25 of £4,000.

Syed's taxable income (after the deduction of the personal allowance) for income tax purposes for the tax year 2025/26 was £29,000.

Required:

(a) **Calculate the capital gains tax payable by Syed for the tax year 2025/26. (9 marks)**

(b) **State the due date of payment for the capital gains tax on Syed's disposal of the residential investment property. (1 mark)**

(Total: 10 marks)

CAPITAL GAINS TAX RELIEFS: INDIVIDUALS

70 TONY

Tony sold his unincorporated business, which he had owned for several years, in February 2026.

He sold the entire business, which included two chargeable business assets, a factory and a plot of land used for parking staff vehicles. The factory had cost £200,000 and was sold for £800,000 and the land had cost £213,000 and was sold for £180,000. Structures and buildings allowances were not available on the factory.

Tony has not previously sold any other business assets and has made no other disposals in the tax year 2025/26.

Required:

Calculate Tony's capital gains tax liability for the tax year 2025/26 on the disposal of his business assuming that business asset disposal relief is claimed. (5 marks)

71 LUKNE

Lukne is a sole trader. On 19 December 2025 she sold an asset, which had always been used in her business, to her daughter Becky for £80,000. The asset had cost Lukne £70,000 in May 2013 and it had a market value of £100,000 on the day of the sale.

Business asset disposal relief is not available on this disposal.

Required:

Calculate Lukne's chargeable gain arising on the disposal of the asset in the tax year 2025/26, assuming that both Lukne and Becky make any beneficial claims to reduce the tax payable immediately on the sale.

Your answer must clearly identify the amount of any relief claimed and the base cost of the asset for Becky. **(5 marks)**

72 TIGRAN

Tigran sold his 60% holding in X Ltd, an unquoted trading company, on 14 January 2026, realising a gain of £1,300,000. Tigran has owned the shares and been a full-time employee of X Ltd for the last eight years. Tigran also made a gain of £9,000 on the disposal of a residential property on 31 May 2025.

Tigran's taxable income for the tax year 2025/26 is £25,000. He has never claimed any business asset disposal relief (BADR) in the past.

Required:

(a) **Explain why Tigran's disposal of the shares in X Ltd qualifies for BADR.** **(4 marks)**

(b) **Calculate Tigran's capital gains tax payable for the tax year 2025/26 assuming BADR is claimed.** **(5 marks)**

(c) **State the date(s) when the tax is due to be paid.** **(1 mark)**

(Total: 10 marks)

73 ELIF

Elif purchased a chargeable non-business asset in September 2011 for £18,000. It was destroyed by a flash flood in November 2025. Elif replaced the asset in March 2026 at a cost of £28,000, having received £29,500 compensation from an insurance company.

Required:

(a) **Calculate the chargeable gain arising in the tax year 2025/26, assuming all beneficial elections are made.** **(3 marks)**

(b) **State the base cost of the replacement asset.** **(2 marks)**

(Total: 5 marks)

74 PEDRO

Pedro purchased his main residence on 1 July 2005 for £54,500 and spent £10,000 on an extension in July 2012.

He moved into the property immediately and occupied it until he moved abroad to take up employment on 1 September 2007. He returned to the UK and reoccupied the property on 1 May 2012. He remained in the property until 1 January 2013 when he moved to another UK city on a temporary work secondment.

On 1 January 2018 he returned to the property. On 1 September 2021 he moved to his parents' home to take care of his sick mother. The property was finally sold on 1 July 2025 for £160,000. Pedro never returned to the property after 1 September 2021.

Required:

(a) **Using a tabular format, state, giving reasons in each case, the exempt and non-exempt periods for private residence relief (PRR). (8 marks)**

(b) **Calculate the chargeable gain, after reliefs, arising in the tax year 2025/26 on the sale of the house. (2 marks)**

(Total: 10 marks)

75 PAMELA

Pamela has her own business selling computer games. On 1 September 2025 she sold a shop for £80,000, which had cost her £42,000 on 1 May 2008.

In June 2025 she had purchased a new shop for £72,000.

Both shops were used 100% for business purposes. Structures and buildings allowances were not available on the shops.

Required:

On the assumption that Pamela always claims any reliefs available:

(a) **Calculate her chargeable gain (before the annual exempt amount) arising in the tax year 2025/26 on the disposal of the old shop, and (4 marks)**

(b) **State the base cost of the replacement shop for capital gains tax purposes. (1 mark)**

(Total: 5 marks)

76 PETRA

Petra runs a successful business and in February 2026 she sold one of her business premises to her son Peter for an agreed price of £120,000. The building was actually worth £245,000.

Petra had purchased the building for £80,000 in 1998. Petra and Peter have made a joint election for gift holdover relief.

Structures and buildings allowances were not available on the building.

Required:

(a) **Calculate Petra's chargeable gain on the disposal of the building. (4 marks)**

(b) **State Peter's base cost of the building for future capital gains tax purposes. (1 mark)**

(Total: 5 marks)

77 PATRICIA

Patricia, who is a higher rate taxpayer, has run a pottery business for a number of years. In October 2025 she sold a workshop for £160,000, which had cost £40,000 in June 2013.

In November 2025 she sold a painting that has always been on display in her showroom for £20,000. It had cost £12,000 in May 2014.

In December 2025 Patricia purchased a retail shop for £140,000, which qualifies as a business asset and a forklift truck for use in the business for £15,000.

Structures and buildings allowances were not available on the buildings.

Required:

Calculate Patricia's capital gains tax payable for the tax year 2025/26 on the assumption that Patricia always claims any reliefs available. (5 marks)

78 ADELE

Adele purchased a painting in May 2012 for £24,500. It was destroyed by fire in December 2025. Adele received £29,000 compensation from an insurance company in January 2026 and immediately reinvested £28,000 in another painting to replace the one destroyed.

Required:

(a) **Calculate the chargeable gain arising in the tax year 2025/26, assuming she made all available elections. (4 marks)**

(b) **State the base cost of the replacement painting. (1 mark)**

(Total: 5 marks)

79 POLA

Pola purchased a house, as her only residence, on 1 June 2016 and occupied it immediately. Between 1 May 2017 and 31 August 2025 Pola was required, by her employer, to take up a temporary post in another UK city.

On 31 August 2025 Pola sold her house, without ever reoccupying it, and went to live in Scotland due to work commitments.

Required:

(a) **State, giving reasons, in respect of Pola's period of absence between 1 May 2017 and 31 August 2025, the dates of each period covered by, or not covered by, private residence relief (PRR).**

Note: The calculation of PRR relief is NOT required. (3 marks)

(b) **State the due date(s) for the tax payable in respect of the disposal of the house and the final payment of capital gains tax for the tax year 2025/26. (2 marks)**

(Total: 5 marks)

80 SANDRA

Sandra has run a small manufacturing business for several years.

On 16 August 2025 she sold a factory, which had always been used in her business, for £220,000 realising a capital gain of £80,000.

On 10 June 2025 Sandra had invested £210,000 in fixed plant and machinery, which was to be used in her business.

Sandra wishes to claim all available reliefs.

Required:

(a) Calculate Sandra's chargeable gain arising in the tax year 2025/26 on the disposal of the factory. (2 marks)

(b) State when any deferred gain will become chargeable. (3 marks)

(Total: 5 marks)

81 SUSANNAH

Susannah purchased her main residence in London on 1 May 2012 for £147,000 and sold it on 31 October 2025 for £390,000.

Susannah lived in the house until 31 July 2013 when she moved abroad to work in her company's head office. Susannah returned to the UK on 1 August 2019 but was required by her company to work in Manchester. Susannah returned to work in London and reoccupied her residence from 1 January 2024 until it was sold on 31 October 2025.

Required:

Calculate Susannah's chargeable gain (if any) on the disposal of her main residence.

Note: Your answer should include a table showing detailed workings of any relief given.

(5 marks)

82 HALINA

Halina disposed of the following assets during the tax year 2025/26:

30 September 2025

Halina sold a house for £282,200, which had been purchased on 1 October 2003 for £186,000. Halina has never lived in the house and has always rented it out on long-term lettings.

7 July 2025

Halina sold 15,000 of her 20,000 £1 ordinary shares in Straight Ltd that she had acquired for £48,000. The sale proceeds were £62,400.

Halina has never worked for Straight Ltd.

15 October 2025

Halina sold a small business she had been running part time for many years. The only chargeable asset in the business was a warehouse and this resulted in a gain of £3,700.

Halina has taxable income of £23,945 for the tax year 2025/26. She also has a brought forward capital loss of £7,200.

Required:

Compute Halina's capital gains tax liability for the tax year 2025/26. (10 marks)

83 ANDREA

Andrea purchased shares in an unquoted trading company in March 2008 for £40,000. In November 2025, Andrea sold the shares to her daughter Michelle for £55,000, when their value was £60,000.

Andrea and Michelle jointly claimed relief for a gift of business assets.

Required:

(a) **Calculate the chargeable gain incurred by Andrea on the sale of shares to Michelle in November 2025. (4 marks)**

(b) **State the date by which the claim for relief for a gift of business assets must be made by Andrea and Michelle. (1 mark)**

(Total: 5 marks)

84 BRODIE

Brodie disposed of the following assets during the tax year 2025/26:

Shares in an unquoted trading company

Brodie reduced his 60% shareholding in Xtrema Ltd by selling 40,000 of his 60,000 £1 ordinary shares on 1 June 2025 for £32,000. He had bought all 60,000 shares in January 2017 for £30,000. Brodie had been an employee of the company since January 2017.

Residential property

Brodie sold a residential property on 15 August 2025 for £516,000, which had been purchased on 19 December 2014 for £457,300. Brodie had never lived in the property and had always rented it out to tenants.

Car

Brodie sold his car on 19 November 2025 for £7,000. He bought the car in May 2018 for £13,500.

Brodie's taxable income (after the deduction of the personal allowance) for income tax purposes for the tax year 2025/26 was £15,670. He also has a brought forward capital loss of £7,100.

Required:

Calculate the capital gains tax payable by Brodie for the tax year 2025/26. (10 marks)

CORPORATION TAX

85 PACIFIC PLC

Pacific plc has always prepared accounts to 31 March annually. During the year ended 31 March 2026 the trading accounts showed a profit before income taxes of £850,000. Included in these accounts were the following items:

Payments

1 Entertainment of £4,000, comprising £2,500 spent on customers and £1,500 spent on the company's own staff.

2 Repairs of £25,000. This amount included a figure of £20,000 to repair a warehouse, which was purchased in August 2025. The warehouse had been badly damaged by a fire before Pacific plc had purchased it. The repair was necessary to put the warehouse into a usable condition. The remaining £5,000 was spent on general office repairs.

3 Loan note interest of £9,000. This represents interest on £100,000 of 9% loan notes issued to other companies to fund the purchase of plant and machinery used in the business.

4 Lease rental payments of £2,000 per annum each for two cars. The cars have CO_2 emissions of 42g/km and 67g/km respectively.

5 Purchase of some plant and machinery in June 2025 costing £100,000.

Receipts

6 Insurance proceeds of £40,000 in respect of a claim for lost profits whilst the factory was closed by a minor flood.

7 £14,000 representing the profit on the sale of a packing machine sold in September 2025. The machine had been purchased in 2016 and had been used in the business since that date.

Required:

Explain the action required, if any, to adjust the profit before income taxes of Pacific plc for tax purposes because of the items listed above.

Your answer should clearly state your reasons for the action you are proposing and whether you will be adding back, deducting or leaving the relevant figures unadjusted.

You are not required to calculate the actual final profit figure. (15 marks)

86 CARGO LTD

Cargo Ltd is a trading company.

In the year to 31 March 2026 the company had the following transactions in non–current assets:

Purchases		
18 August 2025	A car for a director's use	£26,000
14 February 2026	New plant	£37,000
Sales		
20 August 2025	Car (original cost £18,000, CO_2 emissions 170 g/km)	£7,000

The car bought in August 2025 was used 20% for business and 80% privately and has CO_2 emissions of 62g/km.

As well as the above, the company had traded in an old car for a newer model in November 2025. The old car had cost £10,000 in January 2021 with CO_2 emissions of 47g/km and had a trade in value of £3,000. The company paid additional £11,000 cash for the new model. This car is used 100% for business purposes and has CO_2 emissions of 37g/km.

The balances on the pools as at 1 April 2025 were:

Main pool	£248,000
Special rate pool	£9,000

Required:

Calculate the maximum capital allowances available to Cargo Ltd for the year ending 31 March 2026. Ignore VAT. (10 marks)

87 STONEY PAVING LTD

Stoney Paving Ltd prepares accounts to 31 March each year.

The tax written down value of the main pool as at 1 April 2025 was £1,276,000.

During the year ending 31 March 2026 the company invested in numerous integral features for the factory at a total cost of £1,020,000, a car with CO_2 emissions of 49g/km, costing £24,000 and another car with zero emissions, costing £32,600.

An old machine was sold for £4,000 on which 130% super deduction had been claimed (the sales proceeds are less than the original cost).

Required:

Calculate the maximum capital allowances available for the year ended 31 March 2026. Ignore VAT. (5 marks)

88 UK FABRICS LTD

UK Fabrics Ltd has always drawn up its accounts to 31 March each year.

The following information is provided in respect of the year ending 31 March 2026:

	£	£
Sales revenue		3,428,000
Less: Cost of sales		(1,600,000)
Gross profit		1,828,000
Profit on sale of a non-current asset (Note 1)		141,000
Rent received (Note 2)		168,000
Depreciation	70,000	
Wages	320,000	
Power and lighting costs	48,000	
Increase in specific allowance for receivables	18,000	
Miscellaneous expenses (Note 3)	28,000	
		(484,000)
Profit before income taxes		1,653,000

Notes:

1 The profit shown is the gain, after accounting for depreciation, on the sale of an unwanted showroom in August 2025.

2 The rent received is in respect of an office block leased to another UK resident company.

3 Miscellaneous expenses comprise:

	£
Legal fees in respect of trade debt collection	5,000
Customer entertainment	2,000
Gifts of food hampers to customers valued at £60 each	3,000
Legal fees in respect of the renewal of 40-year lease on its factory	3,500
Parking fines incurred by delivery drivers on deliveries	250
Staff training courses on use of company's computer system	1,000
Office expenses (all allowable)	13,250
	28,000

4 The capital allowances for the year ended 31 March 2026 have been calculated as £304,000.

Required:

Calculate the tax adjusted trading profit (after capital allowances) for the year ended 31 March 2026. (10 marks)

89 DANDY PLC

Dandy plc is a UK resident company with two 60% owned subsidiaries.

For the company's accounting year ended 31 March 2026 it made a profit before income taxes of £115,000. Included in this figure were the following items:

Income

1 £4,500 dividend from a company in which it owns 40% of the shares.

2 £6,300 dividends each from the two 60% owned subsidiaries.

3 £20,000 insurance proceeds in respect of lost profit as a result of the temporary closure of its factory.

4 £8,000 rent. The annual amount due is £9,000. The tenant did not pay the balance of £1,000 due as at 31 March 2026 until April 2026.

5 £10,000 loan note interest income in respect of £250,000 loan notes issued at an interest rate of 4% per annum.

Expenditure

1 £8,000 interest paid. This is in respect of an £180,000 loan borrowed in 2020 at 5% interest per annum. The borrowed money was used to buy the factory in which Dandy plc now conducts its business. The amount of interest outstanding at 31 March 2026 was paid in April 2026.

2 £6,000 interest paid. This is in respect of an £120,000 loan borrowed in 2016 at 5% interest per annum. The borrowed money was used to buy a factory, which is now being let to a third party.

3 £3,000 donation to Oxfam, a national charity.

In addition to this, and NOT included in the accounts, the company had a chargeable gain of £9,000 in the year and a capital loss brought forward of £3,000 on 1 April 2025.

The company claimed capital allowances of £16,000 for the year ended 31 March 2026.

Required:

For the year ended 31 March 2026:

(a) Calculate the tax adjusted trading profit. **(7 marks)**

(b) Calculate the corporation tax liability. **(8 marks)**

(Total: 15 marks)

90 THOMPSON BROTHERS LTD

Thompson Brothers Ltd is a UK resident company. Up to 2025 the company had always prepared its accounts to 31 March annually but because of new accounting policies, the company decided to change its accounting reference date to 31 December.

The adjusted trading profit before capital allowances for the nine-month period ended 31 December 2025 was £974,307.

Other income and expenditure received and paid in the same period was:

Income	
Dividends from UK companies	£18,000
Rental income (Note 1)	£10,000
Loan note interest (Note 2)	£6,000
Expenditure	
Interest for late payment of tax	£2,000
Qualifying charitable donation to a UK registered charity	£7,000

Notes:

1 The rent was received in two equal amounts on 1 June 2025 and 1 December 2025 and was in each case in respect of the following six months.

2 Loan note interest is received six-monthly on 30 June and 31 December each year and is in respect of a holding of £120,000 5% loan notes.

The tax written down value on the company's main pool as at 1 April 2025 was £140,000. During the period ended 31 December 2025 the company purchased plant for £775,000 in May 2025, and a new car costing £22,000 in December 2025. The car is used 60% for business and 40% privately by one of the directors. This car has CO_2 emissions exceeding 50g/km. An old machine, which had originally cost £28,000, was sold for £23,000 in November 2025. No claim had been made on this machine for first year allowances.

Required:

(a) **Calculate Thompson Brothers Ltd's total capital allowances for the nine-month period ended 31 December 2025. Ignore VAT.** **(8 marks)**

(b) **Calculate the corporation tax liability for Thompson Brothers Ltd for the nine-month period ended 31 December 2025.** **(7 marks)**

(Total: 15 marks)

91 PARKER PLC

Parker plc is a large UK resident company for the purpose of corporation tax payments. In the accounting year ended 31 March 2026 it had estimated its taxable total profits to be £1,600,000. The company had taxable total profits amounting to £1,800,000 in the year to 31 March 2025.

Required:

In respect of the accounting period ended 31 March 2026:

(a) **Calculate the corporation tax liability.** **(1 mark)**

(b) **State the due dates of payment of the tax and the amount of each of those payments.** **(3 marks)**

(c) **State how the company must pay its tax.** **(1 mark)**

(Total: 5 marks)

92 YELLOW LTD

Yellow Ltd is a UK registered company.

On 1 April 2025, Yellow Ltd's tax written down values brought forward were as follows:

Main pool	£76,000
A short-life asset (SLA) (purchased in August 2024 for £8,000)	£6,560

During its eight-month accounting period ended 30 November 2025 Yellow Ltd had the following capital transactions:

Purchases

1 May 2025	Second-hand machine for £750,000 (this machine is to be treated as a short life asset)
2 August 2025	New plant and machinery for £500,000

Disposal

5 April 2025	Furniture for £20,000, which was lower than cost. A claim for the 130% super deduction was made when the furniture was initially purchased.
16 October 2025	The SLA purchased in August 2024, sold for £2,400

Required:

Calculate the maximum capital allowances claimable by Yellow Ltd for its eight-month accounting period ended 30 November 2025. (10 marks)

93 SCARLET LTD

Scarlet Ltd is a UK resident company. The company has always prepared its accounts to 31 March each year. Due to a change in accounting procedures the company decided to change its accounting reference date to 30 June.

The following are Scarlet Ltd's results for the 15 months ended 30 June 2026:

Adjusted trading profit (before capital allowances)			£1,400,500
Property business profit			£105,000
Chargeable gains			
–	14 August 2025	disposal	£28,000
–	2 May 2026	disposal	£4,000
Allowable capital loss			
–	12 April 2026	disposal	(£5,000)
Qualifying charitable donation to a UK registered charity paid on 30 June 2026			(£8,000)

The property business profit was earned evenly over the entire period and is based on the actual amount of rents due.

The tax written down value of the company's main pool brought forward on 1 April 2025 was £800,000. There were no capital transactions affecting the capital allowances pool during the 15 months ended 30 June 2026.

Required:

(a) **Calculate the corporation tax liability for Scarlet Ltd for each of its two accounting periods in the 15 months ended 30 June 2026.** **(13 marks)**

(b) **State the due date(s) of payment of the tax calculated in part (a).** **(1 mark)**

(c) **State the due date(s) for filing the company's corporation tax return(s) covering the period to 30 June 2026.** **(1 mark)**

Assume FY2025 rates continue. **(Total: 15 marks)**

94 FGV LTD

FGV Ltd prepared accounts for the 12-month period of account ended 31 March 2026. Information taken from the accounts for the period showed the following:

	£	£
Gross profit		694,500
Dividends		18,000
Interest from non-trading activities		15,000
		727,500
Depreciation	42,000	
Salaries	316,000	
Director's remuneration	60,000	
Interest on loans:		
– to buy a machine used in the business	5,000	
– to buy an investment property	4,000	
Donation to a national charity	1,500	
Gifts to customers:		
– 200 mouse mats	2,000	
– 200 bottles of wine	5,000	
Entertainment of customers	2,000	
		(437,500)
Profit before income taxes		290,000

Note: All of the gifts to customers had the company name displayed on them.

FGV Ltd claimed capital allowances of £62,700 for the year ended 31 March 2026.

In addition, FGV Ltd made a chargeable gain of £82,000 in August 2025 and had a trading loss of £39,000 and an allowable capital loss of £17,000 which were both brought forward as at 1 April 2025. (The trading loss was incurred in the year ended 31 March 2025.)

Required:

Calculate the corporation tax payable by FGV Ltd for the year ended 31 March 2026. Your answer should identify any item which is not taxable and state why it is not included in your calculation.

Note: When calculating the tax adjusted trading profit you should start your computation with the profit before income taxes figure of £290,000 and indicate by the use of a zero (0) any items which do not require adjustment. **(15 marks)**

95 ZVC LTD (ADAPTED)

ZVC Ltd is a UK company and prepares financial statements annually to 31 March.

During the period of account ended 31 March 2026 ZVC Ltd had the following income:

	£
Tax adjusted trading income	80,000
Property income	14,000
Non-trade interest	11,000

Included in the property income figure above was £2,000 rent for March 2025. Rent of £3,000 and interest of £1,000 were still receivable for March 2026. Neither of these amounts are included in the figures listed above.

In addition to the above, ZVC Ltd sold a building for £400,000 in March 2026. The building cost £100,000 in September 1995 and ZVC Ltd incurred incidental costs of acquisition of £20,000. The building had been extended at a cost of £51,920 in November 2018. Structures and buildings allowances were not available.

ZVC Ltd made a qualifying charitable donation of £3,500 in January 2026.

A £42,000 trading loss, a capital loss of £22,000 and a £5,000 property loss, all of which arose in the year ended 31 March 2025, were brought forward as at 1 April 2025.

Required:

Calculate the corporation tax payable by ZVC Ltd for the year ended 31 March 2026 and state the due date of payment.

Note: In answering this question the following indexation factor may be used:

September 1995 to December 2017: 0.847 **(15 marks)**

96 POPPY LTD

Poppy Ltd has always prepared accounts to 31 March annually. In 2025 Poppy Ltd decided to change its accounting reference date to 31 May and produced accounts for the 14 months ended 31 May 2026.

The results for the 14-month period ended 31 May 2026 were as follows:

	£
Adjusted trading profit (before capital allowances)	1,316,000
Bank interest received (September 2025)	20,000
Interest payable	12,000
Chargeable gain – 14 December 2025	219,900
Allowable capital loss – 2 May 2026	(10,000)

	£
Bank interest income accrued as follows:	
At 1 April 2025	8,000
As at 31 March 2026	9,000
As at 31 May 2026	14,000

Interest payable is in respect of a non-trade related loan. The loan was taken out on 1 June 2025 and interest of £1,000 is payable per month.

The tax written-down value brought forward on the main pool as at 1 April 2025 was £205,000. New machines were purchased on 14 June 2025 for £156,000 and on 20 May 2026 for £104,000. An old machine, which had cost £12,000, was sold for £15,000 on 12 April 2026. There were no enhanced allowances claimed on this machine.

Required:

(a) **Calculate the corporation tax liability for Poppy Ltd for the two accounting periods in the 14-month period ended 31 May 2026. (14 marks)**

(b) **State any unrelieved amounts carried forward as at 31 May 2026. (1 mark)**

(Total: 15 marks)

Assume that the rates of tax and allowances for Financial Year 2025 apply throughout.

97 FIRES LTD

Fires Ltd manufactures electric fires for the UK domestic market and prepares its accounts to 31 March every year.

Fires Ltd is registered for value added tax (VAT) and all of its sales are standard-rated.

Fires Ltd had the following transactions in capital assets during the accounting year ended 31 March 2026:

Purchases:

2 May 2025	A machine for £35,880
6 August 2025	A computer for £9,360
14 October 2025	A car for £16,000

Disposal:

16 September 2025	A machine, which had originally cost £24,000, was sold for £25,200. No claim for enhanced allowances had been made.

All the above figures are **inclusive** of VAT.

The tax written down value of Fires Ltd's main pool on 1 April 2025 was £124,000.

The car purchased on 14 October 2025 has CO_2 emissions of 63g/km and is used 40% for private purposes and 60% for business purposes by the company's managing director.

Required:

Calculate the maximum capital allowances that Fires Ltd can claim for the year ended 31 March 2026. (10 marks)

98 RADIATORS LTD

Radiators Ltd is a UK company. In the accounting year ended 31 March 2026 Radiators Ltd had the following income and expenditure:

Income:

Tax adjusted trading profit	£1,540,000
Interest from a UK bank	£8,000
Chargeable gain	£23,000

Expenditure:

Qualifying charitable donation payment	£4,000
Interest paid	£3,000

The interest paid is the accrued amount for the year to 31 March 2026 and was in respect of a loan used to purchase an investment.

Radiators Ltd had taxable total profits of £1,550,000 in the year ended 31 March 2025.

Required:

(a) **Calculate the corporation tax liability for Radiators Ltd for the year ended 31 March 2026.** **(5 marks)**

(b) **State the due date(s) of payment of the corporation tax.** **(4 marks)**

(c) **State the date the corporation tax return is due for this period.** **(1 mark)**

(Total: 10 marks)

99 STEM LTD

Stem Ltd, a UK company, made the following purchases and disposals of capital items during its nine-month accounting period ending 31 December 2025:

Purchases:

25 June 2025	– Lift in a building for £521,750 (this is a special rate pool item)
7 October 2025	– A new machine for £310,000
2 December 2025	– A car for £20,000 (CO_2 emissions of 60 grams per kilometre)

Disposal:

1 June 2025	– Lift (special rate pool item) for £100,000
14 October 2025	– Plant for £6,000 (original cost £4,000)

The machine purchased on 7 October 2025 was purchased on a hire purchase agreement with 10 monthly payments of £31,000 starting in October 2025. If the machine had been purchased outright the cash price would have been £300,000.

The lift sold on 1 June 2025 had originally cost £400,000. Stem Ltd had claimed 100% AIA on £250,000 of this cost, and 50% FYA on the remaining £150,000.

No enhanced allowances had been claimed on the plant sold on 14 October 2025.

The tax written down values brought forward at 1 April 2025 of Stem Ltd's main pool and special rate pool were £310,000 and £90,000 respectively.

Required:

Calculate the maximum capital allowances that Stem Ltd can claim for the nine-month period ended 31 December 2025. Ignore VAT. (10 marks)

100 BROOKSIDE LTD

Brookside Ltd, which has a 60% owned subsidiary and also holds a 20% share in another company, has always prepared its accounts to 31 May. For operational purposes, the company decided to change its accounting date to 31 March.

The results for the 10-month period ended 31 March 2026 are as follows:

Income:	
Tax adjusted trading profit	£65,000
Non-trade interest	£2,000
Chargeable gain	£7,000
Rental income	£8,000
Dividends received from non-group companies	£15,000
Expenditure:	
Qualifying charitable donation	£2,000

Required:

Calculate the corporation tax liability for Brookside Ltd for the 10-month period ended 31 March 2026. (10 marks)

CORPORATION TAX LOSSES

101 LOSSMAKER LTD

Lossmaker Ltd started to trade and in its first accounting period to 31 December 2025 it made a trading loss of £20,000. In this period it also had property and interest income and made qualifying charitable donations.

Required:

Explain the ways in which the company may utilise this loss and state by when the claims have to be made. (5 marks)

102 LGT LTD

LGT Ltd prepares accounts annually to 31 December. On 31 December 2025 LGT Ltd ceased to trade.

The company's last four sets of financial statements showed the following results:

	Year ended 31 December 2022	**Year ended 31 December 2023**	**Year ended 31 December 2024**	**Year ended 31 December 2025**
	£	£	£	£
Trading profit/loss	40,000	20,000	17,000	(62,000)
Capital gain/loss		(8,000)	7,000	
Qualifying charitable donation	3,000		2,000	

Required:

Assuming that LGT Ltd claims the maximum loss relief in respect of the loss incurred in the year ended 31 December 2025, calculate LGT Ltd's taxable total profit (TTP) for each of the years concerned. Your answer should show the amount of loss unused at 31 December 2025, if any. **(5 marks)**

103 BLUE LTD

Blue Ltd is a UK resident company. The company has recently changed its accounting year end to December.

The company has had the following results for the three accounting periods ending 31 December 2026:

	Year to 31 March 2025	**Year to 31 March 2026**	**Nine months to 31 December 2026**
	£	£	£
Tax adjusted trading profit	20,000	–	40,000
Tax adjusted trading loss	–	(180,000)	–
Property income	9,000	12,000	12,000
Chargeable gain	10,000	–	–
Qualifying charitable donation	(2,000)	(2,000)	(2,000)

Required:

(a) **Calculate the taxable total profits for each of the above periods assuming that Blue Ltd claims relief for the tax adjusted trading loss at the earliest opportunity.**

Assume FY2025 rules continue in future years. **(9 marks)**

(b) **Calculate the amount of corporation tax that will be refunded in respect of the year ended 31 March 2025.** **(1 mark)**

(Total: 10 marks)

104 BULB LTD

Bulb Ltd prepares accounts to 31 March every year.

In its accounting year ended 31 March 2026, Bulb Ltd's income and expenditure was as follows:

Income:

Tax adjusted trading profit	£600,000
Non-trade interest	£20,000
Chargeable gain	£10,000
Rental income actually received in the period	£18,000

£2,000 due for March 2026 was not received until 20 April 2026.

Expenditure:

Non-trade interest	£4,000
Qualifying charitable donation	£6,000

Bulb Ltd had tax adjusted trading losses of £220,000, a property loss of £5,000 and capital losses of £3,000 brought forward as at 1 April 2025.

Required:

Calculate the corporation tax liability for Bulb Ltd for the year ended 31 March 2026 assuming the losses are offset as soon as possible. (10 marks)

CAPITAL GAINS: COMPANIES

105 ST LTD

ST Ltd, a UK resident company, made the following disposal during its accounting period of 12 months ended 31 March 2026.

In August 2015, ST Ltd had sold a factory for £180,000 on which a chargeable gain of £50,000 arose. The factory had been purchased in 1998. Of the proceeds, £150,000 was immediately invested in a major item of fixed plant and the maximum possible gain was deferred. In July 2025 the item of fixed plant was scrapped for nil proceeds.

Required:

Compute the total amount of gains chargeable to corporation tax on ST Ltd for the above transactions in respect of the accounting period ended 31 March 2026. (5 marks)

106 DOVE PLC

Dove plc, a UK resident company, made the following disposals of assets during its 12-month accounting period ending 31 December 2025:

14 April 2025: A factory for £230,000. This had been purchased in May 1991 for £140,000.

17 September 2025: Another factory for £280,000. This had been purchased in June 2004 for £80,000.

The company is also planning to purchase one larger factory to replace the two sold above. The expected cost will be £490,000.

Structures and buildings allowances are not available in respect of any of the factories.

Required:

(a) **Calculate the total chargeable gains/allowable capital losses for the period ending 31 December 2025, before any deferral reliefs. (6 marks)**

(b) **Explain if any of the above gain(s) can be deferred. (4 marks)**

Indexation factors are:

May 1991 – December 2017	1.083
June 2004 – December 2017	0.489

(Total: 10 marks)

107 BOX PLC

Box plc prepares accounts to 31 March each year. In its 12-month period ending 31 March 2026 it sold 13,000 shares in Banana plc on 26 May 2025 for £110,000. Banana plc has one million shares in issue.

These shares had been purchased as follows:

26 May 2007	6,000 shares for	£24,000
24 October 2011	5,000 shares for	£27,500
22 May 2025	2,000 shares for	£12,000

Required:

Calculate the total chargeable gain to be included in Box plc's taxable total profits for the year ending 31 March 2026.

Indexation factors are:

May 2007 – October 2011	0.154
October 2011 – December 2017	0.168

(10 marks)

108 CRATE PLC

Crate plc prepares accounts to 31 March each year. In its 12-month period ending 31 March 2026 it has the following transactions in capital assets:

21 August 2025:

A painting, which had been hanging in the managing director's office, was sold for £5,800. It had been purchased for £8,000 in June 2004. **(2 marks)**

12 January 2026:

Four hectares of land from a larger plot of 12 hectares were sold for £380,000. The 12 hectares had been purchased in March 2000 for £450,000. The remaining eight hectares had a market value of £950,000 on 12 January 2026. **(4 marks)**

14 February 2026

A factory was sold for £250,000 (gross) at auction. The auctioneer charged a fee of 10% of the selling price.

The factory had originally been purchased in June 2004 for £80,000 plus purchase costs of £5,000. It had been extended at a cost of £20,000 in January 2020. Structures and buildings allowances were not available. **(4 marks)**

Required:

Calculate the total net chargeable gains to be included in Crate plc's taxable total profits for the year ending 31 March 2026.

Use the following indexation factors:

March 2000 – December 2017	0.651
June 2004 – December 2017	0.489

(Total: 10 marks)

109 PETAL LTD

Petal Ltd sold 3,000 shares in Bud Ltd on 19 October 2025 for £21,000. Bud Ltd has one million shares in issue.

Petal Ltd had purchased shares in Bud Ltd as follows:

14 June 2007	1,000 shares for £3,000
17 January 2021	3,000 shares for £10,000

Relevant indexation factor is:

June 2007 to December 2017	0.342

Required:

Prepare the share pool in respect of Petal Ltd's holding of shares in Bud Ltd and state the number of shares owned after the disposal on 19 October 2025 together with their cost and indexed cost. (5 marks)

110 NICHOLS PLC

Nichols plc prepares accounts to 31 March 2026. On 30 June 2025, Nichols plc sold 8,000 shares in AD Ltd for £37,000 (net of costs). AD Ltd has one million shares in issue.

The holding in AD Ltd had been acquired as follows:

		Shares	Cost
			£
25 March 1989		6,000	9,000
3 June 1993	Bonus issue of 1 for 3		

Compute the total amount of gains chargeable to corporation tax on Nichols plc for the above transaction in respect of the accounting period to 31 March 2026. (5 marks)

The following indexation factors are supplied:

March 1989 – June 1993	0.256
March 1989 – December 2017	1.476
June 1993 – December 2017	0.972

111 KJP LTD

KJP Ltd sold two factories during its year ended 31 March 2026.

The first factory was sold in February 2026 for £260,000. The factory had cost £210,000 in January 2024. This factory had always been used in KJP Ltd's business.

The second factory was sold in March 2026 for £325,000. The factory had cost £280,000 in February 2024. This factory had been purchased as an investment and was never used in KJP Ltd's business.

A new factory was purchased in May 2026 for £250,000 and will always be used in KJP Ltd's business.

Structures and buildings allowances were not available in respect of any of the factories.

Required:

On the assumption that rollover relief is claimed where possible, calculate KJP Ltd's total chargeable gains for the year ended 31 March 2026. (5 marks)

VALUE ADDED TAX

112 EMMA

Emma is a sole trader and is registered for value added tax (VAT). In the quarter ended 31 March 2026 Emma had the following transactions:

Sales (exclusive of VAT where applicable)

Standard-rated	£450,000
Zero-rated	£20,000
Purchases and expenses	
Purchases of inventory (all standard-rated and exclusive of VAT)	£180,000
Expenses (inclusive of standard-rated VAT where applicable)	
Wages	£120,000
Electricity	£40,000
Motoring expenses (all business)	£15,000

A discount of 4% is offered to select customers if invoices are paid within 30 days. Invoices, representing £25,000 of standard-rated sales and £1,000 of zero-rated sales, were paid within this time during the quarter ended 31 March 2026. These figures are exclusive of VAT.

Debts of £1,200 and £900 (exclusive of VAT at 20%), which were due on 1 February 2025 and 13 October 2025 respectively, were written off by Emma in March 2026.

Required:

Calculate the value added tax (VAT) payable or reclaimable by Emma for the quarter ended 31 March 2026. (10 marks)

113 MONTY

(a) Monty has been trading for the last three years. Their annual standard-rated sales have recently exceeded the VAT threshold of £90,000 but they have failed to notify HM Revenue and Customs.

Required:

Explain the amount(s) of late notification penalty that could be applied. (3 marks)

(b) Broad Ltd is registered for VAT.

Required:

State two types of expenditure on which the input VAT payable by a registered trader is treated as 'blocked' and therefore irrecoverable. (2 marks)

(Total: 5 marks)

114 OMAR

Omar operates a jewellery business and is registered for VAT.

He received an order for a silver and diamond necklace on 14 May 2025. A deposit of £350 was received with the order. The order was completed and delivered on 16 July 2025. An invoice was raised and dispatched on 20 July 2025 and the final (balancing) payment was received on 31 August 2025.

Omar does not operate the cash accounting scheme.

Required:

(a) **State how the tax point for VAT purposes is determined and the date(s) which will apply in this case. (6 marks)**

(b) **State how the VAT tax point is determined for goods supplied on a sale or return basis. (2 marks)**

(c) **State how the VAT tax point is determined for continuous supplies of services. (2 marks)**

(Total: 10 marks)

115 YEE-LING

Yee-ling is a sole trader and has recently registered for value added tax (VAT).

Yee-ling understands that it is important to use the correct deemed date of sale (i.e. the tax point). Recently she sold inventory for £3,000. A £400 payment in advance had been received on 28 May 2025 and the inventory was delivered on 24 June 2025. Yee-ling sent an invoice for the balance due of £2,600 on 2 July 2025 and received this amount from the customer on 1 August 2025.

Yee-ling is not in the cash accounting scheme.

Required:

(a) **State how the tax point (time of supply) is determined for the purposes of VAT. (2 marks)**

(b) **State, giving reasons, the tax point(s) in respect of the above transaction made by Yee-ling. (2 marks)**

(c) **Give one reason why it is important to determine the right tax point. (1 mark)**

(Total: 5 marks)

116 MARTHA

Martha started her own business on 1 October 2025 and has a taxable turnover of £15,100 of standard-rated sales per month.

Required:

(a) **State by when Martha must notify HM Revenue and Customs (HMRC) that she is liable to be registered for value added tax (VAT) and from what date the registration would normally be effective. (6 marks)**

(b) **Explain the circumstances in which Martha will be allowed to recover input VAT incurred on goods purchased and services incurred prior to the date of VAT registration. (4 marks)**

(Total: 10 marks)

117 MARJORIE

Marjorie is a sole trader and is registered for value added tax (VAT). For the quarter ended 31 March 2026 Marjorie had the following results:

	£
Standard-rated sales	260,000
Exempt sales	40,000
Standard-rated purchases	108,000
A new van used for business purposes only	27,000

The sales figures are exclusive of VAT and the purchases and the van are inclusive of VAT.

In addition to the above Marjorie wrote off two debts, one for £2,000 and the other one for £3,000 (both amounts exclusive of VAT). The first debt was for a sale completed in November 2025 and the second for a sale completed in May 2025. Both debts were in relation to standard-rated sales.

Required:

Calculate the amount of VAT Marjorie must pay to HM Revenue and Customs (HMRC) for the quarter ended 31 March 2026. (5 marks)

118 ATHLETIC LTD

Athletic Ltd is a small UK registered company, which is not yet registered for value added tax (VAT). The company started to trade on 1 December 2025 and its forecast total sales for the periods shown are expected to be:

1 December 2025 to 28 February 2026	£23,000
1 March 2026 to 31 May 2026	£30,000
1 June 2026 to 31 August 2026	£60,000

You should assume that all sales are of taxable items, are a mixture of standard and zero-rated, and are made evenly throughout the periods shown. The above figures are exclusive of VAT.

Required:

(a) **State the date by which Athletic Ltd will have to notify HM Revenue and Customs (HMRC) of its need to register for VAT.**

Include workings to support your answer. (3 marks)

(b) **On the basis of your answer to (a), state the date from which Athletic Ltd should charge VAT. (1 mark)**

(c) **On the assumption that Athletic Ltd only makes standard-rated sales and does not join the annual accounting scheme, state the length of the company's normal VAT return period and when the VAT return must be received by HMRC. (2 marks)**

(d) **State two advantages and two disadvantages of registering for VAT voluntarily (i.e. when annual turnover is below the annual registration threshold). (4 marks)**

(Total: 10 marks)

119 EMAIL

You are a junior accountant. Today's date is 16 July 2026.

The company financial accountant has asked you to deal with the VAT return for the quarter ended 30 June 2026.

The VAT payable from the VAT return you have just completed is £11,657.42.

Required:

Draft an email to the financial accountant advising him of the amount of VAT that will be paid or received, how it will be paid, the date due and the impact that the VAT payment may have on the company cash flow and financial forecasts. (5 marks)

120 VECTOR LTD

Vector Ltd is registered for VAT, and is in the process of completing its VAT return for the quarter ended 31 March 2026. The following information is available.

1. Sales invoices totalling £128,000 and £40,000 were issued in respect of standard-rated sales, and zero-rated sales respectively.
2. On 15 March 2026 Vector Ltd received an advance deposit of £4,500 (VAT-inclusive) in respect of a contract that is due to be completed during April 2026. The total value of the contract is £10,000. No sales invoices had been raised in relation to this contract as at 31 March 2026.
3. Standard-rated expenses are £74,800, including £4,200 for entertaining UK customers.
4. On 31 March 2026 Vector Ltd wrote off £12,000 due from a customer as an irrecoverable debt. The debt was in respect of three invoices, each of £4,000, that were due for payment on 15 August, 15 September and 15 October 2025 respectively. Each invoice had VAT of £800 added to make a total payable by the customer of £4,800.
5. On 1 January 2026 the company purchased a car costing £9,800 for the use of its sales manager for both private and business purposes.
6. On 14 January 2026 the company spent £16,500 (VAT-inclusive) on a new piece of plant.

Unless indicated otherwise all of the above figures are exclusive of VAT.

Required:

Calculate the amount of VAT payable by Vector Ltd for the quarter ended 31 March 2026. (10 marks)

121 DOUGLAS

Douglas started to trade as a sole trader on 1 May 2025 selling standard-rated items. For the first 12 months of trading Douglas achieved a taxable turnover of £14,000 per month and gross profit of £9,000 per month.

Required:

(i) Explain by which date Douglas should have notified HM Revenue and Customs (HMRC) of his need to register for value added tax (VAT).

(ii) State from which date Douglas should have been registered for VAT.

(iii) State the maximum penalty for late VAT registration.

(iv) Explain in what circumstances could the penalty be reduced to zero.

(Total: 5 marks)

122 BATTERY LTD

(a) Battery Ltd only sells goods of high value and at present issues sales invoices that show:

1 the invoice date and invoice number

2 the type of supply

3 the quantity and a description of the goods supplied

4 Battery Ltd's name and address, and

5 the name and address of the customer

6 The total VAT-exclusive amount

7 The amount of VAT payable

Required:

State the additional information that Battery Ltd will have to show on its sales invoices in order that these are valid for VAT purposes. (2 marks)

(b) There are two tests for determining compulsory registration for VAT. One is the past turnover test which looks at the taxable turnover of the last 12 months and the other is the future turnover test.

Required:

Explain how the future turnover test is applied. (3 marks)

(Total: 5 marks)

123 CONFUSED LTD

(a) Confused Ltd will commence trading in 2026. The company operates a small aeroplane, and is considering three alternative types of business.

These are:

1 training, in which case all sales will be standard-rated for VAT,

2 transport, in which case all sales will be zero-rated for VAT, and

3 an air ambulance service, in which case all sales will be exempt from VAT.

For each alternative, Confused Ltd's sales will be £91,000 per month (exclusive of VAT), and standard-rated expenses will be £10,000 per month (inclusive of VAT).

Required:

For each of the three alternative types of business

(i) state whether Confused Ltd will be required or permitted to register for VAT when trading commences, and

(ii) calculate the monthly amount of output VAT due and input VAT recoverable.

(8 marks)

(b) Puzzled Ltd has discovered that a number of errors have been made when preparing its VAT returns for the previous four quarters. As a result of the errors, the company will have to make an additional payment of VAT to HM Revenue and Customs.

Required:

Explain how Puzzled Ltd can voluntarily disclose the errors that have been discovered. (2 marks)

(Total: 10 marks)

124 VAT ERRORS

The following table shows four possible error situations.

	Net error	Turnover
	£	£
1	24,567	2,000,000
2	4,568	85,400
3	35,980	4,567,090
4	51,600	10,000,000

Required:

For each of the situations, explain whether the non-deliberate error can be corrected on the next VAT return or whether separate disclosure is required. (10 marks)

125 ASTUTE LTD

Astute Ltd registered for VAT on 1 July 2025. The company has annual standard-rated sales of £350,000. This figure is inclusive of VAT. Because of bookkeeping problems Astute Ltd has been late in submitting its VAT returns.

Required:

Advise Astute Ltd of the conditions that it must satisfy before being permitted to use the VAT annual accounting scheme, and the advantages of joining the scheme. (5 marks)

126 BRIGHT LTD

Bright Ltd voluntarily registered for VAT on 1 January 2026.

The company will have annual standard-rated sales of £75,000 all made to the general public. The company will have annual standard-rated expenses of £13,000 and will buy machinery costing £1,000 each year. All figures are inclusive of VAT at 20%.

The relevant flat rate scheme percentage for the company's trade is 12%.

Required:

(a) **Advise Bright Ltd of the conditions that it must satisfy before being permitted to use the VAT flat rate scheme, the advantages of joining the scheme and when it must leave the scheme. (5 marks)**

(b) **Calculate the potential annual tax saving to Bright Ltd if it uses the flat rate scheme. Ignore the 1% reduction of the flat rate percentage in the first year of VAT registration. (5 marks)**

(Total: 10 marks)

127 CLEVER LTD

Clever Ltd registered for VAT on 1 June 2025. The company has annual standard-rated sales of £250,000. This figure is inclusive of VAT. The company pays its expenses on a cash basis, but allows customers three months credit when paying for sales. Several of Clever Ltd's customers have recently defaulted on the payment of their debts.

Required:

Advise Clever Ltd of the conditions that it must satisfy before being permitted to use the VAT cash accounting scheme, and the advantages of joining the scheme. (5 marks)

128 CITY MERCHANDISE LTD

City Merchandise Ltd prepares value added tax (VAT) returns on a quarterly basis. It does not operate the cash accounting scheme.

During the company's quarter ended 31 March 2026 the following transactions occurred:

Standard-rated sales	£110,000
Zero-rated sales	£30,000
Standard-rated purchases	£60,000

The above three amounts are stated exclusive of VAT where applicable.

The company offers a 5% discount to their three key customers if they pay within 10 days. Only one customer does so and standard-rated invoices totalling £55,000 (VAT-exclusive) were settled in this VAT quarter within the 10-day discount period. All these invoices were issued in the current quarter.

The company also paid the following expenses during the same VAT quarter:

Electricity	£4,000
Wages	£28,000
Machine repairs	£2,500
Entertaining UK customers	£1,400
Entertaining overseas customers	£900
Car to be used exclusively for business	£12,600

The above six expense amounts are stated inclusive of standard-rated VAT where applicable.

Required:

Calculate the VAT payable for the quarter ended 31 March 2026 and state by when this amount must be paid. **(10 marks)**

129 DEFINITIONS

Nuala wishes to know a little more about VAT. You have offered to explain the meaning of taxable persons and taxable supplies to her.

Required:

(a) **What is a taxable person for VAT purposes?** **(1 mark)**

(b) **Name four conditions that must be met before a supply can come within the scope of VAT.** **(4 marks)**

(Total: 5 marks)

130 BADRU

On 1 July 2025, Badru became a value added tax (VAT) registered sole trader making standard-rated supplies to VAT-registered customers.

Prior to her VAT registration, Badru bought a laptop for use in her business on 12 December 2024, incurring VAT on the purchase.

Required:

(a) **State four items which Badru must include on a value added tax (VAT) invoice to her customers.** **(2 marks)**

(b) **State how long Badru must keep her VAT records of supplies made to customers.** **(1 mark)**

(c) **Explain the rules which allow Badru to recover the pre-registration input VAT incurred on the laptop.** **(2 marks)**

(Total: 5 marks)

TAX RETURNS

131 ABRAHAM

Abraham is a sole trader who has been in business for many years. He uses the accruals basis.

Included in his expenses for the year ended 31 March 2026 are the following:

		£
1	Irrecoverable debts written off comprise:	
	Increase in specific provision for impairment losses	800
	Increase in general provision for impairment losses	268
	Trade debts written off	672
	Trade debts recovered	(200)
2	Rent, rates and insurance include:	
	Expenses relating to the flat where Abraham lives	3,000
3	Motor expenses comprise:	
	Van expenses (van used by Abraham exclusively for the business)	1,875
	Car expenses (car used by Abraham exclusively for private purposes)	2,690
4	Wages and salaries include:	
	Abraham's drawings	18,000
5	Miscellaneous expenses include:	
	Gifts of diaries to customers	800
	– costing £7 each and bearing the logo of the business	
	Parking fines incurred by Abraham	280

Required:

State the additional figures that would be entered into the relevant boxes of the tax return below as far as possible using the above information and the information on the return. Boxes 17 to 31 have already been completed. It is not necessary to include any boxes which will be left blank in your answer. (10 marks)

Business expenses

Please read the 'Self-employment (full) notes' before filling in this section.

Box	Total expenses If your annual turnover was below £85,000, you may just put your total expenses in box 31	Box	Disallowable expenses Use this column if the figures in boxes 17 to 30 include disallowable amounts
17	Cost of goods bought for resale or goods used £ 176432.00	32	£ .00
18	Construction industry – payments to subcontractors £ .00	33	£ .00
19	Wages, salaries and other staff costs £ 27680.00	34	£ .00
20	Car, van and travel expenses £ 4565.00	35	£ .00
21	Rent, rates, power and insurance costs £ 15469.00	36	£ .00
22	Repairs and maintenance of property and equipment £ 250.00	37	£ .00
23	Phone, fax, stationery and other office costs £ 956.00	38	£ .00
24	Advertising and business entertainment costs £ .00	39	£ .00
25	Interest on bank and other loans £ .00	40	£ .00
26	Bank, credit card and other financial charges £ .00	41	£ .00
27	Irrecoverable debts written off £ 1540.00	42	£ .00
28	Accountancy, legal and other professional fees £ 1020.00	43	£ .00
29	Depreciation and loss/profit on sale of assets £ 6455.00	44	£ .00
30	Other business expenses £ 1970.00	45	£ .00
31	Total expenses (total of boxes 17 to 30) £ 236337.00	46	Total disallowable expenses (total of boxes 32 to 45) £ .00

132 JACK

Jack runs a sole trader business and uses the accruals basis. He has given you the following information about his capital allowances claim for the year ended 31 March 2026.

	£
Annual investment allowance	22,560
WDA on main pool	12,400
WDA on special rate pool	2,560

Required:

Using this information, state the figures that would be entered into the relevant boxes of the following tax return extract. It is not necessary to include any boxes which will be left blank in your answer. (5 marks)

Tax allowances for vehicles and equipment (capital allowances)

There are 'capital' tax allowances for vehicles, equipment and certain buildings used in your business (do not include the cost of these in your business expenses). Please read the 'Self-employment (full) notes' and use the examples to work out your capital allowances.

49 Annual Investment Allowance
£ .00

50 Capital allowances at 18% on equipment, including cars with lower CO2 emissions
£ .00

51 Capital allowances at 6% on equipment, including cars with higher CO2 emissions
£ .00

52 Zero-emission goods vehicle allowance
£ .00

52.1 Zero-emission car allowance
£ .00

53 The Structures and Buildings Allowance
£ .00

53.1 Freeport and Investment Zones Structures and Buildings Allowance
£ .00

54 Electric charge-point allowance
£ .00

55 100% and other enhanced capital allowances
£ .00

56 Allowances on sale or cessation of business use (where you've disposed of assets for less than their tax value)
£ .00

57 Total capital allowances (total of boxes 49 to 56)
£ .00

Box 58 is not in use

59 Balancing charge on sales of assets or on the cessation of business use (including where Business Premises Renovation Allowance has been claimed) for example, where you've disposed of assets for more than their tax value
£ .00

133 LYNNE

Lynne has traded in partnership with Shirley for many years as social event organisers. Profits are shared in the ratio 3:2 to Lynne and Shirley respectively.

The partnership trading profits for the year ended 31 March 2026 are £230,400, and the partnership received interest of £6,210.

Lynne has a trading loss brought forward of £20,000.

Required:

State the figures that would be entered into boxes 16, 17, 18, 20 and 28 of the extracts of the return below for Lynne as far as is possible using the above information. (5 marks)

Your share of the partnership's trading or professional profits

Please refer to the Partnership Statement to complete these pages and if you need any help, read the 'Partnership (short) notes'. If your partnership's accounting date is not between 31 March and 5 April you will need to apportion your share of the partnership's profits from each accounting period to the tax year – use box 9 to adjust your share of the profit or loss (box 8). If the partnership carries on certain trades or professions, or in certain situations, you may need to make further tax adjustments in boxes 10 to 12. If you have untaxed transition profit from 2023–24 you will need to complete the 'Partnership (full)' page.
If you want to enter a loss, or an adjustment needs to be taken off, put a minus (–) in the box next to the £ sign.

Boxes 6 and 7 are not in use

8 **Your share of the partnership's profit or loss** – from box 11 or box 12 on the Partnership Statement

£ • 0 0

9 **Adjustment where the partnership's accounting period ended before 31 March 2026 or where the partnership's accounting period was not 12 months long**

£ • 0 0

10 **Adjustment for change of accounting practice** – from box 11A on the Partnership Statement

£ • 0 0

11 **Averaging adjustment** – only for farmers, market gardeners and creators of literary or artistic works

£ • 0 0

12 **Foreign tax claimed as a deduction** – only if Foreign Tax Credit Relief is not being claimed on the 'Foreign' pages

£ • 0 0

Boxes 13, 14 and 15 are not in use

16 **Adjusted profit for 2025–26** – see the working sheet in the notes

£ • 0 0

17 **Losses brought forward from earlier years set off against this year's profit (up to the amount in box 16)**

£ • 0 0

18 **Taxable profits after losses brought forward (box 16 minus box 17)**

£ • 0 0

19 **Any other business income not included in the partnership accounts**

£ • 0 0

20 **Your share of total taxable profits from the partnership's business for 2025–26 (box 18 + box 19)**

£ • 0 0

Your share of the partnership's untaxed interest

28 **Your share of untaxed interest** – from box 13 on the Partnership Statement

£ • 0 0

Box 29 is not in use

134 BROADHURST

Broadhurst is in business and has been registered for VAT for several years. His digital VAT records show the following for the quarter ended 31 December 2025. All items are standard-rated except where noted and are stated excluding VAT.

	£
Sales	175,560
Purchases of goods	113,670
Purchase returns	5,249
Purchase of a car (Note)	14,000
Entertaining overseas customers	1,560

In addition, Broadhurst wishes to claim impaired debt relief on an eight months old debt which he has just written off. The debt is £1,760.

Note: The car is to be used by an employee 60% privately.

Required:

Show the figures that Broadhurst should expect to see on the automatically produced MTD (Making Tax Digital) VAT return for the quarter ended 31 December 2025, by entering them into the relevant boxes on the VAT return pro forma shown below.

Enter VAT figures. **(10 marks)**

Box 1	VAT due in this period on sales and other outputs	
Box 4	VAT reclaimed in the period on purchases and other inputs	
Box 5	Net VAT to be paid to HM Revenue and Customs or reclaimed by you	
Box 6	Total value of sales and all other outputs excluding any VAT	
Box 7	Total value of purchases and all other inputs excluding any VAT	

135 RACHAEL

Rachael sold 3 lots of listed shares during the tax year 2025/26. These were her only capital disposals during the tax year 2025/26. None of the disposals qualify for business asset disposal relief.

She has £5,000 of capital losses brought forward.

The summary information from these disposals is:

Shares		**Sale proceeds**	**Cost**
		£	£
May 2025	disposal	20,200	14,000
November 2025	disposal	10,000	8,000
January 2026	disposal	7,000	9,000

Required:

State the figures that would be entered into the relevant boxes of the tax return below as far as is possible using the above information. It is not necessary to include any boxes which will be left blank in your answer. **(10 marks)**

HM Revenue & Customs

Capital Gains Tax summary

Tax year 6 April 2025 to 5 April 2026 (2025–26)

1 **Your name**

2 **Your Unique Taxpayer Reference (UTR)**

You must enclose your computations, including details of each gain or loss, as well as filling in the boxes.

Residential property and carried interest – Please read the notes before filling in this section.

3 **Number of disposals**

4 **Disposal proceeds**

£ · 0 0

5 **Allowable costs (including purchase price)**

£ · 0 0

6 **Gains on residential property in the year, before losses** – do not include gains on carried interest. Any gains on residential property included in boxes 9 and 11 amounts must be included in this total

£ · 0 0

7 **Losses in the year** – any losses included in boxes 9 and 11 amounts must be included in this total

£ · 0 0

8 **If you're making any claim or election, put the relevant code in the box**

9 **Total gains or losses on UK residential property reported on Capital Gains Tax UK Property Disposal returns**

£ · 0 0

10 **Tax on gains in box 9 already charged**

£ · 0 0

11 **Total gains or losses on non-UK residential property or carried interest reported on Real Time Transaction returns**

£ · 0 0

12 **Tax on gains in box 11 already paid**

£ · 0 0

13 **Carried interest (arising basis)** – the amount before any claim or election

£ · 0 0

13A **Carried interest (accruals basis)** – the amount before any claim or election

£ · 0 0

13B **Gains on carried interest in the year** – the sum of boxes 13 and 13A, less any claim or election. Any gains on carried interest included in box 11 amounts must be included in this total

£ · 0 0

Cryptoassets – Please read the notes before filling in this section.

13.1 **Number of disposals**

13.2 **Disposal proceeds**

£ · 0 0

13.3 **Allowable costs (including purchase price)**

£ · 0 0

13.4 **Gains in the year, before losses** – any gains included in box 13.7 amounts must be included in this total

£ · 0 0

13.5 **Losses in the year** – any losses included in box 13.7 amounts must be included in this total

£ · 0 0

13.6 **If you're making any claim or election, put the relevant code in the box**

13.7 **Total gains or losses on the disposal of an asset of this type reported on Real Time Transaction returns**

£ · 0 0

13.8 **Tax on gains in box 13.7 already paid**

£ · 0 0

SA108 2026 Page CG 1 HMRC 12/25

Other property, assets and gains – Gains where Business Assets Disposal Relief (BADR) is being claimed should be included in this section. Please read the notes before filling in this section.

14 **Number of disposals**

15 **Disposal proceeds**

£ · 0 0

16 **Allowable costs (including purchase price)**

£ · 0 0

17 **Gains in the year, before losses** – do not include attributed gains included in box 18. Any gains included in box 21 amounts must be included in this total

£ · 0 0

17.1 **Enter the amount included in box 17 total relating to disposals of non-residential land and buildings**

£ · 0 0

In boxes 17.2 to 17.4, enter the amounts in the box 17 total that relate to a disposal where BADR is being claimed as advised in the guidance notes.

17.2 **Residential property and non-residential land and buildings**

£ · 0 0

17.3 **Listed and unlisted shares and securities**

£ · 0 0

17.4 **Other assets**

£ · 0 0

18 **Attributed gains where personal losses cannot be set off**

£ · 0 0

19 **Losses in the year** – any losses included in box 21 amounts must be included in this total

£ · 0 0

20 **If you're making any claim or election, put the relevant code in the box**

21 **Total gains or losses on the disposal of an asset of this type reported on Real Time Transaction returns**

£ · 0 0

22 **Tax on gains in box 21 already paid**

£ · 0 0

Listed shares and securities – Please read the notes before filling in this section.

23 **Number of disposals**

24 **Disposal proceeds**

£ · 0 0

25 **Allowable costs (including purchase price)**

£ · 0 0

26 **Gains in the year, before losses** – any gains included in box 29 amounts must be included in this total

£ · 0 0

27 **Losses in the year** – any losses included in box 29 amounts must be included in this total

£ · 0 0

28 **If you're making any claim or election, put the relevant code in the box**

29 **Total gains or losses on the disposal of an asset of this type reported on Real Time Transaction returns**

£ · 0 0

30 **Tax on gains in box 29 already paid**

£ · 0 0

SA108 2026 Page CG 2

Unlisted shares and securities – Please read the notes before filling in this section.

31 **Number of disposals**

32 **Disposal proceeds**
£ .00

33 **Allowable costs (including purchase price)**
£ .00

34 **Gains in the year, before losses** – any gains included in box 37 amounts must be included in this total
£ .00

35 **Losses in the year** – any losses included in box 37 amounts must be included in this total
£ .00

36 **If you're making any claim or election, put the relevant code in the box**

37 **Total gains or losses on the disposal of an asset of this type reported on Real Time Transaction returns**
£ .00

38 **Tax on gains in box 37 already paid**
£ .00

39 **Gains exceeding the lifetime limit for employee shareholder status shares**
£ .00

40 **Gains invested under Seed Enterprise Investment Scheme and qualifying for relief**
£ .00

41 **Losses used against income** – amount claimed against 2025–26 income
£ .00

42 **Amount in box 41 relating to share loss relief in 2025–26 to which Enterprise Investment Scheme or Seed Enterprise Investment Scheme Relief is attributable**
£ .00

43 **Losses used against income** – amount claimed against 2024–25 income
£ .00

44 **Amount in box 43 relating to share loss relief in 2024–25 to which Enterprise Investment Scheme or Seed Enterprise Investment Scheme Relief is attributable**
£ .00

Losses and adjustments – Please read the notes before filling in this section.

Losses set against 2025–26 capital gains

45 **Losses brought forward and used in-year**
£ .00

46 **Income losses of 2025–26 set against gains**
£ .00

2025–26 capital losses – other information

47 **Losses available to be carried forward**
£ .00

48 **Losses used against an earlier year's gain**
£ .00

Investors' Relief and Business Asset Disposal Relief (previously 'Entrepreneurs' Relief')

49 **Gains qualifying for Investors' Relief**
£ .00

50 **Gains qualifying for Business Asset Disposal Relief**
£ .00

50.1 **Lifetime allowance of Business Asset Disposal Relief and Entrepreneurs' Relief claimed** – the total amount claimed to date
£ .00

SA108 2026 Page CG 3

136 PANDORA

Pandora sold two blocks of unquoted shares during the tax year 2025/26.

The summary information from these disposals is:

Shares		**Sale proceeds**	**Cost**
		£	£
June 2025	Disposal	35,000	20,000
September 2025	Disposal	15,000	12,000

She also sold a house, (not her main private residence) for £110,000 on 31 May 2025. The house cost £45,000 when bought. Pandora paid £14,880 capital gains tax in June 2025.

Required:

State the figures that would be entered into the relevant boxes of the tax return below as far as is possible using the above information. It is not necessary to include any boxes which will be left blank in your answer. (10 marks)

HM Revenue & Customs

Capital Gains Tax summary

Tax year 6 April 2025 to 5 April 2026 (2025–26)

1 **Your name**

2 **Your Unique Taxpayer Reference (UTR)**

You must enclose your computations, including details of each gain or loss, as well as filling in the boxes.

Residential property and carried interest – Please read the notes before filling in this section.

3 **Number of disposals**

4 **Disposal proceeds**

£ · 0 0

5 **Allowable costs (including purchase price)**

£ · 0 0

6 **Gains on residential property in the year, before losses** – do not include gains on carried interest. Any gains on residential property included in boxes 9 and 11 amounts must be included in this total

£ · 0 0

7 **Losses in the year** – any losses included in boxes 9 and 11 amounts must be included in this total

£ · 0 0

8 **If you're making any claim or election, put the relevant code in the box**

9 **Total gains or losses on UK residential property reported on Capital Gains Tax UK Property Disposal returns**

£ · 0 0

10 **Tax on gains in box 9 already charged**

£ · 0 0

11 **Total gains or losses on non-UK residential property or carried interest reported on Real Time Transaction returns**

£ · 0 0

12 **Tax on gains in box 11 already paid**

£ · 0 0

13 **Carried interest (arising basis)** – the amount before any claim or election

£ · 0 0

13A **Carried interest (accruals basis)** – the amount before any claim or election

£ · 0 0

13B **Gains on carried interest in the year** – the sum of boxes 13 and 13A, less any claim or election. Any gains on carried interest included in box 11 amounts must be included in this total

£ · 0 0

Cryptoassets – Please read the notes before filling in this section.

13.1 **Number of disposals**

13.2 **Disposal proceeds**

£ · 0 0

13.3 **Allowable costs (including purchase price)**

£ · 0 0

13.4 **Gains in the year, before losses** – any gains included in box 13.7 amounts must be included in this total

£ · 0 0

13.5 **Losses in the year** – any losses included in box 13.7 amounts must be included in this total

£ · 0 0

13.6 **If you're making any claim or election, put the relevant code in the box**

13.7 **Total gains or losses on the disposal of an asset of this type reported on Real Time Transaction returns**

£ · 0 0

13.8 **Tax on gains in box 13.7 already paid**

£ · 0 0

SA108 2026 Page CG 1 HMRC 12/25

Other property, assets and gains – Gains where Business Assets Disposal Relief (BADR) is being claimed should be included in this section. Please read the notes before filling in this section.

14 Number of disposals

15 Disposal proceeds

£ .00

16 Allowable costs (including purchase price)

£ .00

17 Gains in the year, before losses – do not include attributed gains included in box 18. Any gains included in box 21 amounts must be included in this total

£ .00

17.1 Enter the amount included in box 17 total relating to disposals of non-residential land and buildings

£ .00

In boxes 17.2 to 17.4, enter the amounts in the box 17 total that relate to a disposal where BADR is being claimed as advised in the guidance notes.

17.2 Residential property and non-residential land and buildings

£ .00

17.3 Listed and unlisted shares and securities

£ .00

17.4 Other assets

£ .00

18 Attributed gains where personal losses cannot be set off

£ .00

19 Losses in the year – any losses included in box 21 amounts must be included in this total

£ .00

20 If you're making any claim or election, put the relevant code in the box

21 Total gains or losses on the disposal of an asset of this type reported on Real Time Transaction returns

£ .00

22 Tax on gains in box 21 already paid

£ .00

Listed shares and securities – Please read the notes before filling in this section.

23 Number of disposals

24 Disposal proceeds

£ .00

25 Allowable costs (including purchase price)

£ .00

26 Gains in the year, before losses – any gains included in box 29 amounts must be included in this total

£ .00

27 Losses in the year – any losses included in box 29 amounts must be included in this total

£ .00

28 If you're making any claim or election, put the relevant code in the box

29 Total gains or losses on the disposal of an asset of this type reported on Real Time Transaction returns

£ .00

30 Tax on gains in box 29 already paid

£ .00

SA108 2026 Page CG 2

Unlisted shares and securities – Please read the notes before filling in this section.

31 **Number of disposals**

32 **Disposal proceeds**

£ · 0 0

33 **Allowable costs (including purchase price)**

£ · 0 0

34 **Gains in the year, before losses** – any gains included in box 37 amounts must be included in this total

£ · 0 0

35 **Losses in the year** – any losses included in box 37 amounts must be included in this total

£ · 0 0

36 **If you're making any claim or election, put the relevant code in the box**

37 **Total gains or losses on the disposal of an asset of this type reported on Real Time Transaction returns**

£ · 0 0

38 **Tax on gains in box 37 already paid**

£ · 0 0

39 **Gains exceeding the lifetime limit for employee shareholder status shares**

£ · 0 0

40 **Gains invested under Seed Enterprise Investment Scheme and qualifying for relief**

£ · 0 0

41 **Losses used against income** – amount claimed against 2025–26 income

£ · 0 0

42 **Amount in box 41 relating to share loss relief in 2025–26 to which Enterprise Investment Scheme or Seed Enterprise Investment Scheme Relief is attributable**

£ · 0 0

43 **Losses used against income** – amount claimed against 2024–25 income

£ · 0 0

44 **Amount in box 43 relating to share loss relief in 2024–25 to which Enterprise Investment Scheme or Seed Enterprise Investment Scheme Relief is attributable**

£ · 0 0

Losses and adjustments – Please read the notes before filling in this section.

Losses set against 2025–26 capital gains

45 **Losses brought forward and used in-year**

£ · 0 0

46 **Income losses of 2025–26 set against gains**

£ · 0 0

2025–26 capital losses – other information

47 **Losses available to be carried forward**

£ · 0 0

48 **Losses used against an earlier year's gain**

£ · 0 0

Investors' Relief and Business Asset Disposal Relief (previously 'Entrepreneurs' Relief')

49 **Gains qualifying for Investors' Relief**

£ · 0 0

50 **Gains qualifying for Business Asset Disposal Relief**

£ · 0 0

50.1 **Lifetime allowance of Business Asset Disposal Relief and Entrepreneurs' Relief claimed** – the total amount claimed to date

£ · 0 0

SA108 2026 Page CG 3

137 HUMMEL LTD

In the year ended 31 March 2026 Hummel Ltd had made sales of £1,000,000 leading to a taxable trading profit of £585,000.

The company also had rental profits of £200,000, interest income of £20,000, chargeable gains of £110,000 and made a qualifying charitable donation of £20,000.

Required:

State the figures that would be entered into the relevant boxes of the return below as far as is possible down to Box 315, 'profits chargeable to corporation tax' (i.e. taxable total profits), using the information above. It is not necessary to include any boxes which will be left blank in your answer. (10 marks)

Tax calculation - Turnover

145	Total turnover from trade	£ .00
150	Banks, building societies, insurance companies and other financial concerns - put an 'X' in this box if you do not have a recognised turnover and have not made an entry in box 145	☐

Income

155	Trading profits	£ .00
160	Trading losses brought forward set against trading profits	£ .00
165	Net trading profits - box 155 minus box 160	£ .00
170	Bank, building society or other interest, and profits from non-trading loan relationships	£ .00
172	Put an 'X' in box 172 if the figure in box 170 is net of carrying back a deficit from a later accounting period	☐

CT600(2026) Version 3 Page 2 HMRC 04/26

Income - continued

175	Annual payments not otherwise charged to Corporation Tax and from which Income Tax has not been deducted	£ . 0 0
180	Non-exempt dividends or distributions from non-UK resident companies	£ . 0 0
185	Income from which Income Tax has been deducted	£ . 0 0
190	Income from a property business	£ . 0 0
195	Non-trading gains on intangible fixed assets	£ . 0 0
200	Tonnage tax profits	£ . 0 0
205	Income not falling under any other heading	£ . 0 0

Chargeable gains

210	Gross chargeable gains	£ . 0 0
215	Allowable losses including losses brought forward	£ . 0 0
220	Net chargeable gains - box 210 minus box 215	£ . 0 0

Profits before deductions and reliefs

225	Losses brought forward against certain investment income	£ . 0 0
230	Non-trade deficits on loan relationships (including interest) and derivative contracts (financial instruments) brought forward set against non-trading profits	£ . 0 0
235	Profits before other deductions and reliefs - net sum of boxes 165 to 205 and 220 minus sum of boxes 225 and 230	£ . 0 0

Deductions and reliefs

240	Losses on unquoted shares	£ . 0 0
245	Management expenses	£ . 0 0
250	UK property business losses for this or previous accounting period	£ . 0 0
255	Capital allowances for the purposes of management of the business	£ . 0 0
260	Non-trade deficits for this accounting period from loan relationships and derivative contracts (financial instruments)	£ . 0 0

CT600(2026) Version 3 Page 3 HMRC 04/26

Deductions and Reliefs - continued

263	Carried forward non-trade deficits from loan relationships and derivative contracts (financial instruments)	£ .00
265	Non-trading losses on intangible fixed assets	£ .00
275	Total trading losses of this or a later accounting period	£ .00
280	Put an 'X' in box 280 if amounts carried back from later accounting periods are included in box 275	
285	Trading losses carried forward and claimed against total profits	£ .00
290	Non-trade capital allowances	£ .00
295	Total of deductions and reliefs - total of boxes 240 to 275, 285 and 290	£ .00
300	Profits before qualifying donations and group relief - box 235 minus box 295	£ .00
305	Qualifying donations	£ .00
310	Group relief	£ .00
312	Group relief for carried forward losses	£ .00
315	Profits chargeable to Corporation Tax - box 300 minus boxes 305, 310 and 312	£ .00
320	Ring fence profits included	£ .00
325	Northern Ireland profits included	£ .00

138 JO LTD

Jo Ltd has taxable total profits of £375,000 for the year ended 31 March 2026.

Required:

State the figures that would be entered into the relevant boxes of the extract from the CT600 form set out below. It is not necessary to include any boxes which will be left blank in your answer. (5 marks)

Tax calculation

326	Number of associated companies in this period	
327	Number of associated companies in the first financial year	
328	Number of associated companies in the second financial year	
329	Put an 'X' in box 329 if the company is chargeable at the small profit rate or is entitled to marginal relief	

Enter how much profit has to be charged and at what rate

	Financial year (yyyy)		Amount of profit		Rate of tax %		Tax
330		335	£	340		345	£ p
		350	£	355		360	£ p
		365	£	370		375	£ p
380		385	£	390		395	£ p
		400	£	405		410	£ p
		415	£	420		425	£ p

CT600(2026) Version 3 Page 4 HMRC 04/26

Tax calculation - continued

Corporation Tax - total of boxes 345, 360, 375, 395, 410 and 425	430	£ .
Marginal relief	435	£ .
Corporation Tax chargeable - box 430 minus box 435	440	£ .

139 LEAFY LTD

Leafy Ltd has taxable total profits of £113,000 for the year ended 31 March 2026. The company has one associated company. No dividends were received during the year.

Required:

State the figures that would be entered into the relevant boxes of the extract from the CT600 form set out below. It is not necessary to include any boxes which will be left blank in your answer. **(5 marks)**

Tax calculation

326 Number of associated companies in this period

327 Number of associated companies in the first financial year

328 Number of associated companies in the second financial year

329 Put an 'X' in box 329 if the company is chargeable at the small profit rate or is entitled to marginal relief

Enter how much profit has to be charged and at what rate

	Financial year (yyyy)		Amount of profit		Rate of tax %		Tax
330		335	£	340		345	£ p
		350	£	355		360	£ p
		365	£	370		375	£ p
380		385	£	390		395	£ p
		400	£	405		410	£ p
		415	£	420		425	£ p

CT600(2026) Version 3 Page 4 HMRC 04/26

Tax calculation - continued

Corporation Tax - total of boxes 345, 360, 375, 395, 410 and 425	430	£ .
Marginal relief	435	£ .
Corporation Tax chargeable - box 430 minus box 435	440	£ .

Section 3

ANSWERS TO MULTIPLE CHOICE QUESTIONS

INTRODUCTION TO THE UK TAX SYSTEM

1 B

> ***Tutorial note***
>
> *VAT is an indirect tax because it is collected from the taxpayer by an intermediary such as a retail shop.*
>
> *The other taxes are direct taxes as they are collected directly from the taxpayer.*

2 B

Statements (1) and (3) are correct. HMRC statements of practice are HMRC's interpretation of the legislation. They have no legal force. National insurance contributions are a revenue tax as they apply to income.

3 D

The UK Parliament passes the annual Finance Act.

4 C

A taxpayer can still appeal to the Tax tribunal even if his, her or their case has been reviewed by another HMRC officer, so statement (2) is false.

The Tax tribunal deals with some cases by correspondence so statement (3) is false.

5 D

> ***Tutorial note***
>
> *Only companies pay corporation tax.*
>
> *Paddy suffers income tax and national insurance contributions on his earnings from employment. He pays VAT when he buys goods and services as a consumer.*

6 B

A taxpayer has 30 days from the issue of the amendment to lodge an appeal.

7 B

Extra statutory concessions are published by HM Revenue and Customs explaining circumstances when it will not apply the letter of the law.

8 C

> ***Tutorial note***
>
> *The Treasury appoint permanent civil servants, as the Board of Revenue and Customs, to administer the UK's taxation system.*
>
> *HMRC issues various types of guidance, setting out its interpretation of the legislation, both on its website and in publications such as Briefs, Statements of Practice, Notices and Guidance notes. They have no legal force and do not remove the taxpayer's right of appeal.*
>
> *The Treasury is the ministry responsible, under the Chancellor of the Exchequer (a government minister), for the imposition and collection of taxation.*

9 D

Capital gains tax applies to capital profits so is not a revenue tax.

TAX ADMINISTRATION

10 D

> ***Tutorial note***
>
> *Form P11D is used to report taxable benefits. It must reach HMRC by 6 July following the relevant tax year.*
>
> *Form P60 is given to each employee by 31 May following each tax year and is a summary of the employee's pay and tax deducted for the previous tax year.*

11 C

> ***Tutorial note***
>
> *Payments on account for 2025/26 are due on 31 January 2026 and 31 July 2026.*
>
> *Each payment is 50% of the 2024/25 income tax and class 4 NICs payable.*
>
> *The balance of tax is due on 31 January 2027 together with any 2025/26 capital gains tax payable plus the first payment on account for 2026/27.*

12 B

Taxpayers have 12 months from the normal filing date of 31 January 2027 to amend their return. The date is the same whether the return is filed electronically or by paper.

13 D

Payments on account = 50% × (£15,000 – £6,100) = £4,450.

Payments on account are not required for capital gains tax except for disposals of residential property. These are due 60 days after the disposal.

> ***Tutorial note***
>
> *Payments on account for 2025/26 are due on 31 January 2026 and 31 July 2026.*
>
> *Each payment is 50% of the 2024/25 income tax payable (i.e. after deducting PAYE) plus the class 4 NICs liability.*

14 A

Payments on account = 50% × £15,600 = £7,800.

The first payment on account on 31 January 2026, during the tax year 2025/26, should have been based on half of the actual 2024/25 liability. Payments on account are not calculated on the estimated liability for the current tax year 2025/26.

15 A

Business records for 2025/26 must be kept until 5 years after the filing date (i.e. 31 January 2032).

The other statements are true.

16 C

Under the common penalty regime, which applies to incorrect returns and late notification of liability, Fran can be penalised on an amount ranging from 0% to 100% of the tax underpaid as a result of the errors.

The amount charged can be reduced depending on the taxpayer's behaviour and co-operation.

17 C

An accountant can only disclose information about a client if the accountant has permission from the client or if the accountant has a legal, regulatory or professional duty to disclose (i.e. in cases of suspected money laundering).

18 B

The tax was due on 31 January 2027 and not actually paid until 10 March 2027.

Interest on late paid tax runs from the due date until the date of payment, so statement (1) is correct.

A 5% penalty is charged if the tax is paid more than 30 days late, so statement (3) is correct.

The immediate £100 penalty in (2) refers to penalties charged for late filing of returns – not late payments.

19 A

A sole trader must retain all records required to make and deliver the tax return for five years after the 31 January following the tax year.

20 B

21 B

An accountant can only disclose information about a client if the accountant has permission from the client or if the accountant has a legal, regulatory or professional duty to disclose (i.e. in cases of suspected money laundering).

The duty of confidentiality continues even after a client relationship has ended.

22 D

The fundamental principles are objectivity, integrity, professional behaviour, professional competence and due care, and confidentiality.

23 B

An accountant should cease to act for a client if the client refuses to disclose the income.

24 D

Tutorial note

Payments on account (POAs) are due for 2025/26 based on the amount paid in 2024/25.

However, no payments on account are required in the following circumstances:

- *tax payable (i.e. tax liability net of PAYE) for the previous year is less than £1,000; or*
- *more than 80% of the income tax liability for the previous year was met by deduction of PAYE. This will mean that most employed people will not have to make payments on account, since more than 80% of their tax liability is likely to be paid through PAYE. However, a taxpayer with only income from self-employment, does not pay PAYE and therefore will not meet the 80% requirement.*

25 D

26 D

Tutorial note

No penalties are applied to the late payment of a payment on account. However, interest may be charged.

TRADING PROFIT, CAPITAL ALLOWANCES AND LOSSES

27 C

Expenditure, which would be allowable once the business has commenced, is allowable if paid in the 7 years before trading commences. The rent and advertising are allowable but the suit is a private expense.

28 B

(£3,200 × 15%) = £480 add back.

15% of car leasing costs are disallowed if CO_2 emissions exceed 50g/km.

As £3,200 has been deducted in the accounts the disallowable amount of £480 must be added back.

29 C

WDA = (£18,000 × 18% × 7/12 × 40%) = £756

Tutorial note

Capital allowances are never restricted for the period of ownership, but are restricted for the length of the accounting period. Only the business proportion of allowances can be claimed.

Key answer tips

Having a short period for capital allowances is a popular type of question. You have to remember to time apportion the WDA and the maximum AIA.

Private use by a sole trader restricts the allowance but remember that for a company there are never any private use restrictions for capital allowances.

30 B

		Main pool	**Special rate pool**	**Allowances**
	£	£	£	£
Non-AIA assets – car (CO_2 > 50g/km)			8,000	
Assets qualifying for AIA	15,000			
AIA				
(Max £1,000,000 × 9/12 = £750,000)	(15,000)			15,000
	–––––	0		
WDA @ (6% × 9/12)			(360)	360
		–––––	–––––	
		0	7,640	
		–––––	–––––	–––––
				15,360
				–––––

Key answer tips

This is another question with a short period for capital allowances. You have to remember to time apportion the WDA and the maximum AIA.

The AIA is never available on cars.

31 D

This is a new zero emission car which qualifies for 100% FYA. The business use percentage is then applied to calculate the deductible allowances for the period. £31,500 × 30% = £9,450.

Tutorial note

AIA is not available on cars. This car does not attract a WDA because it is a zero emission car.

FYAs are never time apportioned.

32 B

All three items are disallowed and must be added back.

Tutorial note

Legal fees for ***renewing*** *a short lease (i.e. less than 50 years) are allowable.*

Car parking fines incurred by ***employees*** *(but not the owner/proprietor) whilst on business are allowable.*

33 C

Loss on the sale of a non-current asset is not an allowable expense (this is dealt with through the capital allowances computation). Entertainment of customers is also not an allowable expense for tax purposes. Staff entertaining is allowable.

34 B

Only the legal fees for the purchase of a new building are not allowable as they are capital expenditure. Staff entertainment is fully allowable, although any amount over £150 per head should be taxed on the employee as an employment income benefit.

The legal fees for defending an action for faulty goods and the bank fee are allowable expenses, as they are revenue in nature and were incurred wholly and exclusively for the purposes of the trade.

35 D

	£
Goods for resale	5,000
Business use portion of computer purchase 3,000 × 60%	1,800
Redecoration costs	1,000
Deductible expenditure	7,800

Tutorial note

Del uses the cash basis to calculate his taxable trading profits, being the default basis unless a claim is made to use the accruals basis. Therefore, the purchase of the computer is deductible, to the extent it is used for business purposes.

The redecoration costs are deductible when paid, not when incurred.

36 A

Mileage allowance deduction = 6,000 × 45p = £2,700

Tutorial note

If flat rate expenses are claimed, no other deductions for running costs or capital allowances can be claimed.

37 D

Maximum AIA for the 14-month period is £1,000,000 × 14/12 = £1,166,667. The additions for the period of £1,100,000 are therefore fully covered by the AIA.

Tutorial note

Capital allowances for a sole trader are prepared for the period of account, in this case a 14 month period.

38 D

Lease payments deductible in full	£4,800

Tutorial note

There is no restriction for lease payments in respect of high emission cars for cash basis users. If Aziz elected to use the accruals basis 15% of the cost of the lease would be disallowable as the car has emissions >50g/km.

39 B

B is the correct answer because late payment interest is a personal liability of the owner of the business rather than the business itself, and is disallowable.

The legal fees in respect of the new shop are capital expenditure and also disallowed.

The write off of trade debts and subscribing to a trade related magazine are both allowable for tax purposes.

40 C

	£
Total premises expenses	12,300
Less: Flat rate disallowable amount	(6,000)
Allowable expenses	6,300

41 A

	Special rate pool £
Year ended 30 June 2026	
TWDV b/f	0
Addition (high emission car)	18,000
WDA @ 6%	(1,080)
TWDV c/f	16,920
Year ended 30 June 2027	
Disposal proceeds	(17,560)
Balancing charge	(640)

42 C

	Main pool	Allowances
	£	£
TWDV b/f	9,300	
Addition: Desk	2,400	
	11,700	
Disposal	(14,700)	
	(3,000)	
Balancing charge	3,000	(3,000)
Total allowances	0	(3,000)

Tutorial note

In the period of account in which the business permanently ceases, the AIA, WDAs and FYAs are not available. Additions and disposals are added to/deducted from the relevant pool and a balancing charge or allowance is calculated.

43 C

Structures and buildings allowance (SBA) can be claimed on qualifying expenditure which includes the cost of the building as well as the renovation cost but not the cost of land.

SBAs can only be claimed from the date the building is brought into use.

(£550,000 + £30,000) × 3% × 5/12 = £7,250

44 C

Structures and buildings allowance (SBA) is not available on the cost of the land. The building was not brought into use until 1 January 2026 so only receives 3 months SBA in the period ended 31 March 2026.

[(£180,000 – £20,000) × 3%] × 3/12 = £1,200

45 C

Structures and buildings allowance (SBA) can be claimed on qualifying expenditure which includes the cost of the building as well as the renovation cost.

SBAs can only be claimed from the date the building is brought into use.

(£250,000 + £20,000) × 3% × 9/12 = £6,075

Examiner's report

Mistakes included not including the cost of the renovation and calculating the SBA from the date of purchase of the building, instead of the date it was brought into business use.

The correct answer was to calculate the SBA based on the cost of the building plus the cost of the renovation, and then to time apportion from the date the building was brought into business use to the end of the assessable period.

46 B

When an asset is hired under a hire purchase (HP) agreement rather than purchased, the amount used in the capital allowances calculation is the cash price regardless of the terms of the HP agreement. Interest payments may be deducted in the statement of profit or loss.

47 C

A trading loss of a sole trader can be set off against the general income of the current and/or previous tax years or against the profits of the same trade in future years. A property loss can only be set off against property income.

48 C

Tax year basis: 6 April 2025 – 5 April 2026

(£95,000 × 5/12) + (£105,000 × 7/12) = £100,833

49 B

Tax year basis: 1 November 2025 – 5 April 2026

£16,000 × 5/8 = £10,000

Tutorial note

A new trader is taxed in the first tax year of trade from the date of starting to trade until 5 April at the end of the tax year. Karishma's first period of account is eight months long, five of which fall before 5 April.

50 B

Tax year basis: 6 April 2025 – 30 June 2025

£2,000 × 3/6 = £1,000

Tutorial note

A trader ceasing to trade is taxed in the final tax year of trade from 6 April to the date of cessation. Mindy's final period of account is six months long, three of which fall after 6 April.

PARTNERSHIPS

51 A

Layla's share of the profits for the year to 31 December 2026:

£60,000 × 1/6 = £10,000

Her trading profits for the tax year 2025/26:

3/12 × £10,000 = £2,500

Key answer tips

The question asks for Layla's trading profits for the tax year 2025/26.

First calculate her allocation of the partnership profits for the period of account.

The profit sharing ratio is 3:2:1. This means that Layla is entitled to 1/6 (1/(3 + 2 + 1)) of the profits from 1 January 2026.

Then apply the tax year basis (1 January 2026 – 5 April 2026) to calculate the trading profits for the tax year.

52 D

y/e 31 December 2025	**Total**	**Henry**
	£	£
p/e 31 July 2025 (£120,000 × 7/12) = £70,000		
PSR (70:30)	70,000	21,000
p/e 31 December 2025 (£120,000 × 5/12) = £50,000		
Salary (£24,000 × 5/12)	10,000	10,000
PSR (80:20)	40,000	8,000
Allocation of profit	120,000	39,000

EMPLOYMENT INCOME

53 D

Only the gift of flowers is exempt.

Tutorial note

There is an exemption for trivial benefits, provided they cost no more than £50 per employee per gift, are not cash or vouchers and are not in recognition of services provided by the employee.

54 C

MV × 20% × 5/12

(£3,600 × 20% × 5/12) = £300

Tutorial note

Special rules exist to tax the benefit for the use of a car, van, first mobile phone and accommodation. For other assets the benefit is calculated as 20% of the market value when first supplied as a benefit.

The benefit is time apportioned if the asset is not made available for the whole of the tax year and business use of the asset can be deducted.

55 A

Employment income is taxed in the year of receipt; the accounting year the bonus relates to is not relevant. Parking provided by the employer is an exempt benefit.

56 B

Key answer tips

Watch out for questions like this where the benefit was not available for the whole year. You need to time apportion the benefit and remember that the employee would only pay 10 months of rent.

	£		£
Basic benefit	2,950		
Expensive accommodation:			
£135,000 – £75,000 = £60,000 × 3.75%	2,250		
	5,200	× 10/12	4,333
Taxable benefit			4,333

Tutorial note

Accommodation benefit is calculated as follows:

1 *Basic benefit = higher of the annual value or rent paid by employer.*

2 *'Expensive' accommodation charge = only applied if the employer owns the property. It is calculated as (cost of the property – £75,000) × official rate of interest. Cost includes all improvements made to the property before the start of the tax year. If the employer has owned the property for more than 6 years before the employee moves in, then the market value at the date the employee moves in is used to replace original cost.*

3 *Any rent paid by the employee is deducted.*

57 B

	£
Cost	32,000
Less: Employee contribution (maximum)	(5,000)
	27,000
Taxable benefit (£27,000 × 17%) (W)	4,590

Working

Appropriate percentage = 17% for a petrol car with CO_2 emissions of 55g/km.

Tutorial note

A contribution by an employee towards the cost of the car is an allowable deduction, but is capped at £5,000.

58 B

The £12 per night exceeds the statutory figure of £10 and therefore the whole amount is a taxable benefit.

59 B

£900 (£10,000 × 9%)

The car has emissions of between 1 and 50g/km so the basic percentage is determined by the electric range. An electric range of 45 miles is between 40 and 69 miles and so the correct percentage is 9%. Provided there is some private use of the car, a full car benefit is charged. The additional 4% supplement for cars that do not meet the RDE2 standard does not apply to hybrid cars.

60 C

Travel to and from your permanent place of work is always classed as private commuting and the cost is not tax deductible.

61 B

The car is provided part way through the year so the benefit must be time apportioned.

Taxable benefit is £5,781 (£18,750 × 37% (W) × 10/12)

Working

Appropriate percentage = 17% (petrol basic) + [(170 – 55) × 1/5] = 40%, but limited to a maximum of 37%.

62 D

D is the correct answer because all of the others are taxable benefits for 2025/26.

The loan is an exempt benefit as it is ≤ £10,000.

A second mobile phone is taxable, as are the provision of medical insurance and the payment of gym subscriptions.

63 C

C is the correct answer because Adin's taxable benefit is computed on the higher of:

- the annual value of the property (i.e. £9,750), or
- the rent paid by the employer (i.e. £32,000).

This figure is then reduced by any employee contribution (i.e. the rent paid by Adin).

The taxable benefit is therefore (£32,000 – £12,000) = £20,000.

64 C

As there has been no private use of the television by any employee prior to the gift to Jules, the market value at the time of the gift is taxed.

The amount is not reduced for the time left in the tax year as it is an outright gift.

65 D

There is no taxable benefit if the sum of all loans to an employee does not exceed £10,000 at any time during the tax year.

66 A

In the case of directors, earnings are treated as received on the earliest of:

- the date of payment
- the date they become entitled to the payment
- the date when the amount is credited in the company's accounts or the date when earnings are determined (in this case, the date depends on – if they are determined before the end of the period of account, then they are treated as received at the end of that period, if they are determined after the end of the period of account, then they are treated as received on the date they are determined).

INVESTMENT INCOME

67 B

	£
Replacement of domestic items relief (replacement bed)	1,200
Repairs	150
Total	1,350

> ***Tutorial note***
>
> *Replacement of domestic items relief is available in respect of replaced furniture and furnishings, but not the initial purchase of furniture (such as the desk).*

68 A

	£
House insurance paid 1 July 2025	1,000
Decoration	0
Total	1,000

> ***Tutorial note***
>
> *Property income for an individual is calculated using the cash basis unless explicitly stated otherwise. Expenses are an allowable deduction in the tax year in which they are paid.*

69 C

Tax on dividends

	£
Nil rate – £500 × 0%	0
Higher rate – £8,500 (£125,140 – £116,140 – £500) × 33.75%	2,869
Additional rate – £8,500 (£17,500 – £9,000) × 39.35%	3,345
Tax liability	6,214

The non-savings income fully uses the basic rate band and most of the higher rate band.

The first £500 of dividend income falls within the nil rate band and is taxed at 0%. The next £8,500 of the dividend income falls in the remaining higher rate band. Note that the dividends falling in the nil rate band also use the remaining higher rate band. The remaining £8,500 of dividend income falls in the additional rate band.

70 C

The £12,000 pension is covered by the personal allowance of £12,570, leaving no taxable non-savings income. Therefore, the savings income (after remaining personal allowance) falls within the starting band of 0%. The tax is therefore:

	Non-savings	**Savings**	**Total**
	£	£	£
Pension income	12,000		12,000
Interest income		4,000	4,000
			16,000
Personal allowance	(12,000)	(570)	(12,570)
Taxable income	0	3,430	3,430
Savings starting rate band (£3,430 × 0%)			0

71 B

	Non-savings	**Dividends**	**Total**
	£	£	£
Taxable income	4,100	9,000	13,100
Non-savings income – basic rate (£4,100 × 20%)			820
Dividend income – nil rate (£500 × 0%)			0
Dividend income – basic rate (£8,500 × 8.75%)			744
Tax liability			1,564

Tutorial note

The dividend nil rate band of £500 is available to all taxpayers.

72 C

Proceeds from NS&I savings certificates are exempt income and profits on the sale of shares are subject to capital gains tax and not income tax.

73 C

	£
Salary	120,000
Dividend income	20,000
Taxable income	140,000

The dividends will be taxed as follows:

£500 × 0%, £4,640 × 33.75% and £14,860 × 39.35%

Note: The remaining higher rate band is £5,140 (£125,140 – £120,000). The £500 dividend nil rate band uses part of the remaining HRB.

74 C

	£
Premium received	50,000
Less: 2% × (45 – 1) × £50,000	(44,000)
Premium taxed as rental income	6,000
Rent received	10,000
Property income	16,000

Note: Always use the cash basis unless the question specifies otherwise.

75 B

	£
Rent received	8,050
Less: Rent-a-room relief	(7,500)
Property income	550

Since rent-a-room relief is greater than the tax allowable expenses this amount is deducted from the rent. It is not possible to deduct both the expenses and rent-a-room relief.

PENSIONS AND NIC

76 A

An employee pays national insurance contributions (NICs) on cash earnings only, not on non-cash benefits.

(£24,000 – £12,570) × 8%	£914

> ***Tutorial note***
>
> *Employee class 1 national insurance contributions are paid on cash earnings and not on non-cash benefits such as a company car.*

77 D

Isa's basic rate band is extended by the grossed up contribution as follows:

(£32,000 × 100/80) = £40,000

The contribution is lower than their relevant earnings for the year (£90,000) and they therefore qualify for tax relief on the full amount.

> ***Tutorial note***
>
> *Tax relief for pension contributions is available on contributions up to the higher of:*
>
> - *£3,600*
> - *Relevant earnings (earnings from employment and self-employment).*
>
> *However, if gross contributions exceed the annual allowance of £60,000 then some of the tax relief can be clawed back. You do not have to know how to calculate this claw back.*
>
> *Relief for personal pension scheme contributions is given firstly by paying the contribution net of 20% tax and then by extending the basic rate and higher rate thresholds by the gross amount of the contributions.*
>
> *If pensions are paid to an occupational (employer's scheme) then the amount of tax relief available is the same, however relief is given by deducting the gross contribution from employment income.*

78 D

	£	£
Basic personal allowance		12,570
Net income	115,000	
Less: Gross personal pension contribution (£5,600 × 100/80)	(7,000)	
	108,000	
Less: Limit	(100,000)	
	8,000	
50% of £8,000		(4,000)
Revised personal allowance		8,570

79 C

With a personal pension scheme the employer and any individual can contribute.

80 D

	£
Bonus month	
(£4,189 – £1,048) × 8%	251
(£4,400 – £4,189) × 2%	4
Employee class 1 contributions	255

Tutorial note

National insurance contributions (NICs) are calculated on a monthly or weekly basis. However, if the employee receives the same amount of salary every week or month, then the calculation of NICs can be simplified and performed on an annual basis.

If the employee receives a bonus in one month then the calculation must be performed on a monthly basis.

The NIC thresholds in the tax tables supplied in the examination are only annual ones. The limits have to be divided by 12 for monthly payments.

	Annual	**Monthly**
Lower limit	*£12,570*	*£1,048*
Upper limit	*£50,270*	*£4,189*

81 D

Employer's class 1 national insurance contributions (NICs) are calculated on cash earnings only, but not benefits. The first £5,000 is exempt and the remainder is charged at 15%.

The NICs are therefore: (£52,000 – £5,000) × 15%	£7,050

82 B

Total earnings received in December 2025 are £11,000 (£3,000 + £8,000)

The NIC thresholds for each month are £12,570/12 = £1,048 and £50,270/12 = £4,189

NICs payable is therefore:

	£
(£4,189 – £1,048) × 8%	251
(£11,000 – £4,189) × 2%	136
	387

83 D

The maximum amount of pension contributions on which tax relief is allowed is the higher of £3,600 and the employee's relevant earnings. The relevant earnings in this case are the employment income (£7,000 + £2,000).

Examiner's report

Many candidates chose option A, limiting the pension contributions to £3,600. This has been an issue in many past exams with candidates being fixated by this figure. Candidates are reminded that £3,600 is the maximum amount of pension contributions allowable for tax relief where the taxpayer has no relevant earnings. Where the taxpayer does have relevant earnings then the amount allowed is the HIGHER of relevant earnings and £3,600. Relevant earnings are employment income (including benefits) and trading income, and do not include savings income or rental income.

84 C

Class 4 national insurance (NIC) is not due on property income.

NICs payable is therefore:

	£
(£50,270 – £12,570) × 6%	2,262
(£54,000 – £50,270) × 2%	75
	2,337

85 A

Examiner's report

Most candidates wrongly thought that the employer contribution would be taxable on the employee. This is incorrect and is in fact an exempt benefit for the employee.

Other candidates incorrectly thought that the employer contributions were not tax deductible in calculating the employer's own taxable trading profits when in fact they are deductible in this situation.

Some candidates wrongly thought that the employer contributions did not count towards the annual allowance of the employee.

The employer contributions are not a taxable benefit for the employee and are neither taxable nor deductible when calculating income tax payable for the employee.

CORPORATION TAX

86 B

	£
Tax adjusted trading profit	20,000
Chargeable gains	15,000
Property business profit	8,000
Taxable total profits	43,000
Corporation tax liability (£43,000 × 19%)	8,170

Tutorial note

Dividends received are not included in taxable total profits. The dividends are added to taxable total profits to get augmented profits £46,000 (£43,000 + £3,000). The augmented profits are compared to the lower limit (£50,000) and upper limit (£250,000). The corporation tax rate applicable is 19%.

87 D

	£
Taxable total profits	67,000
Add: Dividends from non-group companies	4,500
Augmented profits	71,500

Tutorial note

Augmented profits are calculated by adding dividends received from non-associated companies to taxable total profits.

88 B

The corporation tax saved will be based on the original tax paid for the year ended 31 March 2025:

	£
Trading profit	662,200
Property income	80,000
Total profits	742,200
Less: Qualifying charitable donation	(2,000)
Taxable total profits	740,200
FY2024	
Corporation tax liability (£740,200 × 25%)	185,050

Tutorial note

The loss utilised is £742,200, as it is offset against total profits before QCDs. The QCDs are wasted.

The loss is used in the year ended 31 March 2025, which falls in FY2024, when the company paid corporation tax at the main rate of 25%, so the tax saving is calculated at this rate.

89 A

Offset against current period and preceding 12 months provides the earliest relief.

The company must set the loss against total profits (before deducting qualifying charitable donations) arising in the current year first, and then carry back the remaining loss to the previous 12 months.

Any unrelieved qualifying charitable donations are lost.

The remaining loss can be carried forward and is:

(£60,000 – £3,000 – £25,000 – £6,000) = £26,000

90 C

A company has two years from the end of the loss-making period to make a current year claim.

91 C

Grape plc has taxable total profits exceeding £1,500,000 and must therefore pay its tax in instalments. The last instalment is due three months and 14 days from the end of the accounting period.

Tutorial note

Companies with taxable total profits of £1,500,000 or more per year must pay their corporation tax by quarterly instalments. The threshold of £1,500,000 is time apportioned for periods of less than 1 year.

Quarterly instalments for large companies are due on the 14th day of months 7, 10, 13 and 16 after the start of an accounting period. The payments are based on an estimate of the company's corporation tax liability for the year.

Companies do not have to pay by instalments in two situations:

(i) The company was not paying instalments last year and its profits for the current year are no more than £10 million or

(ii) The tax liability is no more than £10,000.

92 B

The return must be submitted within 12 months of the end of the accounting period and the tax paid nine months and one day after the end of the accounting period.

93 A

	£
Trading profits	255,000
Less: QCD	(11,000)
Taxable total profits	244,000
Corporation tax liability (£244,000 × 25%)	61,000

Tutorial note

Qualifying charitable donations such as gifts to national charities are paid gross by companies and deducted in the period when paid.

Dividends received are not included in taxable total profits as they are not taxable. They do however affect the rate of tax payable as they are included in the calculation of augmented profits.

Augmented profits are £271,000 (£244,000 + £27,000) which exceed the upper limit of £250,000. The corporation tax rate applicable is the main rate of 25%.

94 C

	£
Taxable total profits = trading profits	119,000
Corporation tax liability	
(£119,000 × 25%)	29,750
Less Marginal relief:	
(£250,000 – £131,000) × 3/200 × (£119,000/£131,000)	(1,621)
	28,129
Augmented profits:	
Taxable total profits	119,000
Dividends	12,000
Augmented profits	131,000

Tutorial note

Dividends received are not included in taxable total profits. They do however affect the rate of tax payable as they are included in the calculation of augmented profits.

Augmented profits are £131,000. With a lower limit of £50,000 and an upper limit of £250,000, marginal relief is applicable.

Marginal relief is calculated as follows:

(Upper Limit – Augmented Profits) × standard fraction × (TTP/Augmented profits)

95 D

	£
Taxable total profits	34,000
Corporation tax liability	
£34,000 × 25%	8,500
Lower limit (£50,000/4) × 6/12 (Note)	6,250
Upper limit (£250,000/4) × 6/12 (Note)	31,250
Corporation tax rate	25%

Tutorial note

The upper limit and lower limit are divided by the number of associated companies and time apportioned for a short accounting period.

96 B

	£
Trading profits/taxable total profits	195,000
Dividends	25,000
Augmented profits	220,000

Tutorial note

Dividends from group companies are ignored for the purpose of calculating augmented profits. Only dividends from non-group companies are taken into account.

97 C

All companies are required to file their returns electronically and file their accounts using iXBRL. This stands for inline eXtensible Business Reporting Language.

98 D

	£
Tax adjusted trading profit	150,000
Chargeable gains	70,000
Total profits	220,000
Less: Property loss	(50,000)
Less: Trading loss brought forward	(160,000)
Taxable total profits	10,000

99 A

	AIA	Full expense	Main pool	Allowances
Year ended 31 March 2026	£	£	£	£
TWDV b/f			25,000	
Additions qualifying for AIA				
Plant and machinery	1,650,000			
Less AIA	(1,000,000)			1,000,000
Eligible for full expensing		650,000		
FYA @ 100%		(650,000)		650,000
WDA @ 18%			(4,500)	4,500
TWDV c/f			20,500	
Total allowances				1,654,500

100 C

		Special rate pool	Allowances
	£	£	£
TWDV b/f		64,000	
Assets qualifying for AIA – van	19,500		
AIA	(19,500)		19,500
	————		
WDA @ 6%		(3,840)	3,840
		————	
		60,160	
		————	————
			23,340
			————

Examiner's report

The most common mistake was to not give the annual investment allowance (AIA) on the van but instead give the van an 18% writing down allowance (WDA), whilst correctly giving a 6% WDA on the tax written down value of the special rate pool.

The second most common mistake was to not give the AIA on the van but instead give a 6% WDA on the cost of the van, whilst correctly giving a 6% WDA on the tax written down value of the special rate pool.

The correct answer was to give the AIA on the cost of the van and to give a 6% WDA on the tax written down value of the special rate pool.

101 C

A trading loss made in the last 12 months of business (a terminal loss) can be carried back three years against total profits on a LIFO basis.

102 B

The loss on the sale of a van is capital and the donation to a national charity would be treated as a qualifying charitable donation. Both of these would therefore be disallowed for tax purposes. The legal fees are trade related and therefore allowed as a deduction from profit. Therefore, the correct answer is £2,000 + £4,000 = £6,000.

103 D

Where a corporation tax return is filed more than three months but less than six months late, the penalty is £200 but this is increased to £1,000 if it is the third or more consecutive offence.

104 B

Companies must use the accruals basis for taxing property business income. Mortgage interest is not a deductible expense, it is deductible under the loan relationship rules. Therefore, the correct amount is £18,000, i.e. £24,000 – £6,000.

Examiner's report

Property business income for a company is calculated on an accruals basis, unlike the method for individuals which is the receipts basis. In addition to this, interest payable should be netted off with interest received and shown as a separate source of income in the corporation tax calculation, it is not deducted from rental income.

Most candidates chose option A, which was to deduct the total expenses from the total rent due for the year whereas the correct answer was B, being the total rent due for the year minus £6,000 expenses but not the mortgage interest.

105 C

Quarterly payments for companies are calculated by dividing the current year's estimated corporation tax by 4 (for a 12-month accounting period) and paying the instalments on the 14th of the 7th and 10th months of the current period and the 1st and 4th months of the following period.

106 C

A company must retain all records required to make and deliver the tax return for six years after the accounting period. The maximum penalty for failing to keep records is £3,000.

CAPITAL GAINS TAX

107 C

The capital gains tax liability is calculated as follows:

			£
Taxable gains (£21,000 + £11,300)			32,300

Basic rate band remaining:
£37,700 – £21,700 = £16,000

	£		£
Lower rate	16,000	× 18%	2,880
Higher rate	16,300	× 24%	3,912
	32,300		
Capital gains tax liability			6,792

108 C

The chargeable gain arising on the sale of the building equates to the amount of the proceeds not reinvested into a qualifying asset within a qualifying time period. The gain can therefore be calculated as:

(£450,000 – £415,000) = £35,000

Tutorial note

Land and buildings are the most common qualifying assets for rollover relief purposes.

If all the proceeds of sale of a qualifying asset are invested in another qualifying asset in the period from 12 months before the disposal to 36 months afterwards, then the whole of the gain on disposal can be rolled over.

Where some of the proceeds are not reinvested, there is an immediate chargeable gain. The gain chargeable immediately is the lower of:

(i) the gain or (ii) the proceeds not reinvested.

109 D

The asset qualifies as a chattel, but it is not a wasting chattel, and therefore is not exempt.

As the chattel has been sold for more than £6,000 but purchased for less than £6,000, the gain is restricted to 5/3 × (gross sale proceeds – £6,000), as follows:

	£
Gross sale proceeds	7,800
Less: Auctioneer's fee (1%)	(78)
Less: Allowable costs	(2,300)
Chargeable gain	5,422

Restricted to: 5/3 × (£7,800 – £6,000) = £3,000

110 A

The property is Linda's main private residence, and as such qualifies for private residence relief (PRR).

With regard to the period of absences:

The property can be unoccupied for a period of up to three years for any reason (being the 6 months spent away due to repairs following a storm) as long as the property is reoccupied.

The final absence of 7 months falls within the last 9 months of ownership.

Both absences qualify as periods of deemed occupation, therefore no gain is taxable on the disposal of the property.

111 B

	£
Chargeable gain	800,000
Less: Annual exempt amount	(3,000)
Taxable gain	797,000
Capital gains tax (14% × £797,000)	111,580

Tutorial note

Business asset disposal relief (BADR) means that the tax rate on eligible gains is 14% regardless of the level of the taxpayer's income. Taha's disposal qualifies because he is disposing of the whole of his business which he has owned for ≥ 2 years.

112 C

	£
Proceeds	750,000
Cost	(125,000)
Enhancement	(30,000)
Unindexed gain	595,000
IA £125,000 × 0.683	(85,375)
Chargeable gain	509,625

Note: The Indexation allowance is frozen at December 2017. The expenditure on the extension was incurred after December 2017 and does not qualify for the indexation allowance.

113 C

Gift of shares: Value = ½ (4.10 + 4.50) = £4.30 × 1,000 shares = £4,300

Tutorial note

The value of quoted shares when they are disposed of by way of a gift is based on the mid-price of the day's quoted prices, i.e. the average of the day's prices.

114 B

	£
Proceeds	634,000
Cost (£120,000 + £8,000)	(128,000)
	506,000
Indexation allowance:	
0.214 × £128,000	(27,392)
Chargeable gain	478,608

Buying costs are added to the cost of purchase and indexed. Indexation allowance is calculated on the total acquisition costs of £128,000. Indexation allowance is frozen as at December 2017.

115 D

The destruction of an asset and a gift to a friend are both deemed to be disposals for capital gains tax (CGT). The amount of compensation received is generally treated as the disposal proceeds for the asset destroyed. A gift to a friend is deemed to be a disposal at current market value. Therefore, neither of these is exempt from CGT. The sales of gilt-edged securities and the disposals of war medals by those awarded them are both specifically exempted by statute.

Key answer tips

You need to learn which assets are exempt from capital gains tax.

116 C

When a business asset is sold and the proceeds are invested into a depreciating asset (e.g. fixed plant and machinery), the gain on the business asset can be held over until the earliest of:

- the sale of the depreciating asset = 2032
- ceasing to use the depreciating asset in the business = 2032
- the ten year anniversary of the purchase of the depreciating asset = 5 May 2036

The gain never reduces the cost of the depreciating asset.

117 B

	Qualifying for BADR	Not qualifying for BADR
	£	£
Gains	40,000	19,900
Less: Annual exempt amount		(3,000)
Taxable gains	40,000	16,900
Tax rate	14%	24%
Tax	5,600	4,056
Total tax	£9,656	

Tutorial note

Gains not qualifying for BADR are taxed at 18% if they fall in the taxpayer's remaining basic rate band and 24% otherwise.

Gains qualifying for BADR are taxed at 14% regardless of the taxpayer's level of income. However, they are deemed to use up the taxpayer's basic rate band before the non-qualifying gains.

In this question the taxpayer has taxable income of £17,500, which leaves £20,200 (£37,700 – £17,500) of unused basic rate band. As the gains qualifying for BADR exceed £20,200, there is no basic rate band left for the non-qualifying gains and they must be taxed at 24%.

The taxpayer can deduct the annual exempt amount (and any allowable capital losses) from the non-qualifying gains in preference to qualifying gains, which will save the most tax.

118 D

Tutorial note

A *Rollover relief is not available on disposals of shares.*

B *Assil must work for the company to be eligible for BADR.*

C *The shares are sold for their full market value and therefore there is no gift element in the transaction.*

119 D

Tutorial note

A *Rollover relief is only available on disposals of qualifying business assets, not vases. It is also not available on gifts.*

B *BADR is only available on the disposal of qualifying business assets, not antique vases.*

C *Gift holdover relief is only available on the disposal of qualifying business assets, not antique vases.*

120 C

Tutorial note

A *Rollover relief is not available on disposals of shares.*

B *BADR is only available on shares if the individual owns at least 5% of the shares and works for the company.*

C *Gift holdover relief is available on the sale at undervaluation of a qualifying business asset, which includes unquoted trading company shares.*

121 C

The matching order for disposals of shares by an individual is: firstly, those purchased on the same day, followed by those purchased in the next 30 days and then by those shares in the pool. The rights issue is not treated as a separate purchase but forms part of the pool.

122 A

The matching order for disposals of shares by a company: firstly those purchased on the same day, followed by those purchased in the previous nine days and then by those shares in the pool.

123 B

When a chattel (i.e. the painting), costing more than £6,000, is sold for less than £6,000, then the gross proceeds are deemed to be £6,000. The loss is therefore restricted to £6,000 – £400 – £7,000 = £1,400.

Examiner's report

This question examined a disposal of a non-wasting chattel at a loss. This has been examined many times before, therefore candidates would have benefited from studying past exam papers.

As a reminder, the three main issues with non-wasting chattels are:

- If both proceeds and cost are below £6,000 – then the disposal is exempt from capital gains tax (CGT).
- If cost is below £6,000 and gross proceeds are marginally above £6,000 – then the gain is restricted to the lower of the actual gain and 5/3 × (gross proceeds – £6,000).
- If cost is over £6,000 and is sold at a loss – then the actual gross proceeds are deemed to be £6,000, which restricts the allowable loss.

In this case it was the third example that was relevant and therefore the correct answer was £1,400, being deemed proceeds of £6,000 less expenses of £400 less the cost of £7,000.

124 D

The limit of £1 million is a lifetime limit (not an annual one), only 5% of ordinary share capital is required for a personal company (not 10%) and the relief must be claimed within 12 months of the 31 January following the end of the tax year in which the disposal is made.

Examiner's report

This question required knowledge of business asset disposal relief and required the candidates to read the question carefully.

VALUE ADDED TAX

125 A

The flat rate percentage is applied to the full VAT-inclusive turnover including all standard, zero and exempt supplies (i.e. £40,000 × 9% = £3,600).

126 D

		£
Purchases:	£95,000 × 20%	19,000
Van:	£14,400 × 1/6	2,400
Recoverable input VAT		21,400

Note: VAT on the purchase of the car is blocked and cannot be reclaimed as it is used for private purposes.

Tutorial note

When figures are VAT-exclusive, the standard-rated VAT is found by multiplying by 20%.

If the figure is quoted as VAT-inclusive the VAT element is calculated by multiplying by 20/120, usually simplified to 1/6. This is often referred to as the VAT fraction.

Key answer tips

Always check in VAT questions to see whether items are VAT-exclusive or VAT-inclusive.

127 D

The total value of sales (standard-rated and zero-rated) excluding VAT should be included in Box 6 of the VAT return.

128 B

The VAT return must be received within one month and seven days of the end of the relevant quarter.

129 C

The tax point is generally the earliest of: the date of delivery, the invoice date and the cash receipt date. However, if, as in this case, the invoice is issued within 14 days of delivery, and an earlier tax point has not already arisen as a result of a cash receipt, then the invoice date becomes the tax point.

130 C

VAT reclaim is for £285 (£1,710 × 1/6)

Tutorial note

Impairment loss relief can be claimed to recover the output VAT previously paid over to HMRC on invoices which are unpaid. The claim can only be made if certain conditions are met of which the most important here is that 6 months must have passed since the debt was due to be paid. Therefore, only the VAT in respect of the invoice due to be paid in June 2025 can be reclaimed. VAT on the other invoice may be reclaimed in the following quarter to 30 June 2026 provided the invoice is still unpaid.

131 A

The taxable turnover of £150,000 is exclusive of value added tax and includes both zero-rated supplies and standard-rated supplies.

132 B

The VAT payment is due within one month and seven days following the related quarter.

133 C

A business which makes any level of taxable supplies (including zero-rated supplies), can register for VAT. They do not have to wait until turnover exceeds the registration threshold.

A business which only makes exempt supplies cannot register for VAT.

Key answer tips

It is important to read these True/False questions very carefully.

Make sure you know whether you are looking to see if the statements are true or false. Then read each statement carefully.

134 A

Tutorial note

Output VAT is charged on the actual amount received. In this case as the invoice was not paid within 14 days the output tax is calculated on the undiscounted price of £2,000, i.e. £2,000 × 20%.

135 D

Value added tax (VAT) can be recovered on entertainment expenses relating to both employees and overseas customers but not UK customers. VAT can also be recovered on cars provided that they are used 100% for business purposes.

136 D

The *de minimis* limit is the higher of: £10,000 or 1% of turnover (capped at £50,000). Therefore, the correct answer is 1% × £2,500,000 = £25,000.

137 A

The gift is deemed to sell at cost and the £50 limit does not apply. Therefore, the correct VAT is £16, i.e. £80 × 20%.

Examiner's report

A business gift is a taxable supply unless it is less than £50. Where the value of the gift exceeds £50 then the gift is treated as a supply for VAT purposes. The gift is treated as if sold at full cost price, not only on the amount above £50.

138 B

Taxpayers must have a turnover below £1,350,000 exclusive of VAT if they wish to join the cash accounting scheme.

139 D

The flat rate percentage is applied to the full VAT-inclusive turnover including all standard, zero and exempt supplies (i.e. £74,000 × 10% = £7,400).

Examiner's report

Mistakes included thinking that the flat rate percentage did not apply to the exempt supplies of £5,000 or thinking that the flat rate percentage should be applied to VAT-exclusive turnover.

Section 4

ANSWERS TO LONG FORM QUESTIONS

INTRODUCTION TO THE UK TAX SYSTEM

1 APPEALS

Key answer tips

Although multiple choice questions on this area are more likely, you must be prepared for a written question.

Notes for meeting with Eduarda

When a taxpayer disagrees with a decision of HMRC the individual must:

(i) appeal against it in writing within 30 days and,

(ii) if the individual thinks the tax charged is too high then the individual must also apply to postpone any tax due, otherwise all tax will remain payable.

Following this initial appeal, a taxpayer has a choice of two actions.

1 A taxpayer can choose to have the case reviewed by a different HMRC officer to the one who made the original decision. This is a simple and relatively cheap process.

The taxpayer can provide further information about the case if the individual wishes. The review should be completed within 45 days unless HMRC has agreed a different time period with the taxpayer.

The officer conducting the review will then advise the taxpayer whether the officer agrees with the original decision or whether it requires amendment in some way.

2 The taxpayer can accept the decision of the review or if the taxpayer is still unhappy an appeal to the Tax Tribunal can be lodged.

A taxpayer can also appeal directly to the Tax Tribunal if this is not what the individual wishes to have reviewed. In both cases the taxpayer has 30 days from the decision or case review completion to appeal to the Tax Tribunal.

The Tax Tribunal is an independent body administered by the Tribunals Service of the Ministry of Justice.

Key answer tips

In the December 2016 examination there was a question regarding the appeals procedure. In the examiner's report the examining team commented that "the word 'procedure' means the 'way of doing something' not why and when it should be done – therefore answers stating the reason for an appeal could not score marks". It is vital to always answer the question which has been asked, not the one you wish had been asked!

2 DIFFERENT TYPES OF TAXES

Key answer tips

This is an unusual question, but one which should not prove too tricky.

Tax	**Paid to HMRC by**	**On**	**Direct/ indirect**	**Capital/ revenue**
Income tax	Individuals	Employment income Self-employed income Investment income	Direct	Revenue
Corporation tax	Companies	Income and gains	Direct	Capital and revenue
Capital gains tax	Individuals	Disposals of capital assets (e.g. shares)	Direct	Capital
VAT	Businesses and companies	Supply of goods and services	Indirect	Capital and revenue
National insurance contributions	Individuals and businesses	Earnings and self-employed profits	Direct	Revenue

EMPLOYMENT INCOME

3 MARY

Key answer tips

Employment income is a very important topic and is examined frequently. Detailed knowledge of all of the employment benefits is important for this examination.

It is also important to know the key benefits of employment that are exempt for tax purposes as they often feature in such questions and credit is given for recognising and stating that the benefit is exempt. This is an easy mark to gain but is often forgotten and ignored in answers and therefore is an easy mark lost!

> Note the two ways in which the loan benefit can be calculated – both methods need to be considered here.
>
> This question also includes the examination favourite point which is that partial contributions towards private fuel are not deductible.
>
> Pension contributions are also another popular topic.

Taxable benefits

	£	£
Beneficial loan (Note 1)		
Lower of:		
(a) Average method		
$\frac{£40,000+£32,000}{2} \times 3.75\%$	1,350	
Less: Interest paid		
£40,000 × 1% × 3/12	(100)	
£32,000 × 1% × 9/12	(240)	
	1,010	
(b) Precise method		
£40,000 × (3.75% – 1%) × 3/12	275	
£32,000 × (3.75% – 1%) × 9/12	660	
Take the lower	935	935
Car benefit		
(£15,000 × 31% (W) × 7/12)	2,713	
Less: Contribution (£20 × 7)	(140)	
		2,573
Fuel benefit (Note 2)		
(£28,200 × 31% × 7/12)		5,100
Home cinema system		
Two taxable benefits:		
Use (£4,000 × 20%)		800
Gift/sale Higher of:		
(i) Current MV	900	900
(ii) (Market value when first available less benefit taxed for 2022/23 to 2025/26) £4,000 – (4 × (£4,000 × 20%))	800	
Employer pension contributions (Note 3)		
= Exempt benefit		0
Medical treatment (Note 4)		
= Exempt benefit		0
Total taxable benefits		10,308

Working: Appropriate percentage

	%
Basic percentage (diesel – does not meet RDE2 standard) (17% + 4%)	21
Plus: (105 – 55) × 1/5	10
	31

Tutorial note

1 *There are two methods of calculating the taxable benefit for interest free or low interest loans.*

(i) The average method

(Loan at start of tax year + loan at end of tax year)÷ 2 = Average loan

Benefit = Average loan × 3.75% (Official rate) less any interest actually paid.

(ii) The precise method

The precise or accurate method calculates the interest on a monthly basis based on the actual loan outstanding

The taxpayer can choose to use the precise method if it produces a lower benefit.

HMRC can insist on the precise method if it produces a materially larger benefit than the average method.

2 *Partial contributions towards private fuel are not allowable deductions for tax purposes and are therefore irrelevant.*

3 *Employers' contributions to occupational or personal pension schemes are an exempt benefit.*

Remember that the examining team have stated in their examiner's report that if there is an exempt benefit in a question, you should state in your answer that it is exempt to obtain full credit. Do not just leave it out.

4 *Medical treatment costing up to £500 per employee per tax year, which is paid to enable the employee to return to work, is an exempt benefit.*

4 JANA

Key answer tips

A car benefit is a popular examination topic.

Note that the provision of a second car to Jana (which is mainly used by her husband, who does not work in the business), is taxed on Jana.

Total taxable benefits – 2025/26

		£
(i)	Jaguar car – private use (W1)	
	(£26,700 × 29%)	7,743
(ii)	Jaguar car – private fuel	
	(£28,200 × 29%)	8,178
	(50% contribution not relevant – all private fuel must be reimbursed to avoid a charge)	
(iii)	Hybrid-electric car – private use (W2)	
	(£15,000 × 15%)	2,250
(iv)	Hybrid-electric car – private fuel	
	(£28,200 × 15%)	4,230
Total benefits		22,401

Workings

(W1) Jaguar – car benefits

	%
Basic percentage (petrol)	17
Plus: (115 – 55) × 1/5	12
	29

(W2) Hybrid-electric – car benefits

	%
Percentage for a hybrid-electric car with a 20 mile electric range	15

5 MACKENZIE

Key answer tips

An accommodation benefit is a popular examination topic. In answering part (b) it is necessary to consider what type of tax will be payable by the **employer** on benefits provided to an employee.

(a) Accommodation benefit

	£
Annual value	3,600
Additional charge	
(£140,000 (MV) – £75,000) × 3.75% (official rate)	2,438
	6,038

(b) Additional cost of providing benefits

The company will pay class 1A employer's national insurance contributions (NIC) at 15% on all the benefits provided to Mackenzie.

Hence, the additional cost is:

(15% × £6,038) = £906

Tutorial note

1 *For the accommodation benefit, market value is used in place of cost because the company bought the house more than six years before Mackenzie moved in. The improvements carried out prior to the date Mackenzie moved in will be reflected in the market value on that date.*

2 *Note that only employers (not employees) pay class 1A national insurance contributions on taxable benefits.*

6 BENEFITS PLC

Key answer tips

This question requires you to calculate a number of standard benefits, which is a popular examination topic.

Key points to note here are:

Accommodation – the cost exceeds £75,000, so an additional benefit arises.

Assets taken over by the employee – the taxable benefit is the higher of the MV when first made available less amounts already taxed as a benefit, and the market value at the date of the transfer.

Beneficial loan – no benefit arises if total loans to that employee do not exceed £10,000 at any point during the year.

Remember that the general rule for measuring benefits is 'cost to the employer'.

1 **Private accommodation**

Private accommodation provided to a director is taxable based on its annual value, with an additional charge where the accommodation cost is in excess of £75,000. The benefit will be quantified as follows for 2025/26:

	£
Annual value	2,000
Additional benefit:	
3.75% × (£110,000 – £75,000)	1,313
	3,313
Less: Contribution by director	(1,500)
Benefit for P11D	1,813

2 **TV**

Assets taken over by the director will be taxable at the greater of:

- Market value less amount paid = (£800 – £600) £200
- Market value when first available less benefits already taxed less amount paid.

	£	£
MV when first made available	1,500	
Less: Benefits already taxed		
(20% amounts taxed per annum)		
2022/23	(300)	
2023/24	(300)	
2024/25	(300)	
	600	
Less: Amount paid	(600)	
		0

P11D benefit is therefore £200.

3 **Director's loan**

As the loan is below £10,000 there is no benefit charge.

4 **Dishwasher**

The benefit of the gift = the cost to the employer of providing it (i.e. £280).

5 **Medical health insurance**

The cost to the employer of the provision of medical health insurance is entered on form P11D, rather than the price which would have been paid by the employee, i.e. £1,200.

7 RAVI

Key answer tips

Car benefit is a popular examination topic. Remember that the split of business and private use is not relevant to the car benefit. A full benefit is charged if there is any private use of the company car.

	%
Percentage for a hybrid-electric car with a 60 mile electric range	9

List price: (£12,400 + £800 accessories – £1,000 capital contribution) = £12,200

Car and fuel benefit

		£
Car	£12,200 × 9%	1,098
Fuel	£28,200 × 9%	2,538
		3,636

There is no reduction of the fuel benefit for the contribution towards the cost of the private fuel.

Tutorial note

The cost used in calculating the car benefit is the list price plus the cost of any accessories fitted when the car is supplied. Accessories fitted later are added to the cost if they exceed £100.

Where the employer provides fuel for private use the benefit is always calculated using the set fuel benefit charge (£28,200 for 2025/26). The 'cost to the company' general rule does not apply to fuel benefits.

Contributions made by the employee towards the capital cost of the car are deducted from the list price up to a maximum deduction of £5,000.

8 SAMI

> **Key answer tips**
>
> A useful question which covers some of the less commonly tested benefits.
>
> It is important to answer the question and state that exempt benefits are exempt. Do not just leave them out.

Benefits – 2025/26

	£	£	£
Beneficial loan (Note 1)			
(i) Average method:			
$\frac{£25,000 + £15,000}{2} = £20,000$			
(£20,000 × 3.75% × 10/12)		625	
Interest paid:			
(£25,000 × 1% × 6/12)	125		
(£15,000 × 1% × 4/12)	50		
	——	(175)	
		450	
(ii) Precise method:			
£25,000 × (3.75% – 1%) × 6/12 =	344		
£15,000 × (3.75% – 1%) × 4/12 =	138		
	——	482	
The taxpayer will choose the lower figure			450
(HMRC may elect for the precise method – see tutorial note)			
Employer pension contributions (Note 2)			Exempt
Relocation costs			
(£9,500 – £8,000)			1,500
Medical insurance			
Cost to the employer			560
Workplace parking			Exempt
Golf club subscription (Note 3)			1,450
Total benefits			3,960

Tutorial note

1 There are two methods of calculating the taxable benefit for interest free or low interest loans.

1 The average method

Average loan =

(Loan at start of tax year (or when first borrowed) + loan at end of tax year) ÷ 2

Benefit = Average loan × 3.75% (Official rate) less any interest actually paid.

2 The precise or accurate method calculates the interest on a monthly basis based on the actual loan outstanding.

The taxpayer can choose to use the precise method if it produces a lower benefit.

HMRC can insist on the precise method if it produces a materially larger benefit than the average method and HMRC suspects that there has been manipulation of the loan to affect the benefit.

2 Employer pension contributions into either an employee's personal pension plan or the company occupational scheme for an employee are an exempt benefit. Pensions are a popular topic in this examination.

3 Payment of a golf club subscription is a taxable benefit as it is not necessary for Sami to join the golf club in order to carry out the duties of their employment.

9 AMAIA

Key answer tips

This question demonstrates the breadth of knowledge needed in respect of benefits.

Note that the van scale and fuel benefit charges are provided in the tax rates and allowances given to you in the examination, so there are easy marks to achieve for using the figures given to you.

Remember that overseas expenses are wholly taxable if the payments exceed the permitted limit.

Taxable benefits – 2025/26

	£	£
Van scale charge		4,020
Private fuel for van		769
Entertainment system		
Gift = Greater of		
(i) Original cost	1,200	
Less: Use of asset benefits		
2023/24 (£1,200 × 20%)	(240)	
2024/25 (£1,200 × 20%)	(240)	
2025/26 (£1,200 × 20% × 6/12) (see below)	(120)	
	600	
(ii) Current market value	300	
Higher of (i) and (ii)		600
Use of asset for 2025/26 (£1,200 × 20% × 6/12)		120
Overseas expenses (Note 1)		
£14 a night exceeds the statutory limit of £10 per night therefore the full amount is taxable: (£14 × 80)		1,120
Mileage (Note 2)		
(55p – 45p) × 6,000 miles		600
iPad (Note 3)		
Cost to employer		510
Total benefits		7,739

Tutorial note

There are some tricky points in the calculation of the taxable benefits.

1 *The overseas expenses are taxed in full if they exceed the £10 daily limit. It is not the excess over £10 that is taxable but the whole amount. The equivalent daily figure for incidental expenses in the UK is £5 per night.*

2 *Where a taxpayer receives more than the approved mileage allowance the excess is taxed. If the individual receives less than the approved mileage allowance the deficit can be claimed as an allowable deduction from employment income. The approved mileage allowance rates are given in the tax tables.*

3 *Gifts of new assets purchased for an employee by an employer are fully taxable at the cost to the employer.*

10 PEPPY

Key answer tips

This is a tricky question as it encompasses several different complications, such as time apportionment of taxable benefits and contributions toward capital costs and the private use of a car. However, as long as you concentrate on each benefit in turn and read the question carefully these issues should be manageable.

On initially reading the question, highlight important pieces of information, such as dates, so that you do not forget to consider them in your answer.

Remember that if a benefit is exempt, state this in the answer. Do not just ignore it.

Total value of benefits provided to Peppy – 2025/26

Car and fuel benefit

CO_2 emissions 178 g/km, available 9 months of the tax year

	%
Basic percentage (petrol)	17
Plus (175 – 55) × 1/5	24
Appropriate percentage	41
But limited to (Note 1)	37

	£	£
List price	28,000	
Less: Capital contribution (restricted to maximum)	(5,000)	
	23,000	
Car benefit (£23,000 × 37% × 9/12) (Note 2)	6,383	
Less: Contribution towards car (£40 × 9 months)	(360)	
		6,023
Fuel benefit (£28,200 × 37% × 9/12)		7,826
Computer benefit (Note 3)		
(£4,000 × 20% × 5/12)		333
Relocation expenses		
Amount received	10,000	
Less: Tax-free amount	(8,000)	
		2,000
After–school childcare – exempt (Note 4)		0
Total taxable benefits		16,182

Tutorial note

There are several areas that you need to watch in this question.

1 *The maximum percentage for calculating the car benefit is 37%. This information is not given in your tax tables so you must learn it.*

2 *Since the car was provided part way through the year, it is necessary to time apportion the car and fuel benefits. This is something that often catches students out. In addition, the contributions both to the capital cost and the private use of the car need to be handled carefully.*

The key issues with contributions are as follows:

Capital contributions toward the cost of the car are capped at £5,000.

Contributions specifically for the private use of the car can be deducted from the benefit, but partial contributions toward the cost of the private fuel cannot be deducted.

3 *The benefit for the computer also needs to be time apportioned for the period it was available during the tax year.*

4 *Nurseries and similar facilities for older children, after school or during school holidays, that are run by the employer (who must be responsible for finance and management) at the workplace or at other non-domestic premises are not a taxable benefit.*

11 JUANA

Key answer tips

This question covers a wide range of benefits which are frequently tested. Note how you are not given the figure for business mileage directly but have to calculate it.

Where a benefit is exempt, do not ignore it, state that it is exempt to get maximum credit.

Taxable benefits – 2025/26

	£	£
House (Note 1)		
Basic charge:		
Annual value	1,400	
Additional benefit:		
(£195,000 – £75,000) × 3.75%	4,500	
	———	
	5,900	
Less: Employee contribution (£100 × 12)	(1,200)	
	———	4,700
Furniture: (£8,000 × 20%)		1,600

Subsidised canteen (Note 2)	
= Exempt benefit	0
Mileage (Note 3)	
10,000 × (50p – 45p)	500
Total benefits	6,800

Tutorial note

1 *Market value of the house is only relevant if the employer bought the house more than six years before the employee moves in. This is not the case here, so the original cost is used.*

2 *The provision of a subsidised canteen is an exempt benefit provided it is available to all employees. The additional information given in the question is therefore irrelevant. There is no taxable benefit.*

3 *Journeys to and from work are regarded as private motoring so the whole of the 5,000 miles are regarded as private.*

The approved mileage allowance is 45p for the first 10,000 miles of business motoring and Juana is only taxed on the excess over that figure.

12 DAVID

Key answer tips

This covers typical areas of employment income.

Where the car, provided by the employer, has a diesel powered engine, you need to consider how this affects the car benefit calculation.

When you are asked to calculate a loan benefit, and there has been a change in the loan during the year, then you need to calculate the benefit using both the average method and the precise method.

Taxable benefits – 2025/26

Car CO_2 emissions 107 g/km, available all year

	%
Basic percentage (diesel meets RDE2 standard– no supplement) (Note 1)	17
Plus: (105 – 55) × 1/5	10
Appropriate percentage	27
Benefit (£100,000 × 27%)	£27,000

Fuel (Note 1)
(£28,200 × 27%) £7,614

Beneficial loan (Note 2)

Taxed on the greater of:

(i)	**Average method**		£
	$\frac{£15,000 + £12,000}{2} \times 3.75\%$		506
	Less: Interest paid:		
	(£15,000 × 1.5% × 9/12)	169	
	(£12,000 × 1.5% × 3/12)	45	
		——	(214)
			292
(ii)	**Precise method**		
	£15,000 × (3.75% – 1.5%) × 9/12	253	
	£12,000 × (3.75% – 1.5%) × 3/12	68	
		——	321

The taxpayer will choose the lower figure and therefore not elect for the precise method.

HMRC can insist on the precise method, but only usually does so if there is a material difference in the two figures and it suspects there has been manipulation of the loan amount to affect the benefit calculation.

Course fees	(Note 3)	
	Exempt	£0
Computer	(£800 × 20%)	£160
Expenses	(Note 4)	
	Overseas trips – daily amount in excess of £10 therefore the full amount is taxable (£12 × 60 days)	£720
	UK amounts – daily amounts below £5 therefore it is an exempt benefit	£0
Home working allowance		
	(Note 5)	
	Exempt up to £6 per week	£0

Tutorial note

1 *There is no 4% diesel supplement where a diesel car meets the RDE2 standard. Employee contribution towards private fuel is ignored as it does not cover the full cost.*

2 *There are two methods of calculating the taxable benefit for interest free or low interest loans.*

   (i) The average method

   (Loan at start of tax year + loan at end of tax year) ÷ 2 = Average loan

   Benefit = Average loan × 3.75% (Official rate) less any interest actually paid.

   (ii) The precise or accurate method calculates the interest on a monthly basis based on the actual loan outstanding.

   The taxpayer can elect for the precise method if it produces a lower benefit.

   HMRC can insist on the precise method if it produces a materially larger benefit than the average method.

3 *Training course fees are an exempt benefit if the training is relevant to the employee's employment.*

4 *The overseas expenses are taxed in full if they exceed the £10 daily limit. It is not the excess over £10 that is taxable but the whole amount. The equivalent daily figure for incidental expenses in the UK is £5 per night.*

5 *If an employee is required to work at home, then an employer can pay a tax-free home working allowance of up to £6 per week to cover the additional running costs of the home. Higher amounts can be paid towards home working costs if the employee has evidence of the costs.*

13 BERNARD

Key answer tips

A car benefit is a popular examination topic. Be careful with a capital contribution – ensure it is deducted in the correct place and capped appropriately.

Car benefit

	£
List price	32,000
Less: Contribution (maximum)	(5,000)
	27,000
£27,000 × 29% (W)	7,830
£7,830 × ½ (6 months only)	3,915

Working: Benefit percentage

CO_2 emissions	115
Base level	(55)
	60
60/5	12
Base percentage	17
Relevant percentage	29

Examiner's report

This was a five-mark question requiring calculation of a car benefit.

This question was very well answered with many candidates scoring high marks.

The appropriate percentage was calculated well with only a few candidates using the wrong rates, despite these being given in the tax rates and allowances table.

There were two other issues that caused some candidates problems. The maximum personal contribution deduction from cost was £5,000 and the benefit should have been reduced to the period of use (six months).

ACCA Marking scheme

	Marks
Capital contribution deduction	1.0
Benefit for full year	0.5
Time apportionment of benefit	1.0
Excess emissions above base level	1.0
1/5 of excess emissions	1.0
Add base percentage	0.5
Total	**5.0**

PERSONAL TAX

14 YUSIF

Key answer tips

This is a comprehensive test of an income tax computation and typical of a 15 mark question in the examination.

Always read the question very carefully and highlight any income that is exempt or any expenditure that needs grossing up.

Remember to state in your answer whether income is exempt. Do not just leave out exempt income.

Income tax computation – 2025/26

	Non-savings Income	Savings Income	Dividend Income	Total Income
	£	£	£	£
Salary	92,000			
Bonus	8,000			
Benefits	4,350			
	104,350			
Less: Occupational pension contributions (Note) (£400 × 12)	(4,800)			
Employment income	99,550			99,550
Bank interest		3,000		3,000
Dividends			2,000	2,000
NS&I savings certificates				Exempt
Premium Bond winnings				Exempt
Total income	99,550	3,000	2,000	104,550
Less: Personal allowance (W1)	(10,795)			(10,795)
Taxable income	88,755	3,000	2,000	93,755

	£		£
Income tax			
Non-savings income – basic rate (W2)	38,700	× 20%	7,740
Non-savings income – higher rate	50,055	× 40%	20,022
	88,755		
Savings income – nil rate	500	× 0%	0
Savings income – higher rate	2,500	× 40%	1,000
Dividends – nil rate	500	× 0%	0
Dividends – higher rate	1,500	× 33.75%	506
	93,755		
Income tax liability			29,268
Less: PAYE			(27,987)
Income tax payable			1,281

Tutorial note

1 *Relief for occupational pension scheme payments is given by deducting the payments from the employment income in the computation.*

These payments are made gross so no grossing up is required for occupational pension scheme contributions. In the December 2015 examiner's report this point was highlighted, as well as the fact that occupational pension contributions do not increase the tax bands.

2 *NS&I savings certificates and premium bond winnings are exempt income. Remember to state this in the answer to obtain full credit. Do not just ignore them.*

3 *Yusif is a higher rate taxpayer as his taxable income of £93,755 exceeds the extended basic rate band of £38,700. As a higher rate taxpayer he is entitled to a savings income nil rate band of £500. All taxpayers are entitled to a dividend nil rate band of £500.*

Workings

(W1) Restriction of personal allowance

	£	£
Basic personal allowance		12,570
Net income (= Total income)	104,550	
Less: Gross gift aid (£800 × 100/80)	(1,000)	
Adjusted net income	103,550	
Less: Limit	(100,000)	
	3,550	
50% of £3,550		(1,775)
Revised personal allowance		10,795

(W2) Extension of basic rate band

	£
Basic rate band	37,700
Plus: Gross gift aid (£800 × 100/80)	1,000
Extended basic rate band	38,700

Tutorial note

The personal allowance is restricted for taxpayers with adjusted net income over £100,000.

There are two main items that must be deducted from total income to give net income and these are qualifying loan interest payments and trading losses which the taxpayer has chosen to deduct from total income. Neither of these applies in this question.

Net income is then reduced by ***grossed up*** *gift aid and* ***personal*** *pension payments to calculate adjusted net income.*

The ***grossed up*** *gift aid and personal pension contributions also increase the higher and additional rate thresholds.*

15 ANITA AND GREGORY

Key answer tips

This question focuses on the savings income nil rate band, starting rate for savings income and dividend nil rate band.

Anita and Gregory – Tax payable – 2025/26

				£
Anita	Building society interest			18,125
	Less: Personal allowance			(12,570)
	Taxable income			5,555
	Savings income – starting rate	£5,000	× 0%	0
	Savings income nil rate band	£555	× 0%	0
		£5,555		
	Income tax liability			0
				£
Gregory	Taxable income (all dividends)			6,400
	Dividend nil rate band	£500	× 0%	0
	Dividend income – basic rate	£5,900	× 8.75%	516
		£6,400		
	Income tax liability			516

Tutorial note

The first £5,000 of Anita's savings income falls into the starting rate band as she does not have any non-savings income. This is therefore taxed at 0%. Anita is also entitled to a savings income nil rate band of £1,000 as she is a basic rate taxpayer. The remainder of her savings income is therefore taxed at 0% as it all falls within the nil rate band.

All taxpayers are entitled to a dividend nil rate band of £500.

16 CARLOTA

Key answer tips

When preparing the income tax computation in part (a), remember to include any exempt income and state that it is exempt as there will be a mark for this.

Part (b) asks for some information about self-assessment. This is a frequently examined area and you must not neglect these parts of questions which can bring some easy marks.

The examining team have recently commented in their examiner's reports that they have been disappointed with candidates' recent poor performance on such questions – many being unaware of the correct dates, not reading the question properly or omitting the question completely. This is therefore a very likely topic to reappear in future examinations.

(a) Income tax computation – 2025/26

	Non-savings Income	**Savings Income**	**Dividend Income**	**Total Income**
	£	£	£	£
Trading income	4,000			4,000
Transition profit	796			796
Employment income	1,927			1,927
Interest income				
NS&I investment account		70		70
Bank interest		5,806		5,806
Building society interest		6,813		6,813
ISA interest = exempt				0
Dividends			17,000	17,000
Total income	6,723	12,689	17,000	36,412
Less: Personal allowance	(6,723)	(5,847)		(12,570)
Taxable income	0	6,842	17,000	23,842

	£		£
Income tax:			
Savings income – starting rate	5,000	× 0%	0
Savings income – nil rate	1,000	× 0%	0
Savings income – basic rate	842	× 20%	168
	6,842		
Dividend income – nil rate	500	× 0%	0
Dividend income – basic rate	16,500	× 8.75%	1,444
	23,842		
Income tax liability			1,612
Less: PAYE			(292)
Income tax payable			1,320

Tutorial note

The main technical points that you should note in (a) include:

- *The transition profit is taxed along with trading profits*
- *Interest on ISA = exempt*
- *NS&I interest = taxable income*
- *The savings income falling in the first £5,000 of taxable income is taxed at 0%*
- *Basic rate taxpayers are entitled to a savings income nil rate band of £1,000*
- *All taxpayers are entitled to a dividend income nil rate band of £500*
- *As Carlota is not a higher rate taxpayer, her gift aid payment does not affect her tax calculation.*

(b) Due dates for income tax

Payments on account are due on 31 January in the tax year and 31 July following the end of the tax year, i.e. 31 January 2026 and 31 July 2026 for the 2025/26 tax year.

The balance of the income tax liability is due on 31 January following the end of the tax year, i.e. 31 January 2027 for the 2025/26 tax year.

Where the notice to file a tax return is issued later than 31 October following the end of the tax year (through no fault of the taxpayer) then the balance of the income tax liability is due three months after the date of issue of the notice to file a tax return.

Payments on account

Payments on account are calculated by taking half of the income tax liability (less PAYE) of the previous tax year.

17 ZARA

> **Key answer tips**
>
> This question is a typical 15 mark income tax question that includes several sources of income, the reduction of the personal allowance (PA) for high income individuals and the effect of gift aid donations on the basic rate threshold.
>
> Always show a separate working for your calculation of the reduced PA.

Income tax computation – 2025/26

	Non-savings	Savings Income	Dividend Income	Total Income
	£	£	£	£
Salary	99,110			
Benefits	2,290			
	———			
Employment income	101,400			101,400
Property income	820			820
Bank interest		350		350
BSI		450		450
ISA interest = exempt				0
Dividend			300	300
	———	———	———	———
Total income	102,220	800	300	103,320
Less: Personal allowance (W1)	(11,110)			(11,110)
	———	———	———	———
Taxable income	91,110	800	300	92,210
	———	———	———	———

Income tax:	£		£
Non-savings income – basic rate (W2)	38,100	× 20%	7,620
Non-savings income – higher rate	53,010	× 40%	21,204
	———		
	91,110		
Savings income – nil rate	500	× 0%	0
Savings income – higher rate	300	× 40%	120
Dividend income – nil rate	300	× 0%	0
	———		
	92,210		
	———		———
Income tax liability			28,944
Less: PAYE			(28,746)
			———
Income tax payable			198
			———

Workings

(W1) Reduction of personal allowance

	£	£
Basic personal allowance		12,570
Net income (= Total income)	103,320	
Less: Gross gift aid (£320 × 100/80)	(400)	
Adjusted net income	102,920	
Less: Limit	(100,000)	
	2,920	
50% of £2,920		(1,460)
Revised personal allowance		11,110

(W2) Extension of basic rate band

	£
Basic rate band	37,700
Plus: Gross gift aid (£320 ×100/80)	400
Extended basic rate band	38,100

Tutorial note

The personal allowance is restricted for taxpayers with adjusted net income over £100,000.

There are two main items that must be deducted from total income to give net income and these are qualifying loan interest payments and trading losses which the taxpayer has chosen to deduct from total income. Neither of these applies in this question.

Net income is then reduced by grossed up gift aid and personal pension payments to calculate adjusted net income.

The grossed up gift aid and personal pension contributions also increase the higher and additional rate thresholds.

18 CORAL

Key answer tips

A wide ranging question which includes a number of different deductions from employment income, and personal pension contributions which is a popular examination topic.

Remember to include any exempt income and state that it is exempt as there will be marks for this.

Income tax computation – 2025/26

	Non-savings Income	**Savings Income**	**Dividend Income**	**Total Income**
	£	£	£	£
Employment income (W1)	53,250			53,250
Rental income (£4,800 × 1/2)	2,400			2,400
Bank interest		500		500
ISA interest = exempt				0
Dividends			500	500
Prize from lottery = exempt				0
Total income	55,650	500	500	56,650
Less: Personal allowance	(12,570)			(12,570)
Taxable income	43,080	500	500	44,080

Income tax:	£		£
Non-savings income – Basic rate (W2)	42,360	× 20%	8,472
Non-savings income – Higher rate	720	× 40%	288
	43,080		
Savings income – Nil rate	500	× 0%	0
Dividend income – Nil rate	500	× 0%	0
	44,080		
Income tax liability			8,760
Less: PAYE			(7,305)
Income tax payable			1,455

Tutorial note

The key to success is to know how to deal with the various different types of deductions from Coral's salary.

The payroll giving deduction and the professional subscription reduce the amount of employment income, while the personal pension contribution extends the basic rate band of tax by the gross amount of the contribution.

If the pension contribution had been into an occupational scheme, the deduction would have been treated in the same way as the payroll giving and professional subscription deductions.

The examining team have commented that personal and occupational pension contributions are often muddled by students. Make sure you know how to treat each one as these are frequently examined.

Workings

(W1) Employment income

	£
Salary	45,050
Bonus	6,000
Taxable benefits	2,500
	53,550
Less: Payroll giving	(120)
Professional subscription	(180)
Employment income	53,250

(W2) Extended basic rate band

	£
Basic rate band	37,700
Plus: Gross personal pension contribution (£3,728 × 100/80)	4,660
Extended basic rate band	42,360

19 FREDA

Key answer tips

This question contains the usual mix of employment income, investment income and exempt income. You need to be careful with the treatment of the pension contributions made by the employer and employee, a popular topic in 15 mark income tax questions.

Income tax computation – 2025/26

	Non-savings Income	Savings Income	Dividend Income	Total Income
	£	£	£	£
Employment income (W)	51,610			51,610
Bank interest		2,000		2,000
Dividend			1,000	1,000
NS&I account interest		400		400
NS&I certificate interest – exempt				Exempt
Total income	51,610	2,400	1,000	55,010
Less: Personal allowance	(12,570)			(12,570)
Taxable income	39,040	2,400	1,000	42,440
Income tax:				
Non-savings income – basic rate	37,700	× 20%		7,540
Non-savings income – higher rate	1,340	× 40%		536
	39,040			
Savings income – nil rate	500	× 0%		0
Savings income – higher rate	1,900	× 40%		760
Dividend income – nil rate	500	× 0%		0
Dividend income – higher rate	500	× 33.75%		169
	42,440			
Income tax liability				9,005
Less: PAYE				(7,546)
Income tax payable				1,459

Working: Employment income

	£
Salary	45,650
Bonus	8,000
	53,650
Professional fees	(240)
Pension contribution	(1,800)
Employer's contribution	Exempt
Employment income	51,610

Tutorial note

Pension contributions made by an employee to an employer's occupational pension scheme are paid gross and deducted from employment income. Any contributions to the pension scheme made by an employer are an exempt benefit.

The examining team have commented that personal and occupational pension contributions are often muddled by students. Make sure you know how to treat each one as these are commonly examined.

20 DIEGO

Key answer tips

This question requires allocation of the partnership profit and application of the tax year basis so that the correct amount of income can be included in the income tax computation.

Remember to include any exempt income and state that it is exempt as there will be marks for this.

Income tax computation – 2025/26

	Non-savings Income	Savings Income	Dividend Income	Total Income
	£	£	£	£
Partnership profit (W1)	126,340			126,340
NS&I savings certificate interest				Exempt
Premium bond prize				Exempt
NS&I account interest		2,100		2,100
Dividend			8,000	8,000
	———	———	———	———
Total income	126,340	2,100	8,000	136,440
Less: Interest payment (Note)				
(£10,000 × 8%)	(800)			(800)
	———	———	———	———
Net income	125,540	2,100	8,000	135,640
Less: PA (W2) (Note)	0			0
	———	———	———	———
Taxable income	125,540	2,100	8,000	135,640
	———	———	———	———

Tutorial note

1 *A loan to buy plant and machinery for use in a partnership is a qualifying loan. Interest is deducted from total income in the computation.*

2 *Where adjusted net income clearly exceeds £125,140 there is no need to perform a calculation to prove that there will be no personal allowance available. However, a statement is required that there is no personal allowance and the reason why.*

Note that the examining team have stated in their examiner's report that candidates needed to state this fact to get the full mark. Just inserting '£0' in the income tax computation for the personal allowance will not get full marks.

Income tax:

	£		£
Non-savings income – basic rate (W4)	39,700	× 20%	7,940
Non-savings income – higher rate	85,840	× 40%	34,336
	———		
	125,540		
Savings income – higher rate	1,600	× 40%	640
	———		
Higher rate threshold (W4)	127,140		
Savings income – additional rate	500	× 45%	225
Dividend income – nil rate	500	× 0%	0
Dividend income – additional rate	7,500	× 39.35%	2,951
	———		
	135,640		
	———		———
Income tax liability			46,092
			———

Workings

(W1) Diego's partnership profit for 2025/26

	£
Diego's share of partnership profits:	
Year ended 30 April 2025 (£200,300 × 60%)	120,180
Year ended 30 April 2026 (£211,500 × 60%)	126,900
Tax year 2025/26	
(£120,180 × 1/12) + (£126,900 × 11/12)	126,340

Tutorial note

Taxable trading profits of a partnership are calculated in the same way as for a sole trader, under the cash basis (default method) or accruals basis (if so elected).

The taxable profits of the accounting period are then allocated between the partners using the profit sharing ratio of that accounting period.

The tax year basis is then applied to calculate each partner's trading income for the tax year.

Diego is not entitled to a savings income nil rate band as he is an additional rate taxpayer. All taxpayers are entitled to the dividend nil rate band.

(W2) Personal allowance

As Diego's adjusted net income of £133,640 (W3) is in excess of £125,140, there is no personal allowance available to Diego.

(W3) Adjusted net income

	£
Net income	135,640
Less: Gross PPC (£1,600 × 100/80)	(2,000)
Adjusted net income	133,640

(W4) Extended basic rate band

	BR band threshold	**HR band threshold**
	£	£
Basic rate band/higher rate band	37,700	125,140
Plus: Gross PPC (£1,600 × 100/80)	2,000	2,000
Extended basic rate band	39,700	127,140

> ***Tutorial note***
>
> *The grossed up personal pension contributions increase the higher* ***and*** *additional rate thresholds.*
>
> *The examining team have commented that personal and occupational pension contributions are often muddled by students. Make sure you know how to treat each one as these are commonly examined.*

21 GEMING

> **Key answer tips**
>
> This question covers self-employment, employment, property income and other investment income in the calculation of income tax. There is also a gift aid payment which will affect the basic rate band.
>
> Remember to include any exempt income and state that it is exempt as there will be marks for this.

Income tax computation – 2025/26

	Non-savings Income	Savings Income	Dividend Income	Total Income
	£	£	£	£
Salary	38,850			
Occupational pension	(3,000)			
Employment income	35,850			35,850
Trading profit (W1)	12,000			12,000
Property income (W2)	6,800			6,800
Dividends			3,500	3,500
Building society interest		1,800		1,800
NS&I certificate interest – exempt		0		Exempt
Total income	54,650	1,800	3,500	59,950
Less: PA	(12,570)			(12,570)
Taxable income	42,080	1,800	3,500	47,380

Tutorial note

NS&I savings certificates are exempt income. Remember to state this in the answer to obtain full credit. Do not just ignore them.

Income tax payable:

	£		£
Non-savings income – basic rate (W3)	38,700	× 20%	7,740
Non-savings income – higher rate	3,380	× 40%	1,352
	42,080		
Savings income – nil rate	500	× 0%	0
Savings income – higher rate	1,300	× 40%	520
Dividend income – nil rate	500	× 0%	0
Dividend income – higher rate	3,000	× 33.75%	1,013
	47,380		
Income tax liability			10,625
PAYE			(5,270)
Income tax payable			5,355

Workings

(W1) Trading profit for 2025/26

6 April 2025 – 30 September 2025 (£24,000 × 6/12)	£12,000

Tutorial note

When a sole trader ceases trading, the tax year basis means the sole trader is taxed on trading profits arising from 6 April to the date of cessation.

(W2) Property income

	£	£
Rent (cash basis – 7 × £1,100)		7,700
Insurance (paid basis)	300	
Replacement of domestic items relief (£800 – £200)	600	
		(900)
Property income		6,800

The new shed is capital expenditure and is therefore not deductible.

Tutorial note

1 *The default method for calculating property income for an individual is the cash basis. In an examination question you should assume that the cash basis is to be used unless specifically stated to the contrary. This means that the rent due for March 2026 that was never received is not taxed.*

2 *The furniture is eligible for replacement of domestic items relief, with a deduction for the sale proceeds of the old furniture. The new shed, however, is the first purchase of a capital asset and is not eligible for relief. The shed is not an allowable deduction as a capital item under the cash basis as it is an asset provided for use in a residential property.*

(W3) Extended basic rate band

Extension of basic rate band: £37,700 + (£800 × 100/80) = £38,700

Examiner's report

This was the 15-mark question on income tax, examining many of the usual problems and this time the specific issues [included] the receipt of property income.

It was pleasing that many candidates produced good answers and a few candidates scored maximum marks. However, a small minority of candidates had no knowledge of even the basic principles, which was disappointing.

The amount assessed under property income is generally calculated on the receipts and payment basis. Therefore only 7 months' rent was assessable, the final month's rent would be taxed if and when received. Only revenue expenses are deductible, therefore, the amount paid for the new shed was not an allowable expense as this was capital. The cost of similar replacement furniture is allowed, but any amount received for the sale of the old furniture reduces the amount that can be deducted from the rent.

It should also be noted that the amount of taxable property income must be shown as a separate working and not lumped together with other income.

The other areas examined in this question were generally well answered, with most candidates treating the occupational pension contribution, the gift aid and NS&I certificate interest correctly.

ACCA Marking scheme

		Marks
Salary		0.5
Occupational pension deduction		1.0
Dividends		1.0
Building society interest		1.0
NS&I certificate interest		1.0
Personal allowance		1.0
Extension of basic rate band		1.0
Non-savings income – basic rate		0.5
Non-savings income – higher rate		0.5
Savings income – nil rate band		0.5
Savings income – higher rate		0.5
Dividend income – nil rate band		0.5
Dividend income – higher rate		0.5
PAYE		0.5
Trading profit		1.0
Property income	– rent on cash basis	1.0
	– insurance paid basis	1.0
	– replacement of domestic items relief	1.0
	– shed not deductible	1.0
Total		**15.0**

22 STEPHEN

Key answer tips

This question covers employment, partnership profits and other investment income in the calculation of income tax. There are various payments which must be treated correctly as either a deduction from income, extension of the bands or as a relief.

Remember to include any exempt income and state that it is exempt as there will be marks for this.

Income tax computation – 2025/26

	Non-savings Income	Savings Income	Dividend Income	Total Income
	£	£	£	£
Salary (8/12 × £108,000)	72,000			
Professional fees	(400)			
Golf club membership – not deductible	0			
Stephen's contribution to occupational pension	(3,000)			
Employer's contribution – exempt	0			
Employment income	68,600			68,600
Partnership profits (W1)	11,000			11,000
Income from an ISA		0		Exempt
Building society interest		3,000		3,000
Dividends			4,000	4,000
Total income	79,600	3,000	4,000	86,600
Qualifying interest	(2,000)			(2,000)
Net income	77,600	3,000	4,000	84,600
Less: PA	(12,570)			(12,570)
Taxable income	65,030	3,000	4,000	72,030

Tutorial note

1 *Income from an ISA is exempt income. The pension contribution from the employer is exempt. The golf club membership fee is not deductible. Remember to state these in the answer to obtain full credit. Do not just ignore them.*

2 *A loan to buy plant and machinery for use in the employment is a qualifying loan. Interest is deducted from total income in the computation.*

Income tax payable:

	£		£
Non-savings income – basic rate (W2)	45,200	× 20%	9,040
Non-savings income – higher rate	19,830	× 40%	7,932
	65,030		
Savings income – nil rate	500	× 0%	0
Savings income – higher rate	2,500	× 40%	1,000
Dividend income – nil rate	500	× 0%	0
Dividend income – higher rate	3,500	× 33.75%	1,181
	72,030		
Income tax liability			19,153
PAYE			(15,100)
Income tax payable			4,053

Workings

(W1) Partnership profits

	Total	A	B	Stephen
	£	£	£	£
Year ended 31 March 2026				
£38,500 : 3:2:2	38,500	16,500	11,000	11,000

Tutorial note

Taxable trading profits of a partnership are calculated in the same way as for a sole trader.

The trading profits of the accounting period are then allocated between the partners using the profit sharing ratio of that accounting period.

In this case, the accounting period corresponds to the tax year, so no time apportionment is required under the tax year basis.

(W2) Extended basic rate band

Extension of basic rate band: £37,700 + (£6,000 × 100/80) = £45,200

Examiner's report

This was the usual 15-mark question on income tax, examining many of the problems commonly encountered.

Many candidates scored well on this question, but it was still surprising to see that some candidates did not understand the basic principles. Details such as interest, dividends, pension contributions and rates of tax are always examined and therefore candidates should, as a minimum, ensure they have good knowledge of these syllabus areas. This knowledge alone will score a good proportion of the marks available.

Apart from some candidates not knowing the basic principles outlined above the only other major issue was the treatment of the two different pension contributions [by the employee]. Contributions to company schemes should not be grossed up and the figure given in the question [for the employee's contribution] should have been simply deducted from employment income. Contributions to private pension schemes should be grossed up by 100/80 and the gross amount then extends the tax bands.

ACCA Marking scheme

	Marks
Salary	1.0
Professional fees	1.0
Golf club membership fee – not deductible	1.0
Occupational pension deduction	1.0
Employer's contribution – exempt benefit	1.0
ISA interest	0.5
Building society interest	1.0
Dividends	1.0
Qualifying interest	1.0
Personal allowance	1.0
Extension of basic rate band	1.0
Non-savings income – basic rate	0.5
Non-savings income – higher rate	0.5
Savings income – nil rate band	0.5
Savings income – higher rate	0.5
Dividend income – nil rate band	0.5
Dividend income – higher rate	0.5
PAYE	0.5
Apportionment of partnership profits	1.0
Total	**15.0**

23 MORGAN

Key answer tips

This question asks for some information about self-assessment. This is a frequently examined area and you must not neglect these parts of questions which can bring some easy marks.

The examining team have recently commented in their examiner's reports that they have been disappointed with candidates' recent poor performance on such questions – many being unaware of the correct dates, not reading the question properly or omitting the question completely. This is therefore a very likely topic to reappear in future examinations.

(i) Payments on account are due on 31 January in the relevant tax year and 31 July following the relevant tax year.

(ii) Each payment represents 50% of the previous year's income tax and class 4 national insurance contributions (NICs) after giving credit for any tax paid by PAYE. This is the relevant amount.

(iii) No payments on account are due in the following circumstances:

- The relevant amount for the previous year is less than £1,000, or
- More than 80% of the income tax liability for the previous year was met by PAYE, or
- There is no relevant amount in the previous year.

Examiner's report

This was a five-mark theory question requiring details on the payments on account (POA) rules for a sole trader.

Unfortunately, this was poorly answered with very few candidates having the knowledge of the payment dates and the method of calculation. Several candidates confused the rules with those of a company, which are totally different. As a reminder, POAs are due on 31 January **IN** the relevant tax year and 31 July **AFTER** the tax year, each being 50% of the previous year's income tax and class 4 national insurance contributions (NIC) after allowing for credit for any tax paid under PAYE.

It was disappointing that only a few candidates knew the rules for when no POAs are required.

ACCA Marking scheme	
	Marks
Payment on account (POA) due dates	1.0
How POAs are calculated	1.0
No POAs if relevant amount < £1,000	1.0
No POAs if >80% income tax met by PAYE	1.0
No POAs if there is no relevant amount in prior year	1.0
Total	**5.0**

PROPERTY INCOME

24 BERNICE

Key answer tips

Watch out for the rent-a-room relief – the exemption limit of £7,500 is given in the tax tables provided in the examination.

(a) Rental income – normal method

	£
Rent received (£160 × 52)	8,320
Less:	
Household expenses (£1,800 × 10%)	(180)
	8,140
Rental income – rent-a-room relief	
Rent received (as above)	8,320
Less:	
Rent-a-room limit	(7,500)
	820

Bernice will elect for rent-a-room relief

Tutorial note

When a taxpayer lets out a room in an own main residence, rent-a-room relief is available.

If the rents from the letting are ≤ £7,500 then the income is automatically exempt.

If the rents exceed £7,500, then the taxpayer can elect to tax only the excess of the rents over £7,500. This election must be made by 31 January 2028 for the 2025/26 tax year and once made remains in force until it is revoked or the rents fall below £7,500.

In the examiner's report on the June 2013 examination, the examining team commented that a common mistake was to deduct both the expenses and the exempted amount of £7,500 – this is never possible.

(b) Tax implications – employer pension contributions

Pension contributions paid by the employer are a tax-free benefit for Bernice.

For the company, the contributions are deductible in calculating the trading profits subject to corporation tax.

Tutorial note

Pension contributions made by an employee into an employer's occupational pension scheme are paid gross and tax relief is obtained by deducting them from employment income.

Any contributions to the pension scheme made by an employer are an exempt benefit and are tax allowable for the employer.

The examining team have commented that personal and occupational pension contributions are often muddled by students. Make sure you know how to treat each one as these are commonly examined.

25 ADRIANA

Key answer tips

This is a typical rental income calculation. Remember that the cash basis is the default method for the calculation of property income for an individual. It is a furnished letting so you should automatically think about the availability of replacement of domestic items relief.

Property income – 2025/26

	£	£
Rent receivable (cash basis) (Note 1):		
(April – December) (9/12 × £7,200)	5,400	
(January – February) (2/12 × £7,800)	1,300	
	———	6,700
Expenditure:		
Water rates	300	
Insurance	250	
Decoration (£2,250 – £500)	1,750	
Replacement of domestic items relief – kitchen units	3,200	
New TV cabinet	0	
	———	(5,500)
		———
Property income		1,200
		———

Tutorial note

1 *The default method for calculating property income for an individual is the cash basis. In an examination question you should assume that the cash basis is to be used unless specifically stated to the contrary. This means that the rent received on 2 May 2026, even though it was due on 6 March 2026, is not taxed until it is received, i.e. in the tax year 2026/27. Likewise, expenses are deductible when paid. So the £500 decoration costs paid in March 2025 will have been deducted in the property income calculation for the previous tax year, i.e. 2024/25.*

2 *The free-standing kitchen units are eligible for replacement of domestic items relief, as they are a replacement of existing furniture with the modern equivalent. The TV cabinet, however, is the first purchase of a capital asset and is not eligible for relief. The TV cabinet is not an allowable deduction as a capital item under the cash basis as it is an asset provided for use in a residential property.*

26 HASNAA

Key answer tips

This is a good test of your knowledge of rental income computations. Watch out for the treatment of the unpaid rent.

Property income – 2025/26

		£	£
Rent – cash basis (Note):			
30 April 2025 – 30 November 2025	(£800 × 8)	6,400	
31 January 2026 – 28 February 2026	(£880 × 2)	1,760	
		———	8,160
Less: Expenditure			
Contents insurance	Paid January 2026	800	
Letting agent's commission	(£8,160 × 10%)	816	
Repairs		250	
Water rates		300	
Garage (Building = not allowable) (Note)		0	
Replacement of domestic items relief	(£1,200 – £100)	1,100	
		———	(3,266)
			———
Property income			4,894
			———

Tutorial note

The default method for calculating property income for an individual is the cash basis. In an examination question you should assume that the cash basis is to be used unless specifically stated to the contrary. This means that only rents received in the tax year are included in the computation. Similarly, only expenses actually paid in the tax year are deductible.

Under the cash basis there is generally no distinction between capital and revenue expenditure for tax purposes. However, certain assets such as cars and land and buildings are specifically disallowed. As the garage is a building it is not an allowable deduction.

The fridge-freezer, being an asset provided for use in a residential property is also not an allowable deduction. However, it is eligible for replacement of domestic items relief since it is a replacement. However, only the cost of the modern equivalent item is eligible for relief, and it is reduced by the proceeds received for the disposal of the old fridge.

27 ROBERTA

Key answer tips

Take care with the premium received on the granting of a short lease.

Paula is taxed on the full amount (less 2% for each year apart from the first) in the year of receipt.

However, Roberta's relief is spread over the period covered by the lease. The relief is available as Roberta uses the accruals basis to calculate her trading profits.

In addition, relief for the first year must be time-apportioned as the lease was only entered into part way though Roberta's accounting period.

(a) Paula: Property income taxable 2025/26

	£
Premium	20,000
Less: 2% × (26 – 1) × £20,000	(10,000)
	10,000
Rental income – cash basis – received May 2025	800
Property income	10,800

(b) Roberta: Trading profit deduction in the year ended 31 December 2025

	£
Premium $\frac{£10{,}000}{26} \times 8/12$	256
Rent in y/e 31 December 2025 (£800 × 8/12)	533
Trading profit deduction	789

Tutorial note

Lease premiums are only partly chargeable to income tax. The amount to be deducted from the premium in order to leave the taxable amount is calculated using the formula:

2% × (n–1) × Premium where n= the length of the lease in years.

This formula is not given in the examination and must be learned.

The taxable amount is then included in property income for the period together with any rents.

The default method for calculating property income for an individual is the cash basis. In an examination question you should assume that the cash basis is to be used unless specifically stated to the contrary. Therefore, the full annual rent of £800 is also taxable as it was received in the tax year.

Part (b) can only be done once part (a) has been completed. The amount that can be deducted from trading profit is the taxable amount, calculated in part (a), divided by the length of the lease. This must be done on an accruals basis as it is for a trading deduction under that basis.

This topic was examined in December 2014 and December 2017 and in both cases the examiner's report indicated that it was not dealt with well. In December 2017 the examiner's report noted that very few candidates knew that the payer of the premium, who uses the property for business purposes, can deduct the amount of the lease premium taxable as property income on the landlord, spread over the life of the lease.

28 JOHANN

Key answer tips

In part (a) the question only asks for the annual amount that the tenant can deduct from his business profits, but it is necessary to first calculate the amount taxed on the landlord.

Part (b) deals with rent-a-room relief although in this case it is better to elect to ignore the exemption as a loss is created.

(a) Johann – Lease deduction

	£
Premium	18,000
2% × (10 – 1) × £18,000	(3,240)
Property income taxable on the landlord	14,760
Johann's deduction: (£14,760 ÷ 10)	£1,476 p.a.

Tutorial note

Lease premiums are only partly chargeable to income tax. The amount to be deducted from the premium in order to leave the taxable amount is calculated using the formula:

2% × (n–1) × Premium where n= the length of the lease in years.

This formula is not given in the examination and must be learned.

The taxable amount is then included in property income for the period together with any rents.

The amount that can be deducted from trading profit is the taxable amount divided by the length of the lease.

This topic was examined in December 2017 and the examiner's report noted that very few candidates knew that the payer of the premium, who uses the property for business purposes, can deduct the amount of the lease premium taxable as property income on the landlord, spread over the life of the lease.

(b) Gilbert – rental income

		£
Rents received	(£75 × 52)	3,900
Less: Household expenses	(£15 × 52)	(780)
Replacement furniture relief		(3,390)
Property income loss		(270)

Tutorial note

As the annual rents are below £7,500 the rental income is exempt under rent-a-room relief.

However, the taxpayer can elect to ignore the relief and calculate property income in the usual way. This is advantageous here as a loss arises which can be used against other rental income or carried forward for use against rental income in the future.

The replacement of carpets and curtains is eligible for replacement of domestic items relief.

29 AYANA

Key answer tips

This looks like a straightforward rental income computation but you need to be careful.

Ayana is taxed on rents received and expenses paid in the tax year. However, she lives in the property for one month so adjustment for private use must be made for the annual expenses like water rates and insurance.

No adjustment is needed for expenses that relate solely to letting, for example, the agent's fees.

The approved mileage allowances available for mileage in relation to the property business are given in the tax tables.

Property income – 2025/26

	£	£
Rent (£1,200 × 11 months)		13,200
Less: Expenses		
Insurance (£240 × 11/12)	220	
Agents fees (12% × £13,200)	1,584	
Approved mileage rate (800 × 45p)	360	
		(2,164)
Property income		11,036

Tutorial note

Ayana has lived in the property herself for one month. This means that 1/12 of the expenses relating to the property must be disallowed.

The expenses of letting, such as the agent's fees and mileage, do not need to be apportioned.

Ayana has the option of claiming either, capital allowances and actual running costs on a car used in her property business, or claiming a flat rate deduction for motor expenses using the approved mileage allowances of 45p and 25p per mile.

TRADING PROFIT

30 OLGA

Key answer tips

This question covers a number of key examination areas for a sole trader who uses the cash basis but the question does not specifically state that this basis is being used. The cash basis is the default method unless the sole trader elects to use the accruals basis. Therefore, in the examination you should assume the cash basis is being used unless told otherwise.

Read the information given carefully. Do not include receipts and payments that are not made during the year but remember to pick up the easy marks for showing these items with a zero, as this question instructs.

Watch out for expenses that are disallowed, even when they have been paid.

Trading profit – year ended 31 March 2026

	£
Sales receipts	45,000
Amount owed at year end	0
Less: Office insurance costs – amount paid 1 July 2025	(2,000)
Land	0
Office equipment	(4,000)
Client entertaining	0
Allowable costs paid (£15,000 – £1,000)	(14,000)
Trading profit	25,000

Tutorial note

1 *Sales receipts are taxable even those relating to sales made in the previous year, but received in the current year. Amounts owed at the year end are not taxable.*

2 *Allowable expenses are deducted in the period when paid, so the office insurance costs paid on 1 July 2025 are deductible, regardless of the period they cover.*

3 *There is no distinction between capital and revenue expenditure under the cash basis and so the payment for the office equipment is deducted in full. Capital allowances are not claimed under the cash basis (except for cars). However, capital expenditure on land and buildings is not allowable.*

4 *Client entertaining costs are not deductible.*

31 TANYA

Key answer tips

This is a good revision question covering a number of key examination areas for a sole trader who uses the accruals basis.

Note the treatment of the leased car where the standard 15% disallowance must be made as it is a high emission car (> 50g/km), as well as a disallowance for private use.

Tax adjusted trading profit – year ended 31 October 2025

	£
Net profit per accounts	6,649
Less: Bank interest	(280)
Profit on sale of cash register	(100)
	6,269
Add: Electricity (£380 × 40%) (private element)	152
Car expenses (£600 × 25%) (private element)	150
Lease rental – emissions > 50g/km (£1,000 × 15%)	150
Lease rental – private use (£1,000 – £150) × 25%	213
Depreciation	450
General shop repairs	0
Repairs – new counters (capital)	600
Administrative expenses	0
Rent (£4,800 × 40%) (private element)	1,920
Donations – Conservative Party	200
– Chamber of Commerce	0
	10,104
Less: Capital allowances	(600)
Tax adjusted trading profit	9,504

Tutorial note

1 *Car leasing costs are normally allowable. However, under the accruals basis, if the car has CO_2 emissions exceeding 50g/km then 15% of the leasing costs must be disallowed. In this question there is also a disallowance for 25% private use.*

Alternative method of calculating the lease adjustments:

Allowable amount = (£1,000 × 85% × 75%) = £638

Disallowable amount = (£1,000 – £638) = £362

= same as (£150 + £213 = £363) in the model answer (except for rounding)

2 *The new shop counters have been disallowed as capital items and would qualify for capital allowances. However, you do not need to make an adjustment for this as the question gives you the capital allowances and says that they have been calculated taking into account any relevant information in the notes.*

ACCA Marking scheme	
	Marks
Net profit per accounts	0.5
Bank interest	0.5
Gain on sale of cash register	0.5
Electricity	1.0
Car expenses	1.0
Lease rental – 15%	1.0
Lease rental – private use	1.0
Depreciation	0.5
General shop repairs – no adjustment	0.5
Repairs – counters	0.5
Administrative expenses – no adjustment	0.5
Rent	1.0
Donations – Conservative Party	0.5
– Chamber of Commerce – no adjustment	0.5
Capital allowances	0.5
Total	**10.0**

32 DUNCAN

Key answer tips

This capital allowances calculation involves a nine-month accounting period.

This means you need to remember to time-apportion the AIA and WDA.

The sale of a private use asset requires the calculation of a balancing adjustment. The new private use car with emissions exceeding 50g/km is only entitled to a 6% WDA.

		Main pool	Private use car (1)	Private use car (2)	Allowances
	£	£	£	£	£
TWDV b/f		52,000	12,000		
Additions without AIA:					
17 March 2026				27,000	
Additions with AIA:					
14 January 2026	180,000				
AIA (max £1,000,000 × 9/12 = £750,000)	(180,000)				180,000
		0			
Disposals:					
6 July 2025		(38,000)			
12 December 2025			(13,000)		
		14,000	(1,000)	27,000	
Balancing charge			1,000 × 60%		(600)
WDA @ (18% × 9/12)		(1,890)			1,890
WDA @ (6% × 9/12)				(1,215) × 50%	608
TWDV c/f		12,110	0	25,785	
Total allowances					181,898

Tutorial note

1 *Cars with CO_2 emissions of > 50g/km are entitled to a 6% WDA.*

2 *If any car has private use by the owner (not an employee) then it is depooled and kept in a column on its own. This means there is always a balancing charge or allowance when the car is sold. Only the business use of the WDA or balancing adjustment can be claimed.*

*Both the June 2018 and December 2018 examiner's reports noted that the incorrect treatment of cars with private use is a common mistake. The examining team have stated that 'future candidates should note that the private use percentage never reduces the cost or proceeds figure' included in the capital allowances computation. The **full** cost of the car must be added to and the **full** proceeds on disposal deducted from a separate column for the car.*

*Another common error identified by the examining team in the June 2018 exam was the incorrect calculation of the WDA. The **full** WDA must be deducted from the private use asset column with the private use percentage only restricting the actual allowance claimed.*

3 *The accounting period is only nine months long, so the AIA and WDA must be time apportioned.*

4 *Capital allowance questions, particularly for periods which are not 12 months long are popular in the examination.*

In the June 2014 examiner's report the examining team commented that many students made errors. They stated that the common questions that candidates should be asking themselves are:

"Which items receive annual investment allowance (AIA)?

In which pool should items be placed?

Is the AIA and writing down allowance (WDA) restricted?

Which rate of WDA should be applied?

Are amounts restricted by private use?"

The examining team considers that "if these questions are considered carefully then the majority of marks would be earned with minimal effort".

Examiner's report

This was a 10-mark question requiring the calculation of capital allowances for a 9-month period. This question was well attempted by the majority of candidates.

The main issues were that the two cars should have been treated separately (each being used partly for private purposes), and both the annual investment allowance (AIA) and the writing down allowance (WDA) should have been restricted to 9/12 of the annual amounts.

All rates were given in the Tax Rates and Allowances table, therefore candidates should not have had a problem using the correct rates for the different assets given in the question. Unfortunately, a few candidates did not take the time to check this and used the wrong rates for the wrong assets.

Candidates are reminded that the answer to this type of question should follow the standard layout shown in all recommended text books and therefore presented in a columnar format.

ACCA Marking scheme	
	Marks
Additions without AIA	1.0
Additions with AIA	0.5
Max AIA	1.0
Disposals	2.0
Balancing charge	1.5
WDA – main pool	1.5
WDA – private use car	2.0
Total allowances	0.5
Total	**10.0**

33 SUSAN

Key answer tips

Marks are available in this question for listing out the allowable items and explaining why they are not adjusted. Keep your explanations very brief.

Tax adjusted trading profit – year ended 31 December 2025

		£
Net profit		32,600
Add:	Wages (drawings)	24,000
	Son's wages	0
	Shop rent	0
	Electricity (£4,400 × 60%)	2,640
	Business rates	0
	Depreciation	1,000
	Car expenses (£1,800 × 70%)	1,260
	Irrecoverable trade debt	0
	Parking fine	400
	Legal fees for renewal of short lease	0
	Legal fees (personal expenditure)	50
	Donations to trade associations	0
	Goods for own use (at selling price)	1,250
		63,200
Less: Capital allowances		(800)
Tax adjusted trading profits		62,400

Items not adjusted for:

- Son's wages = reasonable remuneration for services provided to the business. All other employees are paid the same rate.
- Shop rent = wholly and exclusively for the purposes of the trade
- Business rates = wholly and exclusively for the purposes of the trade
- Irrecoverable trade debt written off – a specific debt identified that will not be paid = allowable
- Legal fee for the renewal of short lease (less than 50 years) = specifically allowable
- Trade donation = wholly and exclusively for the purposes of the trade

Tutorial note

1 *Wages to family members are allowed if they are reasonable (i.e. no more than another employee who is not a family member would receive).*

2 *Parking fines incurred by the owner of the business are always disallowed.*

3 *Inventory for own use must be charged to the trader at selling price not just cost. As the items had not yet been charged to Susan, then full selling price must be added to increase the profits. If Susan had paid for the cost of the items or the cost had been charged to her drawings account then only the profit element would need to be added when calculating the tax adjusted trading profit.*

34 JI-HO

Key answer tips

A tricky question as it requires VAT adjustments before the capital allowances can be calculated. In addition, the period is 14 months long meaning that the WDA and maximum AIA must be scaled up (something that only happens with sole traders and partnerships).

Capital allowances – 14 m/e 31 December 2025

		Main pool	**Private use car**		**Allowances**
	£	£	£		£
Purchases no AIA			14,000		
Purchases (with AIA)					
P & M (£85,920 × 100/120)	71,600				
Computer (£6,144 × 100/120)	5,120				
	76,720				
AIA (Max £1,000,000 × 14/12 = £1,166,667)	(76,720)				76,720
		0			
WDA @ (18% × 14/12)			(2,940)	× 60%	1,764
TWDV c/f		0	11,060		
Total allowances					78,484

Tutorial note

1 Cars with CO_2 emissions of 50g/km or less are entitled to an 18% WDA and, if they have no private use, they are added to the main pool.

However, if any car has private use by the owner (not an employee) then it is de-pooled and kept in a column on its own.

*Both the June 2018 and December 2018 examiner's reports noted that the incorrect treatment of cars with private use is a common mistake. The examining team have stated that 'future candidates should note that the private use percentage never reduces the cost or proceeds figure' included in the capital allowances computation. The **full** cost of the car must be added to and the **full** proceeds on disposal deducted from a separate column for the car.*

*Another common error identified by the examining team in the June 2018 exam was the incorrect calculation of the WDA. The **full** WDA must be deducted from the private use asset column with the private use percentage only restricting the actual allowance claimed.*

2 When a trader is VAT registered the individual can reclaim input VAT on all assets except cars used partly privately. Capital allowances are claimed on the net of VAT cost except for cars with any private use. These cars are added to the appropriate column in the computation at their VAT-inclusive cost.

The December 2017 examiner's report commented that "candidates should have known that VAT in relation to the purchase of cars can never be reclaimed if there is any private use at all. Therefore, the starting point for calculating writing down allowance is the VAT-inclusive cost...."

3 To find the net of VAT figure from a VAT-inclusive figure you multiply by 100/120. Note that 100/120 simplifies to 5/6 so this fraction can be used instead.

4 The period is 14 months long so the WDA and maximum AIA are scaled up. Note that this rule is different from that for a company.

5 Capital allowance questions, particularly for periods which are not 12 months long are popular in the examination.

In the December 2014 examination in which question 3 tested a 15 month period for a sole trader, the examining team commented that the answers were generally unsatisfactory. They stressed that "capital allowances should be calculated for the whole period with AIA and WDA being calculated as 15/12 of the annual amounts. Many candidates confused these rules with those for a company and consequently calculated the allowances in two separate periods."

LOSSES

Key answer tips

In the June 2013 examiner's report the examining team were disappointed with candidates' attempts at the income tax losses question and remarked that "For those candidates who had learnt this area it was an easy six marks, however far too many had very little understanding of this area".

This topic is an important area in tax and candidates need to make sure that they learn and apply the rules carefully and accurately.

Common mistakes included:

- Simply netting the trading loss against income in the same year without reference to the need for a claim to be made.
- Using the trading loss in the previous year against trade income only.
- Using the trading loss against total income in the following year.
- Not showing the amount of loss carried forward as required by the question.

35 KEVIN

Key answer tips

This question has two separate income tax computations for husband and wife. In Kevin's computation relief is given for a trading loss arising in the following tax year.

The house provided by Susan's employer qualifies as job-related accommodation and therefore the benefit is not taxable. This also has an effect on the amount of ancillary services which can be taxed, which is limited to 10% of her other earnings from her employment.

(a) Income tax computation – 2025/26

	Non-savings Income	Savings Income	Total Income
	£	£	£
Trading profit	15,000		15,000
Bank interest		1,237	1,237
	15,000	1,237	16,237
Less: Loss relief (Note)	(15,000)	(1,237)	(16,237)
Taxable income	0	0	0
Income tax liability	0	0	0

Savings income nil rate band

Kevin would be entitled to a savings income nil rate band of £1,000 as he is a basic rate taxpayer. However, by making a claim against total income in the tax year 2025/26 the savings income nil rate band is wasted.

> ***Tutorial note***
>
> *A current year trading loss may be relieved against the total income of the tax year in which the loss arises and/or the preceding year.*
>
> *Thus the trading loss of the year ended 31 March 2027 (2026/27) may be set against the total income of 2026/27 and/or 2025/26.*
>
> *However, the requirement explicitly stated to assume that Kevin claims relief for his loss against his 2025/26 income. As the examining team stated in their December 2013 report, "if the question says make a claim then you must do this."*
>
> *By making a claim against total income both the personal allowance and the savings income nil rate band are wasted.*

(b) Remaining loss

The trading loss remaining is £3,763 (£20,000 – £16,237).

This loss is available for relief in:

- 2026/27 against total income, or
- in future years it can be deducted from the first available future trading profits from the same trade.

(c) Susan

Income tax computation – 2025/26

	£
Salary	25,000
House (Note 1)	Exempt
House services (Note 2) (no restriction as less than 10% of £25,000)	1,500
Employment income	26,500
Less: Personal allowance	(12,570)
Taxable income	13,930
Income tax liability (£13,930 × 20%)	2,786

Notes:

1 As the occupation of the house is 'job-related' there is no charge.

2 Where there is no charge for 'job-related' accommodation any charge for ancillary services is restricted to 10% of the other net emoluments (excluding the charge for ancillary services).

Tutorial note

There is no taxable benefit for the accommodation itself if the accommodation is job-related. To qualify as such it must be:

1 *necessary for the proper performance of the employee's duties (e.g. a caretaker); or*

2 *provided for the better performance of the employee's duties and, for that type of employment, it is customary for employers to provide living accommodation (e.g. hotel worker); or*

3 *provided due to a special threat to the employee's security and the employee resides in the accommodation as part of special security arrangements.*

There is a limit on the amount taxable as a benefit in respect of expenses and furnishings where the employee's accommodation is job-related.

The taxable limit is 10% of net emoluments (salary plus benefits, other than the accommodation expenses in question, less any expenditure deductible against employment income).

36 BI

Key answer tips

Trading losses are covered in this question. Questions about trading losses often require a written explanation rather than calculations.

Brief notes are requested. These should have headings.

Tax years in which loss can be used

- The trading loss can be set against total income of the same tax year (i.e. 2025/26) and/or the preceding tax year (i.e. 2024/25). The trading loss can be used in either of these two years, in any order.

- Alternatively, or if any trading loss remains after the above claim(s), the trading loss can be carried forward and set against trading profit from the same trade. The trading loss can be carried forward indefinitely, but must be set off as soon as there are trading profits.

Income it can be used against

- Total income is income from all sources before deducting reliefs or the personal allowance.

  A claim against total income is the lower of:

  (i) the trading loss

  (ii) the amount of total income.

  Partial claims are not possible.

  The trading loss is offset before the personal allowance which may mean that the personal allowance is wasted.

- If the trading loss is carried forward it can only be set against trading profit arising from the same trade. There are no partial claims.

Planning points

- Avoid wasting the personal allowance – look at the level of total income for the two tax years where such a claim is possible. If the total income for the year is lower than the personal allowance, then the claim should not be made.

  For example – in 2025/26 Bi has no trading income (loss) and only £4,000 of other non-savings income. Hence a loss claim in that year would not be advisable.

- Aim to save the most tax – If there is a choice of years in which to use the trading loss then use the loss in the year in which it will save the most tax. Always aim to save tax at the highest marginal rate.

  For example – in Bi's case she is not a higher rate taxpayer in either 2024/25 or 2026/27 so would save tax at 20% in both years.

- Relieve the trading loss as early as possible – if there is a choice of years, then other things being equal choose the earlier year.

  Carrying back the trading loss to the preceding tax year results in a repayment of tax in respect of that tax year.

Tutorial note

It is important to practice this type of written question. The December 2016 examiner's report concluded that "candidates should not rely on numerical questions to pass the paper. MCQs and theoretical questions will enable the broad spectrum of this syllabus to be examined and, therefore, it is essential that candidates practise these types of questions."

37 NICOLE

Key answer tips

This question involves first calculating the trading loss for a tax year using time apportionment under the tax year basis. Remember that a time apportioned profit reduces the time apportioned loss available. In other questions, the trading loss for the tax year may be given in the question.

After calculating the trading loss for the tax year, you can consider how it should be used.

When a trading loss is to be used 'as early as possible' this means a claim should be made against total income starting with the claim against total income for the tax year preceding the year of loss.

Don't forget to give the date of the loss claim as asked.

(a) Calculation of trading loss – 2025/26

(£40,000 (loss) × 9/12) – (£6,600 (profit) × 3/12) = £28,350 loss

(b) Use of trading loss

Claims against total income are possible in 2025/26 and/or 2024/25.

However, it is not worth making a claim for 2025/26 as the income is covered by the personal allowance.

	2024/25	2025/26
	£	£
Trading profit		
2024/25	21,850	
2025/26		0
Savings income	3,000	3,000
Total income	24,850	3,000
Less: Loss relief	(24,850)	0
Net income	0	3,000
Less: PA	0	(3,000)
Taxable income	0	0

(c) Date by which loss relief claim must be made

31 January 2028

Tutorial note

Trading losses can be offset against total income of the tax year of loss and/or the preceding year. The claims can be made in any order.

It is not possible to restrict the claim to use up the personal allowance in a year when the claim is made. This means that if a claim is made for 2024/25 the trading loss must be offset against the total income and the PA is unavoidably wasted. The savings income nil rate band of £1,000 would also be wasted. However, a claim will still save a significant amount of tax and is therefore worthwhile.

The requirement stated that Nicole is keen not to waste her personal allowance if this can be avoided. Therefore, a claim against total income in 2025/26 should not be made. In the December 2015 examination the requirement stated that loss relief should only be claimed when it was beneficial to do so, therefore it was important not to claim relief in a year in which a claim would only result in a waste of the personal allowance. In the examiner's report, the examining team said that "candidates are advised to ensure that they are comfortable with the different rules on how losses can be used for income tax purposes. The rule is different when a trading loss is carried forward – here the loss MUST be used against trading income even if this results in a loss of the personal allowance."

The claim for prior year loss relief must be made within 12 months of 31 January following the tax year in which the loss arose, i.e. by 31 January 2028 for a loss arising in 2025/26. The actual date must be stated, not the rule.

38 MICHELLE

Key answer tips

This question requires use of the loss in the 'most beneficial manner' and the answer should include an explanation of any claims not made. Such an explanation can be kept brief, and may be shown on the computation as below. When more than one tax year is involved in a loss question it is best to present the different years side by side.

	2023/24	2024/25	2025/26
	£	£	£
Trading income	22,000	0	16,000
Loss brought forward			(16,000)
Property income	4,000	3,000	6,000
Total income	26,000	3,000	6,000
Current year loss relief claim not beneficial – personal allowance would be wasted			
Less: Loss carried back	(26,000)		
Net income	0	3,000	6,000
Less: PA	Wasted	(3,000)	(6,000)
Taxable income	0	0	0
Trade loss			44,000
Loss carried back			(26,000)
Loss carried forward and claimed in 2025/26			(16,000)
Carried forward to 2026/27			2,000

Examiner's report

This was a five-mark question on the use of losses for a sole trader.

The question required candidates to use the loss in the most efficient manner and, therefore, if the use meant that the personal allowance (PA) was wasted, then the loss should not have been used. This was the case for the tax year 2024/25 where the taxable income was below the PA. The loss, therefore, should have been carried back to the tax year 2023/24 against total income before the PA and the remaining amount carried forward to the tax year 2025/26 and used against trading income only.

Once again an easy mark was lost by candidates not stating the amount of loss to be carried forward to the tax year 2026/27, as was required in the question.

ACCA Marking scheme	
	Marks
Trading income	0.5
Loss brought forward	1.0
Property income	0.5
Current year loss not beneficial with explanation	1.0
Loss carried back	1.0
Personal allowance	0.5
Loss carried forward to 2026/27	0.5
Total	**5.0**

Tutorial note

Trading losses can be offset against total income of the tax year of loss and/or the preceding year. The claims can be made in any order.

It is not possible to restrict the claim to use up the personal allowance in a year when the claim is made. This means that if a claim is made for 2023/24 the trading loss must be offset against the total income and the PA is unavoidably wasted. However, a claim will still save a significant amount of tax and is therefore worthwhile.

The requirement stated that Michelle claims loss relief in the most beneficial manner. Therefore, a claim against total income in 2024/25 should not be made as this would waste the personal allowance. In the December 2015 examination the requirement stated that loss relief should only be claimed when it was beneficial to do so, therefore it was important not to claim relief in a year in which a claim would only result in a waste of the personal allowance. In the examiner's report, the examining team said that "candidates are advised to ensure that they are comfortable with the different rules on how losses can be used for income tax purposes. The rule is different when a trading loss is carried forward – here the loss MUST be used against trading income even if this results in a loss of the personal allowance."

PARTNERSHIPS

39 SEAN AND LAUREN

Key answer tips

This question initially involves a straightforward partnership allocation of profits. There are no salaries or interest on capital and the new partner starts at the beginning of the period.

Note it does not matter if the total column is shown as the first or last column.

Make sure you complete the question. After allocating the profits between partners, calculate each partner's trading profit for the tax year 2025/26, under the tax year basis. A joining partner is taxed on profits arising from the date of joining the partnership to 5 April.

Allocation of partnership trading profit

	Total	Sean	Lauren	Helena
	£	£	£	£
Year ended 31 December 2025	18,000	9,000	9,000	
Year ended 31 December 2026	25,000	10,000	10,000	5,000

Trading profits for tax year 2025/26

Sean and Lauren

2025/26	(£9,000 × 9/12) + (£10,000 × 3/12)	£9,250

Helena

2025/26	£5,000 × 3/12	£1,250

Tutorial note

1 *When dealing with partnerships, it is important to split the trading profit for the accounting period (as calculated for tax purposes) between the partners using the profit sharing arrangements in force during the accounting period, and then apply the tax year basis rules individually to each partner.*

2 *Helena joins the partnership on 1 January 2026 so cannot share in the trading profits before that date. In the tax year of joining, 2025/26, she is taxed on her share of the profits arising from 1 January 2026 to 5 April 2026. The existing partners, Sean and Lauren, are taxed on their shares of the profits arising in the tax year from 6 April 2025 to 5 April 2026.*

40 MCBETH, MCDUFF AND MCBRIDE

Key answer tips

This question involves a change in the members of a partnership where the change occurs part way through the accounting period.

Before you allocate the trading profits between the partners, you must time apportion the profits according to the number of months in the accounting period falling before and after the change.

Remember also to time apportion the salaries and the interest on capital as they are usually quoted as annual figures.

Note it does not matter if the total column is shown as the first or last column.

Allocation of partnership trading profit – y/e 31 December 2025

	Total	McBeth	McDuff	McBride
	£	£	£	£
1 Jan – 31 Oct 2025 (Note 1)				
Salary (× 10/12)	24,000	8,000	8,000	8,000
Interest (2% × 10/12)	900	400	300	200
Profit (2:1:1)	20,100	10,050	5,025	5,025
(Note 2)	45,000	18,450	13,325	13,225
1 Nov – 31 Dec 2025 (Note 1)				
Salary (× 2/12)	3,200		1,600	1,600
Profit (1:1)	5,800		2,900	2,900
(Note 2)	9,000		4,500	4,500
Total (Note 2)	54,000	18,450	17,825	17,725

Tutorial note

1 *In the December 2012 examination, the allocation of profits requiring the splitting of the accounting period into two was tested. Note that the examiner's report indicated that many candidates missed an easy half mark by not adding the two separate period allocations together to give the final totals for each partner.*

In the answer above, the sub-total for each partner is shown also, but in fact it is not necessary to show the sub-total for each period as this number is never required for any calculation for tax purposes. It is the total allocation for each partner that is important.

Time could therefore be saved by not subtotalling, but ensuring that the final totals are clearly shown. See the solution to the next question for the optimum layout to minimise effort and maximise marks!

2 *This area was also tested in the December 2014 examination where the examiner's report commented that common errors included "errors in splitting the period before and after a change in the profit sharing agreement or allocating a full annual salary and interest on capital to partners for a period which was not 12 months in length".*

41 CHARLES, MEG AND RODNEY

Key answer tips

This question covers the allocation of partnership profits where the change happens part way through the accounting period.

Remember that both salaries and interest on capital must be time apportioned when the period is split due to a change in the profit sharing arrangements, as the annual amount will be quoted in the question.

Note it does not matter if the total column is shown as the first or last column.

Allocation of partnership trading profits

	Total	Charles	Meg	Rodney
	£	£	£	£
(1 Jan 2025 – 30 June 2025)				
Salary (× 6/12)	9,000	5,000	4,000	
Interest on capital (× 6/12)	1,200	500	400	300
Profit share (1:1:1)	49,800	16,600	16,600	16,600
	60,000			
(1 July 2025 – 31 December 2025)				
Interest on capital (× 6/12)	900	500	400	
Profit share (1:1)	59,100	29,550	29,550	
	60,000			
Total	120,000	52,150	50,950	16,900

Tutorial note

1 *In the December 2012 examination, the allocation of profits requiring the splitting of the accounting period into two was tested. Note that the examiner's report indicated that many candidates missed an easy half mark by not adding the two separate period allocations together to give the final totals for each partner.*

Note that it is not necessary to show the sub-total for each period as this number is never required for any calculation for tax purposes. It is the total allocation for each partner that is important.

Time could therefore be saved by not subtotalling, but ensuring that the final totals are clearly shown. The solution above shows the optimum layout to minimise effort and maximise marks.

2 *This area was also tested in the December 2014 examination where the examiner's report commented that common errors included "errors in splitting the period before and after a change in the profit sharing agreement or allocating a full annual salary and interest on capital to partners for a period which was not 12 months in length".*

42 CAROL, WENDY AND BOB

Key answer tips

This question covers the allocation of a partnership trading loss where there is no change in partnership agreement during the accounting period.

It is important to know that whether the partnership is profitable or loss-making, the method of allocation is the same.

With a partnership, the partners' salaries and interest on capital are merely ways of splitting out the trading profits or losses and are not expenses to be charged against trading profits. They must be allocated to the partners first and then the balance of the results for that period (whether profits or losses) are allocated in the agreed profit sharing ratios.

Note it does not matter if the total column is shown as the first or last column.

Allocation of partnership trading loss

Year to 31 January 2026

	Carol	Wendy	Bob	Total
	£	£	£	£
Salary	10,000			10,000
Interest (4%)	1,600	800	400	2,800
Balance (3:1:1)	(55,680)	(18,560)	(18,560)	(92,800)
	(44,080)	(17,760)	(18,160)	(80,000)

Tutorial note

When the partnership makes a trading loss, the allocation still starts with the salary and interest on capital. This increases the balance of trading loss to be shared between the partners.

In this question the balance of trading loss to be shared between the partners is £92,800 (£80,000 + £10,000 + £2,800).

43 PETER, SAM AND MARTHA

Key answer tips

With a partnership, the partners' salaries are a way of allocating the trading profits and are not expenses to be charged against trading profits.

This question covers a commonly examined partnership situation – a change in the partnership part way through an accounting period.

This requires the trading profits before and after the change to be time apportioned so they may be allocated between the partners using the correct sharing arrangements.

Note it does not matter if the total column is shown as the first or last column.

Make sure you complete the question and calculate the leaving partner's trading profits for the tax year of departure, using the tax year basis.

Allocation of partnership trading profits

Year to 31 December 2024

	Peter	Sam	Martha	Total
	£	£	£	£
Salary	10,000	10,000	10,000	30,000
Balance (40:40:20)	12,000	12,000	6,000	30,000
	22,000	22,000	16,000	60,000

Year to 31 December 2025

	£	£	£	£
(1 January 2025 – 30 September 2025)				
Salary (× 9/12)	7,500	7,500	7,500	22,500
Balance (40:40:20)	4,500	4,500	2,250	11,250
				33,750
(1 October 2025 – 31 December 2025)				
Salary (× 3/12)	2,500	2,500	–	5,000
Balance (50:50)	3,125	3,125	–	6,250
				11,250
Totals	17,625	17,625	9,750	45,000

Martha's trading profits for tax year 2025/26

2025/26	£9,750 × 6/9	£6,500

Tutorial note

1 *When dealing with partnerships, split the trading profit for the accounting period between the partners using the profit sharing arrangements in force during the accounting period. The next stage is to apply the tax year basis individually to each partner.*

2 *In the December 2012 examination, the allocation of profits requiring the splitting of the accounting period into two was tested. Note that the examiner's report indicated that many candidates missed an easy half mark by not adding the two separate period allocations together to give the final totals for each partner.*

Note that it is not necessary to show the sub-total for each period as this number is never required for any calculation for tax purposes. It is the total allocation for each partner that is important in order to then calculate the amount taxable in a tax year.

Time could therefore be saved by not subtotalling, but ensuring that the final totals are clearly shown. The solution above shows the optimum layout to minimise effort and maximise marks.

3 *This area was also tested in the December 2014 examination where the examiner's report commented that common errors included "errors in splitting the period before and after a change in the profit sharing agreement or allocating a full annual salary and interest on capital to partners for a period which was not 12 months in length".*

4 *A partner leaving in the tax year will be subject to tax on the profits allocated to them from 6 April to the date of departure. For Martha, who leaves on 30 September, nine months into an accounting period, this means six months of those nine months of profit are taxed in the tax year of departure.*

PENSIONS AND NIC

Key answer tips

In the June 2013 examiner's report, the examining team said that "many candidates were not aware of how to use the [pension] contributions. Net contributions paid to a personal pension plan must be grossed up by 100/80 and then used to extend both the basic and upper bands – not deducted from income."

In December 2013 they made a similar comment and stated that "contributions paid to an occupational pension plan must be deducted from employee's salary – they must not be grossed up and used to extend the income tax bands. Candidates continually confuse the use of personal plan contributions and occupational plan contributions."

In June 2014 they stated that one of the main problems in question 1 was "the issue of personal pension plan contributions".

Always make sure you know whether you are dealing with occupational or personal pension contributions and that you are applying the appropriate rules.

Regarding national insurance contributions (NICs), it is important to only answer the question you have been asked – for example, do not calculate employer's NICs if only the employee's NICs are required.

44 AVERY

Key answer tips

Be careful! When the question asks for the total national insurance contributions, don't forget the class 1A which the company has to pay on the value of benefits provided to employees.

National insurance contributions (NIC) – 2025/26

	£
Avery	
Employee's class 1	
(£48,000 – £12,570) × 8%	2,834
Modern Fashions Ltd	
Employer's class 1	
(£48,000 – £5,000) × 15%	6,450
Less: NIC employment allowance (Note)	(6,450)
	0
Class 1A	
£2,400 × 15%	360
Total NICs paid by employer	360

Tutorial note

As Avery is the only employee the employment allowance is offset against the employer's class 1 NIC liability on her salary, and in this case reduces that liability to nil.

Class 1A NICs are payable by the employer only, not the employee. It is an annual charge payable on the value of benefits provided to employees for the previous tax year. The employment allowance cannot be used against class 1A NICs. Class 1A NICs are payable by 19 July (22 July if paid electronically) each year in arrears.

45 KARLA

Key answer tips

Pension contributions are an important form of saving for the future for many taxpayers.

Note that you are only required to have an awareness of the annual allowance but are not required to calculate any tax charge as a result of exceeding it.

(a) Maximum tax relief

Karla can contribute any amount into a personal pension scheme. However, tax relief is only available up to the amount of relevant earnings for the current tax year (i.e. £37,000).

(b) Annual allowance

If Karla had higher earnings, say £80,000, then her pension contribution might exceed the annual allowance of £60,000 which is the limit on tax allowable contributions. If this happened an additional tax charge would be added to Karla's tax liability.

(c) Method of tax relief

Personal pension premiums are paid net of basic rate tax.

Higher and additional rate relief is given by increasing the basic and higher rate thresholds by the gross pension contribution.

(d) Dividend income

If Karla's only income was dividend income, this is not relevant earnings. Therefore, the maximum gross contribution for which tax relief is available is £3,600.

Tutorial note

It is important to understand the difference in the way that relief is given for personal and for occupational pension contributions. The examining team frequently comments that students muddle these two areas.

Relief for personal pension contributions is given by paying the contribution net and increasing the basic and higher rate thresholds.

Relief for occupational pension contributions is given by paying the contribution gross and then deducting them from the figure of employment income in the income tax computation. This reduces taxable income and hence saves the same amount of tax as a personal pension scheme contribution.

Either way, the maximum gross amount of contribution on which tax relief is available, is the higher of £3,600 and 100% of relevant earnings (subject to the annual allowance available).

46 PETER

Key answer tips

This question requires you to calculate class 1 NICs on a monthly basis.

Since you are only given the annual NIC thresholds in your tax tables you must find the monthly figures by dividing the annual figures by 12.

Remember to clearly show your treatment of each item of Peter's employment package as requested.

National insurance contributions – 2025/26

Class 1 NICs payable by employee and employer on cash earnings i.e. salary and bonus.

Pension contributions are not an allowable deduction against earnings for national insurance purposes.

Calculations must be based on Peter's earning period (i.e. monthly).

Monthly thresholds:

Employee	£12,570/12 = £1,048
	£50,270/12 = £4,189
Employer	£5,000/12 = £417

Peter received £2,210 for 11 months and £9,710 for one month.

Employee class 1 (Peter)	£
(£2,210 – £1,048) × 8% × 11 months	1,023
(£4,189 – £1,048) × 8% × 1 month	251
(£9,710 – £4,189) × 2% × 1 month	110
	1,384

Employer's class 1 (Sports (UK) Ltd)	£
(£2,210 – £417) × 15% × 11 months	2,958
(£9,710 – £417) × 15% × 1 month	1,394
	4,352

Tutorial note

Note that there is no upper threshold for employer's NICs.

Key answer tips

The question asks you to ignore the employment allowance so do not waste time deducting it.

Employer's class 1A (Sports (UK) Ltd)

Payable by employer only on taxable benefits i.e. medical insurance

Employer provided childcare is an exempt benefit.

£200 × 15%	£30

47 PAUL

Key answer tips

This question requires you to write brief notes. Make sure you use headings or numbered points to break up your answer.

Meeting notes

1 The maximum contribution per tax year on which tax relief is available is the higher of £3,600 or 100% of earned income, subject to the annual allowance.

2 Method of obtaining tax relief:

If an occupational scheme – the actual payments are deducted from employment income, therefore obtaining full tax relief at source.

If a personal plan – the amount is paid net of tax at 20%. Higher rate and additional rate relief (if applicable) is given by increasing the basic rate and higher rate thresholds by the amount paid grossed up by 100/80.

3 Company contributions are exempt benefits.

They are, however, deductible for the purposes of corporation tax.

The total of the employee and employer contributions is compared to the annual allowance to see if an excess contribution charge is payable by the employee.

Key answer tips

It is important to understand the difference between the way relief is given for occupational scheme contributions and personal pension scheme contributions.

48 NORMAN

Key answer tips

This is a straightforward NI contribution calculation for a self-employed individual.

As the rates and thresholds are given in the tax tables provided in the examination, students should score well here.

National insurance contributions

	£
Class 4	
(£50,270 – £12,570) × 6%	2,262
(£52,000 – £50,270) × 2%	35
	2,297

Payment dates

Payments, based on 50% of prior year class 4 liability, paid with self-assessment for income tax on 31 January 2026, 31 July 2026, with any balance paid on 31 January 2027.

Tutorial note

The pension contribution does not obtain relief from national insurance contributions.

49 LEON

Key answer tips

This question states that the employees do not receive benefits. Therefore, do not waste time mentioning class 1A NICs as there will not be any marks for this.

Use a table layout to present your answer to a question like this.

National insurance contributions (NICs)

Class	**Calculation based on:**	**Payable to HMRC by:**
In respect of employees:		
Class 1 (employee)	Cash earnings	19th of month following payment to employee (22nd if paid electronically)
Class 1 (employer's)	Cash earnings	19th of month following payment to employee (22nd if paid electronically)
In respect of Leon:		
Class 4	Taxable trading profits Less trading loss relief claimed	Payments on account – 31 January in the tax year – 31 July following the tax year Payments on account are based on the previous year's liability Balance – 31 January following tax year

Tutorial note

Note that electronic payments for class 1 give an extra 3 days to pay.

The NIC employment allowance of £10,500 is deducted from the amount of employer's class 1 NICs payable to HMRC. It is an annual limit, and if the total employer's class 1 NICs for the year is less than or equal to £10,500 then the liability is nil.

50 JAVIER

Key answer tips

This is a NI contribution calculation for a self-employed individual. However, the first step is to calculate the trading profits for the tax year, under the tax year basis.

As the rates and thresholds are given in the tax tables provided in the examination, students should score well on the NIC calculation.

	£
Class 4 NICs	
(£50,270 – £12,570) × 6%	2,262
(£53,000 (W) – £50,270) × 2%	55
	2,317

Payable as follows:

Payments, based on 50% of prior year class 4 liability, paid with self-assessment for income tax on 31 January 2026, 31 July 2026, with any balance paid on 31 January 2027.

Working

Trading profit for tax year 2025/26:

(£51,000 × 9/12) + (£59,000 × 3/12) £53,000

INCOME TAX ADMINISTRATION

51 MATILDA

Key answer tips

Brief notes only are required, so do not write too much. Only cover what is asked for and do not include any other issues.

Action concerning employment of friend

- Must register with HMRC as an employer.
- Start PAYE scheme and deduct correct tax from employee earnings.
- Apply national insurance – both employee and employer contributions – dependent on total amounts paid.
- Annual employer's contributions can be reduced by the NIC employment allowance of £10,500. If employer's NICs are less than £10,500 the employer's liability is nil.
- PAYE tax and NICs are usually payable to HM Revenue and Customs by the 19th of each month (22nd for electronic payments), in respect of the previous tax month (i.e. the month ending on 5th).

Tutorial note

Registration with HMRC as an employer is not necessary if Matilda's friend will be earning less than the weekly PAYE and NIC thresholds (i.e. will not be liable for tax or NIC).

52 KARTER

Key answer tips

This question deals with forms and due dates which are always popular examination topics. You need detailed knowledge in this area.

Forms and due dates for submission

(a) P60 – 31 May 2026

(b) P11D – 6 July 2026

(c) Submission of electronic tax return – 31 January 2027

53 NOAM

Key answer tips

You will almost certainly be tested on the income tax payment system somewhere in your examination. Make sure you are happy with the various payment dates.

Tax payments – 2025/26

Payments on account
Estimated using 2024/25 figures = (£5,800 × ½) = £2,900

	£
31 January 2026	2,900
31 July 2026	2,900
31 January 2027 (Balance £6,400 – £5,800)	600

Tutorial note

Payments on account are required for taxpayers such as the self-employed; who unlike employees do not have most of their taxes paid by PAYE.

Instalments are due on 31 January in the tax year and 31 July following the tax year with any balancing payment required payable on 31 January following the tax year. For 2025/26 the relevant dates are 31 January 2026, 31 July 2026 and 31 January 2027.

The payments on account are:

50% of the tax payable for the previous year (i.e. tax liability after deducting any PAYE) plus 50% of the class 4 NICs for the previous year.

Payments on account do not apply to capital gains tax (gains relating to residential property are an exception to this and a payment on account is due within 60 days of disposal).

Note on 31 January 2027, the first payment on account for 2026/27 equal to (£6,400/2) £3,200 is also due.

54 ALTHEA

Key answer tips

Always read questions very carefully. This question looks similar to the previous one but is actually testing a different rule.

2025/26 Income tax liability

No payments on account were required for 2025/26 as more than 80% (W) of the previous year's tax liability was paid by PAYE. The income tax payable for 2025/26 is payable as follows:

Balance	31 January 2027	(£10,400 – £4,800)	£5,600

2026/27 Income tax liability

Payments on account (POAs) for 2026/27 are due as ≤ 80% (W) of the previous year's tax liability was paid by PAYE.

The first POA for 2026/27 of £2,800 ((£10,400 – £4,800) ÷ 2) is also due on 31 January 2027.

The total income tax due on 31 January 2027 is £8,400 (£5,600 + £2,800).

Working

2024/25 = (£7,000/£8,600 × 100%) = 81.4% which is > 80%.

2025/26 = (£4,800/£10,400 × 100%) = 46.2% which is ≤ 80%.

Tutorial note

POAs are due for 2025/26 based on the amount payable for 2024/25.

In the report on the June 2014 examination the examining team commented that performance in this area was disappointing. Very few candidates knew the rules for when payments on account are not required.

No payments on account are required in the following circumstances:

– *the tax payable (i.e. liability after deducting PAYE) for the previous year is less than £1,000; or*

– *more than 80% of the tax (i.e. income tax and class 4 NIC) for the previous year was paid via PAYE. This will mean that most employed people will not have to make payments on account, since more than 80% of their tax liability is likely to be paid through PAYE. Note that this question does not involve class 4 NIC therefore only income tax is considered when calculating the percentage.*

55 RICHARD

Key answer tips

You should learn the names, functions and due dates of all the common PAYE forms.

(a) The form required is the P45.

(b) Richard must submit the following details online every month.

The information must be submitted on or before the day he pays his employees:

- amount paid to employees,
- deductions such as income tax and national insurance contributions,
- starter and leaver dates if applicable.

Richard will have to use an RTI enabled software package to run his payroll which will automatically generate the reports needed.

56 ESTHER

Key answer tips

This question tests the income tax and national insurance payment rules. This is a popular examination topic.

Be sure to answer all parts of the question asked – this question asks for a calculation of payment on account amounts, and for the dates of both the payments on account and the balancing payment.

	£
The amounts of payments on account due for the tax year 2025/26	
Income tax payable	7,490
Class 4 national insurance contributions	3,370
	10,860
Payments on account (£10,860/2)	5,430

The dates on which payments on account for the tax year 2025/26 are due

31 January 2026

31 July 2026

The date on which the balancing payment for the tax year 2025/26 will be due

31 January 2027

Examiner's report

One of the weakest responses [in the exam] related to [this] question concerning the payments on account and balancing payment payable by a sole trader.

Candidates were confused as to the amounts payable and did not know the due dates for payments. Candidates are reminded that the rules relating to tax administration are an important part of the syllabus as this level and, since they are regularly tested, they should not be overlooked.

Tutorial note

Payments on account are required for taxpayers such as the self-employed; who do not pay most of their tax through the PAYE system.

Instalments are due on 31 January in the tax year and 31 July following the tax year with any balancing payment required payable on 31 January following the tax year. For 2025/26 the relevant dates are 31 January 2026, 31 July 2026 and 31 January 2027.

The payments on account are:

50% of the tax payable for the previous year (i.e. tax liability after deducting any PAYE) plus 50% of the class 4 NICs for the previous year.

Payments on account do not apply to capital gains tax (gains relating to residential property are an exception to this and a payment on account is due within 60 days of disposal).

57 LIN

Key answer tips

This question also tests the income tax and national insurance payment rules.

Although the first instalment of 2026/27 tax will be due on 31 January 2027 you are told to ignore this.

Payment dates – 2025/26

Income tax and class 4 national insurance contributions (NIC) are payable in instalments. Capital gains tax (CGT) is payable in full on 31 January following the relevant tax year.

	£
First payment on account – 31 January 2026:	
50% of 2024/25 total income tax payable and class 4 contributions	
(£16,000 + £3,000) × 50%	9,500
Second payment on account – 31 July 2026:	
Calculated as above	9,500
Final payment – 31 January 2027:	
Balance of income tax and class 4 contributions	
[(£19,300 + £3,500) – (£9,500 × 2)]	3,800
Plus: CGT	2,300
	6,100

Tutorial note

Payments on account are required for taxpayers such as the self-employed; who do not pay most of their tax through the PAYE system.

Instalments are due on 31 January in the tax year and 31 July following the tax year with any balancing payment required payable on 31 January following the tax year. For 2025/26 the relevant dates are 31 January 2026, 31 July 2026 and 31 January 2027.

The payments on account are:

50% of the tax payable for the previous year (i.e. tax liability after deducting any PAYE) plus 50% of the class 4 NICs for the previous year.

Payments on account do not apply to capital gains tax (gains relating to residential property are an exception to this and a payment on account is due within 60 days of disposal).

CAPITAL GAINS: INDIVIDUALS

58 YE-JUN

Key answer tips

This question has a variety of disposals, as is usually the case with capital gains tax questions.

Part disposals and non-wasting chattels are common assets in questions.

Remember to read the requirements carefully and only answer what is required. Note in this case the total of net chargeable gains is required, before deducting the annual exempt amount and not the taxable gain (i.e. after the annual exempt amount and capital losses brought forward), and not the capital gains tax payable.

Total net chargeable gains – 2025/26

	£	£
14 July 2025		
Proceeds	240,000	
Less: Fees (5% × £240,000)	(12,000)	
Net proceeds	228,000	
Less: Allowable cost		
$\frac{£240,000}{£240,000 + £400,000} \times £360,000$	(135,000)	
Chargeable gain		93,000
14 December 2025		
Gross proceeds (£9,009 × 100/90)	10,010	
Less: Fees (10% × £10,010)	(1,001)	
Net proceeds	9,009	
Less: Cost	(3,916)	
Chargeable gain	5,093	
Chargeable gain cannot exceed: (£10,010 – £6,000) × 5/3 = £6,683		
Lower chargeable gain applies		5,093
6 February 2026		
Proceeds	9,500	
Less: Cost	(42,000)	
Allowable loss		(32,500)
Total net chargeable gains		65,593

Tutorial note

1 *Part disposals are popular examination questions. The cost of the land sold must be found by applying the part disposal formula to the cost:*

Cost × A/A + B

Where A = gross sales proceeds, and

B = market value of the part of the asset remaining.

The examining team have put in the number of hectares sold out of the total number of hectares purchased to tempt you into using those to split the cost instead!

2 *The non-wasting chattel marginal gain rules apply when the proceeds > £6,000 and the cost ≤ £6,000.*

The gain is the lower of:

(i) The gain calculated as normal

(ii) 5/3 × (Gross proceeds – £6,000)

59 JOHN AND IMRAN

Key answer tips

In part (a) of the question you have to calculate capital gains tax liability remembering that only gains falling in the basic rate band are taxed at 18%.

The second part tests the difference between the treatment of allowable capital losses incurred in the current tax year and those brought forward.

Remember to read the requirements carefully and only answer what is required. Note that in part (a) the capital gains tax payable is required.

(a) John

Capital gains tax – 2025/26

			£
Investment property			92,000
Shares			14,000
Table			3,000
Total chargeable gains			109,000
Less: Allowable capital loss in the year			(5,000)
Less: Annual exempt amount			(3,000)
Taxable gains			101,000
	£		£
Lower rate	8,200	× 18%	1,476
Higher rate	92,800	× 24%	22,272
	101,000		
Capital gains tax liability			23,748

Working: Remaining basic rate band available

	£
Basic rate band	37,700
Less: Taxable income	(29,500)
Basic rate band available for taxing gains	8,200

Tutorial note

Chargeable gains are taxed at three possible rates:

(i) *14% if the gain qualifies for BADR (regardless of the level of income)*

(ii) *18% for any part of other gains falling below the basic rate threshold*

(iii) *24% for balance of other gains*

The amount qualifying for the lower rate of 18% is calculated as follows:

	£
Basic rate band	*37,700*
Less: Taxable income	*(X)*
Remaining basic rate band available	*X*

(b) Imran – Capital loss carried forward to 2026/27

	£
Chargeable gains for the year	15,000
Less: Allowable capital loss for the year	(2,000)
Net chargeable gains for the year	13,000
Less: Annual exempt amount	(3,000)
Net chargeable gains after AEA	10,000
Less: Capital loss b/f (restrict)	(10,000)
Taxable gains	0

	£
Capital loss b/f	13,000
Less: Used in year	(10,000)
Capital loss c/f	3,000

Tutorial note

Chargeable gains and allowable losses incurred in the same tax year must be netted off.

*Capital losses brought forward are offset **after** the annual exempt amount has been deducted from the net chargeable gains for the year (i.e. current year gains less current year losses). Capital losses brought forward are therefore not wasted against current year net chargeable gains which are covered by the annual exempt amount.*

The balance of unused losses can be carried forward again.

60 LETHABO

Key answer tips

This question has a variety of disposals, as is usually the case with capital gains tax questions. Part disposals, non-wasting chattels and exempt assets are commonly tested.

Remember to read the requirements carefully and only answer what is required. Note in this case the total net chargeable gains is required, not the taxable gain (i.e. after the annual exempt amount), and not the capital gains tax payable.

Total net chargeable gains – 2025/26

	£	£
Farmland		
Proceeds	90,000	
Less: Allowable cost		
$(£54,000 + £3,000) \times \frac{90,000}{90,000 + 180,000}$	(19,000)	
Chargeable gain		71,000
Car = Exempt		0
Painting		
Deemed proceeds	6,000	
Less: Probate value	(8,200)	
Allowable capital loss		(2,200)
Total net chargeable gain		68,800

Tutorial note

1 *Part disposals are popular in examination questions. The cost of the land sold must be found by applying the part disposal formula to the cost and the incidental costs of acquisition:*

Costs × A/A + B

Where A = gross sales proceeds, and

B = market value of the part of the asset remaining.

The examining team have put in the number of hectares sold out of the total number of hectares purchased to tempt you into using those to split the cost instead!

2 *Cars are exempt assets even if they are veteran or vintage cars.*

3 *Special loss rules apply for non-wasting chattels when proceeds ≤ £6,000 and the cost > £6,000.*

The allowable capital loss is calculated assuming gross sale proceeds of £6,000.

When an asset is inherited the probate value (market value at the date the asset was inherited) should be used for cost in a future disposal.

61 AMEER

Key answer tips

It is important to learn the share valuation rule, as this is not provided in the tax tables, and to be comfortable with applying it to the information in the question.

Capital gains tax – 2025/26

	£	£
Bronze statuette		
Proceeds	7,200	
Less: Cost	(4,100)	
Chargeable gain	3,100	
Gain cannot exceed: (£7,200 – £6,000) × 5/3	2,000	
Take the lower chargeable gain		2,000
Gift of shares		
Proceeds (143p × 12,000)(W1)	17,160	
Less: Cost	(5,300)	
Chargeable gain	11,860	11,860
Total gains		13,860
Less: Annual exempt amount		(3,000)
		10,860
Less: Capital loss b/f		(800)
Taxable gains		10,060
Capital gains tax (24% × £10,060)		2,414

Working: Share value

Average= ½ × (140p + 146p) =143p

Tutorial note

1 *The non-wasting chattel marginal gain rules apply when the proceeds > £6,000 and the cost ≤ £6,000.*

The gain is the lower of:

(i) The gain calculated as normal

(ii) 5/3 × (Gross proceeds – £6,000)

2 *A gift is treated as a disposal with proceeds equal to market value. In the case of quoted shares the market value is the mid-price (i.e. average) of the day's quoted prices.*

Neither gift holdover relief nor BADR is available as ABC plc is not Ameer's personal company. He owns less than 5% of the shares.

3 *Capital gains tax is paid at 24% on gains where there is no basic rate band available after taxing income. Although Ameer will be paying tax at the additional rate on his income, the maximum capital gains tax rate is still 24% on these gains.*

62 DONALD

Key answer tips

This question involves using the matching rules for the disposal of shares by an individual, including the 30 day rule and then share pooling.

In the December 2012 examiner's report the examining team were disappointed that very few candidates knew the identification rules for an individual. "Many incorrectly used the rules for companies (which are different!) and others simply added the purchases together and calculated one gain".

It is important that you know the distinction between the rules for individuals and companies and how to apply them to calculate gains on share disposals.

This question asks for the chargeable gain, therefore it is not necessary to deduct the annual exempt amount (which would give taxable gains) or to calculate capital gains tax. Do not waste time doing more than the question has asked for.

Matching rules

			Number of shares	
1	**Same day acquisitions**			**0**
2	**Next 30 days**			
	30 July 2025	Purchase		**500**
3	**Share pool**			
	14 October 2011	Purchase	4,000	
	18 May 2015	RI (1 for 2)	2,000	
			6,000	
	10 December 2017	BI (1 for 5)	1,200	
			7,200	
	14 July 2025	Sale	(3,500)	**3,500**
			3,700	
				4,000

Calculation of individual gains – 2025/26

	£	£
Next 30 days purchase (500 shares)		
Sale proceeds (£18,000 × 500/4,000)	2,250	
Less: Cost	(2,100)	
Chargeable gain		150
Share pool (3,500 shares)		
Sale proceeds (£18,000 × 3,500/4,000)	15,750	
Less: Cost (W)	(5,347)	
Chargeable gain		10,403
Total chargeable gain		10,553

Working: Share pool

		Number of shares	Cost
			£
14 Oct 2011	Purchase	4,000	6,000
18 May 2015	Rights issue 1 for 2	2,000	5,000
		6,000	11,000
10 Dec 2017	Bonus issue 1 for 5	1,200	0
		7,200	11,000
14 July 2025	Sale (£11,000 × 3,500/7,200)	(3,500)	(5,347)
		3,700	5,653

Tutorial note

When dealing with the sale of shares by an individual you should first consider the share identification rules. Disposals are matched with:

(i) Shares purchased on the same day

(ii) Shares purchased within the next 30 days

(iii) Shares in the share pool i.e. all the shares acquired before the sale date.

In this question there are no purchases on the same day but nonetheless you should mention the rule and show that you know these rules before calculating the gains.

Purchases of shares and rights issues are added to the pool at cost. Bonus issues have no cost so the only entry in the pool is in the number column. The question gives you the market value of the shares at the time of the bonus issue but this is not used.

Disposals are removed from the pool at average cost:

(Number of shares disposed of/Total shares in the pool before sale) × Pool cost

63 ALBERTO

Key answer tips

This question covers a part disposal and a non-wasting chattel sold at a loss. You also need to calculate capital gains tax. When calculating the balance of any basic rate band remember to deduct the taxable income. Do not miss the easy mark for stating the due payment date. Always look out for the separate payment date in respect of residential property (60 days after the disposal), although that is not relevant in this question.

(a) Calculation of individual gains – 2025/26

Statuette	£
Proceeds	48,000
Less: Incidental costs of disposal	(1,000)
Net disposal proceeds	47,000
Less: Allowable cost:	
$£32,000 \times \frac{48,000}{48,000 + 85,000}$	(11,549)
Chargeable gain	35,451
Painting	
Deemed proceeds	6,000
Less: Cost of painting	(8,700)
Allowable loss	(2,700)

(b) Alberto – Calculation of capital gains tax – 2025/26

	£
Gain on disposal of statuette (above)	35,451
Less: Allowable capital loss on painting (above)	(2,700)
Net chargeable gains	32,751
Less: Annual exempt amount	(3,000)
Net chargeable gains after AEA	29,751
Less: Loss brought forward	(1,000)
Taxable gains	28,751

Capital gains tax

£		£
5,270	× 18% (W)	949
23,481	× 24%	5,635
28,751		
Tax payable		6,584
Payment date		31 Jan 2027

Working: Remaining basic rate band

	£
Basic rate band	37,700
Less: Taxable income	(32,430)
Remaining basic rate band	5,270

Tutorial note

1 *Part disposals are popular in examination questions. The cost of the asset sold must be found by applying the part disposal formula to the cost:*

Cost × A/A + B

Where A = gross sales proceeds, and

B = market value of the part of the asset remaining.

2 *Chargeable gains are taxed at three possible rates:*

(i) 14% if the gain qualifies for BADR (regardless of the level of income)

(ii) 18% for any part of other gains falling below the basic rate threshold

(iii) 24% for balance of other gains

The amount qualifying for the lower rate of 18% is calculated as follows:

	£
Basic rate band	*37,700*
Less: Taxable income	*(X)*
Basic rate band available	*X*

64 KATRIN

Key answer tips

This question includes the more unusual topic of compensation as well as the more common topics of a part disposal and exempt assets.

Chargeable gains – 2025/26

	£
Land	
Net proceeds (£30,000 – £2,000)	28,000
Less: Cost	
$£80,000 \times \frac{£30,000}{£30,000 + £190,000}$	(10,909)
Chargeable gain	17,091
Vase – Non-wasting chattel	
Both proceeds and cost are less than £6,000	Exempt
Car	
All cars are exempt	Exempt
Painting	
Insurance proceeds	18,000
Less: Cost	(10,000)
Gain	8,000
Less: Amount not reinvested and chargeable now (£18,000 – £15,000)	(3,000)
Amount deferred via no gain/no loss election and deducted from the base cost of the new asset	5,000
Chargeable gain (i.e. amount not reinvested)	3,000

Tutorial note

1 *Part disposals are popular in examination questions. The cost of the part of the asset sold must be found by applying the part disposal formula to the cost:*

Cost × A/A + B

Where A = gross sales proceeds, and

B = market value of the part of the asset remaining.

2 *The complete destruction of an asset is a disposal for capital gains purposes. If compensation is received this becomes the proceeds figure in the calculation of the gain on the disposal. The date of disposal is the date the insurance is received.*

If the compensation is used to buy a replacement asset within 12 months an election can be made to treat the disposal as a no gain/no loss disposal.

If all of the compensation is used to replace the asset then no gain is charged now. Instead the gain is deducted from the cost of the replacement asset carried forward.

If some of the compensation is not spent on replacing the asset then part of the gain is charged now. This part is the lower of:

(i) the total gain

(ii) the compensation not spent

The balance of the gain is deducted from the cost of the replacement asset carried forward.

65 JUAN

Key answer tips

This question includes the share pooling rules for an individual but is reasonably straightforward as it does not have the complication of a share purchase on the same day or within the 30 days following the disposal.

The painting is a non-wasting chattel which is sold for > £6,000 so you must remember to apply the 5/3 rule.

Cars are exempt even if they are valuable vintage cars.

Chargeable gains – 2025/26

		£	£
Shares	Proceeds	28,000	
	Less: Cost (W)	(23,600)	
			4,400
Painting	Proceeds	7,500	
	Less: Cost	(3,500)	
	Chargeable gain	4,000	
	Chargeable gain cannot exceed: 5/3 × (£7,500 – £6,000)	2,500	
	Lower chargeable gain taken		2,500
Car	Exempt		0
Total chargeable gains			6,900

Working: Share pool

	Number	£
May 2009	4,000	8,180
August 2011	3,000	9,600
June 2016	3,500	7,000
	10,500	24,780
Disposal (£24,780 × 10,000/10,500)	(10,000)	(23,600)
	500	1,180

Tutorial note

1 *When dealing with the sale of shares by an individual you should first consider the share identification rules. Disposals are matched with:*

(i) Shares purchased on the same day

(ii) Shares purchased within the next 30 days

(iii) Shares in the share pool i.e. all the shares acquired before the sale date.

In this question there are no purchases on the same day or within the next 30 days so the disposal all comes out of the share pool.

Purchases of shares and rights issues are added to the pool at cost. Bonus issues have no cost so the only entry in the pool is in the number column.

Disposals are removed from the pool at average cost:

Number of shares disposed of/Total shares in the pool before sale × Pool cost

2 *The non-wasting chattel marginal gain rules apply when the proceeds > £6,000 and the cost ≤ £6,000.*

The gain is the lower of:

(i) The gain calculated as normal

(ii) 5/3 × (Gross proceeds – £6,000)

3 *Cars are exempt assets even if they are veteran or vintage cars.*

66 BANDILE

Key answer tips

This question covers the usual mix of a non-wasting chattel, a part disposal and an exempt asset. Note that you are asked to calculate capital gains tax and state the due date of payment so make sure you do not miss the easy marks for these. Always look out for the separate payment date in respect of residential property (60 days after the disposal), although that is not relevant in this question.

Capital gains tax – 2025/26

		£	£
Antique table	Deemed proceeds	6,000	
	Less: Selling expenses	(300)	
	Net proceeds	5,700	
	Less: Cost	(8,000)	
	Allowable capital loss		(2,300)
Painting	Sale proceeds	28,000	
	Less: Selling expenses	(200)	
	Net proceeds	27,800	
	Less: Cost $\frac{£28,000}{£28,000 + £140,000} \times £60,000$	(10,000)	
	Chargeable gain		17,800
Victoria Cross medal – Exempt as it is a decoration for valour			0
Total chargeable gains			15,500
Less: Annual exempt amount			(3,000)
Net chargeable gains after AEA			12,500
Less: Capital loss b/f			(2,000)
Taxable gains			10,500
Capital gains tax (£10,500 × 24%)			2,520

Due date: 31 January 2027

Tutorial note

1 *The antique table is a non-wasting chattel which is sold for less than £6,000 and cost more than £6,000. This means that the gross proceeds (before selling expenses) are deemed to be £6,000.*

2 *Part disposals are popular in examination questions. The cost of the part of the asset sold must be found by applying the part disposal formula to the cost:*

Cost × A/A + B

Where A = gross sales proceeds, and

B = market value of the part of the asset remaining.

3 *The medal awarded for valour is exempt because Bandile did not purchase it but received it as an inheritance. If a medal is purchased then it is not exempt if the purchaser later sells it.*

67 BARTHOLOMEW

Key answer tips

This question covers the calculation of capital gains tax which includes the use of a loss on a disposal in the current year. Be careful to calculate the remaining basic rate band before applying the rates of tax to the gains.

Capital gains tax liability for 2025/26

	£
Residential property	27,000
Chattels	16,000
Total gains	43,000
Less: Losses	(2,000)
Net chargeable gains	41,000
Less: Annual exempt amount	(3,000)
Taxable gains	38,000

	£		£
Lower rate	21,700	× 18%	3,906
Higher rate	16,300	× 24%	3,912
	38,000		
Capital gains tax liability			7,818

Working

Bartholomew's unused basic rate is £21,700 (£37,700 – £16,000).

68 HANS

Key answer tips

This question has a variety of disposals, as is usually the case with capital gains tax questions. Non-wasting chattels are common assets in questions, but assets which have been damaged or destroyed are less common.

You also need to calculate capital gains tax. Do not miss the easy mark for stating the due payment date.

Capital gains tax – 2025/26

		£
Painting (Note 1)	Proceeds	7,600
	Less: Expenses	(400)
	Net proceeds	7,200
	Less: Cost	(4,500)
	Gain under normal rules	2,700
	Restricted to:	
	5/3 (£7,600 – £6,000)	2,667
Armour (Note 2)	Insurance proceeds	42,000
	Scrap value	14,000
		56,000
	Less: Cost	(74,000)
	Allowable loss	(18,000)
Antique	Proceeds	140,000
	Less: Cost	(60,000)
	Chargeable gain	80,000

Net gains (Note 3)	Painting	2,667
	Antique	80,000
	Armour	(18,000)
Total chargeable gains		64,667
Less: Annual exempt amount		(3,000)
Taxable gains		61,667
Hans is a higher rate taxpayer therefore 24% tax applies		
Capital gains tax (£61,667 × 24%)		14,800
Due date of payment		31 January 2027

Tutorial note

1 *The non-wasting chattel marginal gain rules apply when the proceeds > £6,000 and the cost ≤ £6,000.*

The gain is the lower of:

(i) The gain calculated as normal

(ii) 5/3 × (Gross proceeds – £6,000)

2 *Damage to an asset is a disposal for capital gains purposes. If compensation is received this becomes the proceeds figure in the calculation of the gain on the disposal. The date of disposal is the date the insurance is received. In this case the damaged asset was immediately sold, therefore there are also scrap proceeds to include.*

3 *Current year losses should be netted off against current year gains before the deduction of the annual exempt amount.*

Examiner's report

This was a 10-mark question requiring the calculation of gains and losses on the disposal of three different assets. These calculations were done well, however, the subsequent use of the loss and the use of the annual exempt amount were unsatisfactory.

The painting sold for marginally more than £6,000 required an alternative calculation of 5/3rds of the gross proceeds above £6,000 – many candidates did not do this.

When calculating the loss on the damaged set of armour, the scrap value and the insurance proceeds should have been added together to give the total proceeds, before deducting the original cost to give a loss of £18,000.

Finally, the loss should have been deducted from the total gains, before the deduction of the annual exempt amount.

Once again, an easy mark was lost by candidates who did not state the date of payment, as required by the question.

ACCA Marking scheme	
	Marks
Painting	
Proceeds	0.5
Expenses	0.5
Cost	0.5
Restricted to 5/3 (Proceeds – £6,000)	2.0
Armour	
Insurance proceeds	0.5
Scrap value	0.5
Cost	0.5
Antique	
Proceeds	0.5
Cost	0.5
Capital gains tax	
Net chargeable gains	1.0
Annual exempt amount	1.0
CGT payable	1.0
Due date	1.0
Total	**10.0**

69 SYED

Key answer tips

This question has a variety of disposals, as is usually the case with capital gains tax questions. Exempt assets are common in questions.

You also need to calculate capital gains tax. Be careful to calculate the remaining basic rate band before applying the rates of tax to the gains.

(a) Capital gains tax – 2025/26

		£
Qualifying corporate bonds	Exempt	0
Residential property	Proceeds	316,000
	Less: Cost (probate value)	(105,000)
	Chargeable gain	211,000
Antique	Proceeds	15,000
	Less: expenses of sale	(1,000)
	Less: cost	(23,000)
	Capital loss	(9,000)
Net gains	Residential property	211,000
	Antique (current year loss)	(9,000)
		202,000
	Less: Annual exempt amount	(3,000)
	Less: Capital loss brought forward	(4,000)
		195,000

Basic rate band remaining: £37,700 – £29,000 = £8,700

£8,700 × 18%	1,566
£(195,000 – 8,700) = £186,300 × 24%	44,712
Capital gains tax payable	46,278

(b) Payment date

Due date of payment on residential investment property is within 60 days of the date of disposal i.e. by 31 December 2025.

Tutorial note

Chargeable gains are taxed at three possible rates:

(i) 14% if the gain qualifies for BADR (regardless of the level of income)

(ii) 18% for any part of other gains falling below the basic rate threshold

(iii) 24% for balance of other gains

Examiner's report (adapted for rate changes since this question was set)

In part (a) some candidates calculated a capital gain on the disposal of the qualifying corporate bonds when these were exempt from capital gains tax. Candidates often used the original cost of the property rather than the probate value as the cost figure in their capital gains calculation. Generally, candidates scored well on calculating the loss on disposal of the antique.

When it came to calculating the capital gains tax, candidates often assumed that because the taxpayer was a basic rate taxpayer, the whole gain on the property should be charged at 18%. Only the better prepared candidates were able to work out the basic rate band remaining and apply 18% and 24% rates accordingly.

In part (b) many candidates guessed wrongly at this date or just ignored this part completely. Only a very small minority knew the 60-day rule.

ACCA Marking scheme	
	Marks
Qualifying corporate bonds	1.0
Residential property	
Proceeds	0.5
Cost – probate value	1.0
Antique	
Proceeds	0.5
Expenses of sale	0.5
Cost	0.5
Capital gains tax	
Net gain	1.0
Annual exempt amount	1.0
Capital loss brought forward	1.0
Basic rate band remaining	1.0
Basic rate	0.5
Higher rate	0.5
Payment date	1.0
Total	**10.0**

CAPITAL GAINS TAX RELIEFS: INDIVIDUALS

Key answer tips

In the June 2012 examiner's report, the examining team said that "Future candidates are reminded that the examination will always include a question involving one of the four reliefs in the syllabus; rollover relief, gift holdover relief, business asset disposal relief or private residence relief".

All the reliefs covered in the FTX syllabus have been examined regularly, involving both written questions (for example testing the conditions for a relief to apply) and calculations of the reliefs available.

The examining team commented in their December 2014 report "written answers will continue to be examined and candidates are advised to prepare for these".

70 TONY

Key answer tips

This question tests the very important business asset disposal relief (BADR).

In this question you are told that the relief is claimed but watch out for questions where it simply says that 'all beneficial reliefs are to be claimed'. In that case you have to work out which reliefs are applicable.

Capital gains tax – 2025/26

		£	£
Factory:	Proceeds	800,000	
	Less: Cost	(200,000)	
	Chargeable gain		600,000
Land:	Proceeds	180,000	
	Less: Cost	(213,000)	
	Allowable loss		(33,000)
Net chargeable gains			567,000
Less: Annual exempt amount			(3,000)
Taxable gains			564,000
Capital gains tax (£564,000 × 14%)			78,960

Tutorial note

BADR results in a tax rate on the first £1 million of qualifying gains of 14%, regardless of the taxpayer's level of income.

Disposals that qualify for BADR include:

- *the whole or part of a business carried on by the individual either alone or in partnership*
- *shares **provided** the:*
  - *shares are in the individual's 'personal trading company', and*
  - *the individual is an employee of the company (part time or full time).*

*Broadly an individual's **personal company** is one in which the individual holds at least 5% of the voting rights.*

Tony has sold his entire business which he has owned for more than two years; hence the disposal qualifies for BADR.

71 LUKNE

Key answer tips

This question tests gift holdover relief which is available for outright gifts or sales at undervalue of qualifying business assets.

Chargeable gain – 2025/26

	£
Market value of asset gifted	100,000
Less: Cost	(70,000)
Capital gain	30,000
Less: Gift holdover relief (balancing figure)	(20,000)
Chargeable gain (W)	10,000
Base cost of asset to Becky	
Market value of asset gifted	100,000
Less: Gift holdover relief	(20,000)
Base cost	80,000

Working: Chargeable gain now	£
Actual proceeds received	80,000
Less: Cost	(70,000)
Chargeable gain	10,000

Tutorial note

If an asset is given away, sold at an undervalue or sold to a connected person, then market value must be used for the disposal proceeds in the gain calculation and this also becomes the deemed 'cost' for the donee.

Gift holdover relief is available for:

- *Assets used in the trade of the:*
  - *donor (i.e. where the individual is a sole trader), or*
  - *donor's personal company*
- *Shares and securities of trading companies provided that the:*
  - *shares or securities are those of the individual's personal company or*
  - *shares or securities are not quoted on either a recognised stock exchange or the unlisted securities market.*

*An individual's **personal company** is one in which a taxpayer holds at least 5% of the voting rights.*

If the asset is gifted then provided both donor and donee elect, the gain is not charged now but is deferred and transferred to the donee by reducing the individual's base cost by the amount of the gain deferred.

If the disposal is a sale at undervalue and the actual proceeds received exceed the original cost, then part of the gain is charged now.

The amount charged now is the lower of:

(i) the gain

(ii) (proceeds actually received – original cost)

The balance of the gain is deferred and reduces the base cost of the asset for the donee.

72 TIGRAN

Key answer tips

The first part of this question requires an explanation of why the share disposal qualifies for BADR. Keep your explanation brief and use bullet points where appropriate.

The second part of the question tests the situation where the taxpayer has gains, some of which qualify for BADR and some which do not.

Remember to state the due date of payment as this is an easy mark. Always look out for the separate payment date in respect of residential property (60 days after the disposal).

(a) BADR

Tigran's disposal of shares qualifies for BADR because:

- the shares are in an unquoted trading company and
- Tigran has worked for the company and owned at least 5% of the shares for the previous two years.

Tutorial note

As shown in the December 2014 examination, you must be prepared to state the conditions for obtaining reliefs, not just calculate their effect.

(b) Capital gains tax payable – 2025/26

	Gains qualifying for BADR	Gains not qualifying for BADR
	£	£
Chargeable gains	1,300,000	9,000
Less: Annual exempt amount		(3,000)
Taxable gains	1,300,000	6,000
Capital gains tax		
£1,000,000 × 14%		140,000
£300,000 × 24%		72,000
£6,000 × 24%		1,440
		213,440

Tutorial note

BADR is available on the first £1 million of qualifying gains. It results in a tax rate on the gains of 14%, irrespective of the taxpayer's level of taxable income.

Where there are both gains qualifying for BADR and those which do not qualify, the annual exempt amount is deducted from non-qualifying gains. Tax is charged at 24% on the non-qualifying gains as the gains which qualify for BADR are deemed to use up the remaining basic rate band.

(c) Payment date

A payment on account is due in respect of the gain on the residential property within 60 days of the disposal i.e. by 30 July 2025.

The final balance of capital gains tax is due to be paid by 31 January 2027.

Tutorial note

You do not need to be able to calculate the amount due for the payment on account on the residential property disposal. You do need to know when it is due.

73 ELIF

Key answer tips

This question covers an area of the syllabus that you might not be too familiar with, but which works in a similar way to rollover relief. As most of the compensation has been used to replace the asset, a no gain/no loss election can be made and the gain deducted from the cost of the replacement asset.

The amount chargeable now is the extent to which the insurance proceeds are not reinvested in replacing the asset.

(a) Chargeable gain – 2025/26

	£
Insurance proceeds	29,500
Less: Cost	(18,000)
Capital gain	11,500
Deferred via no gain/no loss election to replacement (balancing figure)	(10,000)
Chargeable gain (£29,500 – £28,000)	1,500

(b) Base cost of replacement asset

	£
Cost	28,000
Less: Gain deferred via no gain/no loss election	(10,000)
Base cost	18,000

Tutorial note

The complete destruction of an asset is a disposal for capital gains purposes.

If compensation is received this becomes the proceeds figure in the calculation of the gain on the disposal.

The date of disposal is the date the insurance monies are received.

If the compensation is used to buy a replacement asset within 12 months an election can be made to treat the disposal as a no gain/no loss disposal.

If all of the compensation is used to replace the asset then no gain is charged now. Instead, the gain is deducted from the cost of the replacement asset carried forward.

If some of the compensation is not spent on replacing the asset, part of the gain is charged now.

This part is the lower of the

(i) total gain

(ii) compensation not spent on replacing the asset.

The balance of the gain is deducted from the cost of the replacement asset carried forward.

74 PEDRO

Key answer tips

This question tests the deemed occupation rules for a private residence.

This question uses these terms 'exempt' and 'non-exempt' instead of 'occupation and deemed occupation' and 'non-occupation' (see key answer tip below).

(a) Actual and deemed periods of occupation

Period	Occupation (exempt) months	Non-Occupation (not exempt) months	Reason
1.7.2005 – 31.8.2007	26		Actual occupation as living in property
1.9.2007 – 30.4.2012	56		Deemed occupation – working abroad (any periods)
1.5.2012 – 31.12.2012	8		Actual occupation as living in property
1.1.2013 – 31.12.2016	48		Deemed occupation – working in UK (maximum 4 years)
1.1.2017 – 31.12.2017	12		Deemed occupation – any reason (up to 3 years)
1.1.2018 – 31.8.2021	44		Actual occupation as living in property
1.9.2021 – 30.9.2024		37	Chargeable. Can't be counted as a period of deemed occupation as Pedro did not re-occupy the property afterwards
1.10.2024 – 30.6.2025	9		Deemed occupation – last 9 months
Totals	203	37	

Tutorial note

A taxpayer's private residence is exempt for the periods when it is occupied or deemed occupied. Otherwise the period is not exempt.

The last 9 months of ownership are always deemed occupation (and therefore exempt) even if the taxpayer has another residence during that time.

Other deemed residence (i.e. exempt) periods are:

(i) Any period working abroad – this covers Pedro's time abroad.

(ii) Up to a total of 4 years working elsewhere in the UK.

(iii) Up to a total of 3 years for any reason.

However, to be exempt, these periods must be preceded at some time by actual occupation and followed by actual occupation (except occupation after the absence is not insisted on for (i) and (ii) if by reason of employment the taxpayer cannot return to the residential property due to being moved elsewhere to work).

This means that the 3 years for any reason cannot be applied to the time Pedro moves to his parents' house as he does not return to his own house.

Key answer tips

In the December 2012 examiner's report, the examining team were disappointed that the question on PRR was either extremely poorly answered or not attempted.

"The biggest issue was the meaning of 'exempt' and 'non-exempt'. If the question asks for an exempt period for PRR it is asking for a period which is covered by PRR and is therefore not subject to tax whereas the reverse is true for a non-exempt period where the period is not exempted from tax".

This question similarly uses these terms and requires explanations as to why a period is exempt or not exempt.

In the June 2014 examination report, the examining team stated that reasons had to be given to earn full marks. In the December 2016 examination report, they stated that only copying the dates given in the question did not score any marks.

(b) Chargeable gain after relief

	£
Proceeds	160,000
Less: Cost	(54,500)
Extension	(10,000)
Chargeable gain before relief	95,500
Less: PRR relief (203/240 × £95,500)	(80,777)
Chargeable gain after relief	14,723

Tutorial note

The capital cost of improving an asset can be deducted in calculating the chargeable gain.

75 PAMELA

Key answer tips

This question tests rollover relief for business assets.

This is the only capital gains relief available to companies so has twice as much chance of being tested.

(a) Chargeable gain – 2025/26

	£
Proceeds	80,000
Less: Cost	(42,000)
Capital gain	38,000
Less: Rollover relief (balance)	(30,000)
Chargeable gain (W)	8,000

(b) Base cost of replacement shop

	£
Cost of new shop	72,000
Less: Rolled over gain	(30,000)
Base cost	42,000

Tutorial note

Rollover relief is available where the proceeds of sale of qualifying business assets are reinvested in other qualifying business assets.

In December 2014 the examining team commented that "a few candidates did not appear to know that rollover relief applies to business assets only and not to investment property".

Pamela has not reinvested all the proceeds so cannot rollover all of the gain.

The gain that is chargeable now is equal to the lower of the:

(i) proceeds not reinvested

(ii) total gain.

The examining team commented in their report on the June 2013 examination that some candidates get the amount not reinvested and the rollover relief "the wrong way around and continue to defer the amount not reinvested instead of the balance of the gain."

Working: Chargeable gain now

	£
Proceeds	80,000
Less: Amount reinvested in new shop	(72,000)
Chargeable gain = Amount not reinvested	8,000

76 PETRA

Key answer tips

This question tests the relief for the gift/sale at an undervalue of a business asset. Remember that full gift holdover relief is not available when the actual proceeds received exceed the original cost.

(a) Petra – Chargeable gain

	£
Proceeds	245,000
Less: Cost	(80,000)
Capital gain	165,000
Less: Gift holdover relief	(125,000)
Chargeable now (£120,000 – £80,000) (Note)	40,000

(b) Base cost for Peter

	£
Market value	245,000
Less: Gift holdover relief	(125,000)
Base cost	120,000

Tutorial note

If an asset is given away, sold at an undervalue or sold to a connected person, then market value must be used for the disposal proceeds in the gain calculation and this also becomes the deemed 'cost' for the donee.

Gift holdover relief is available for:

- *Assets used in the trade of the:*
  - *donor (i.e. where the individual is a sole trader), or*
  - *donor's personal company*
- *Shares and securities of trading companies provided that the:*
  - *shares or securities are those of the individual's personal company, or*
  - *shares or securities are not quoted on either a recognised stock exchange or the unlisted securities market.*

*An individual's **personal company** is one in which the taxpayer holds at least 5% of the voting rights.*

If the asset is gifted then provided both donor and donee elect, the gain is not charged now but is deferred and transferred to the donee by reducing the individual's base cost by the amount of the gain deferred.

If the disposal is a sale at undervalue and the actual proceeds received exceed the original cost, then part of the gain is charged now.

The amount charged now is the lower of:

(i) the gain

(ii) (Proceeds actually received – Original cost)

The balance of the gain is deferred and reduces the base cost for the donee.

77 PATRICIA

Key answer tips

This is a question involving rollover relief which tests knowledge of qualifying assets and the application of the relief when not all the proceeds are reinvested.

Capital gains tax payable – 2025/26

Workshop	£	£
Proceeds	160,000	
Less: Cost	(40,000)	
Capital gain	120,000	
Less: Rollover relief	(100,000)	
Chargeable now = amount not reinvested (Note)	20,000	20,000
Painting	£	
Proceeds	20,000	
Less: Cost	(12,000)	
Capital gain	8,000	8,000
Total gains		28,000
Less: Annual exempt amount		(3,000)
Taxable gain		25,000
Capital gains tax (£25,000 × 24%)		6,000

Tutorial note

Rollover relief is available where the proceeds of sale of qualifying business assets are reinvested in other qualifying business assets.

The following are the main categories of qualifying assets:

- *land and buildings that are both occupied and used for trading purposes*
- *fixed (i.e. not movable) plant and machinery*
- *goodwill (for individuals only).*

The painting and the forklift truck are not qualifying assets.

Patricia has not reinvested all the proceeds from the sale of the workshop in qualifying assets so cannot rollover all of the gain.

The gain that is chargeable now is equal to the lower of the:

(i) proceeds not reinvested (£160,000 – £140,000 = £20,000)

(ii) capital gain (£120,000).

The gain remaining chargeable is not eligible for BADR because Patricia has not sold her entire business.

78 ADELE

Key answer tips

This question covers an area of the syllabus that you might not be too familiar with; compensation receipts. However, the syllabus and exam format enable a wide variety of topics to be tested so you must be familiar with this area. In fact the rules for compensation receipts are not difficult to deal with as they follow very similar rules to rollover relief.

The insurance proceeds which are not reinvested in the replacement asset are taxed immediately and the rest of the gain is deferred against the base cost of the new asset via a no gain/no loss election.

(a) Chargeable gain – 2025/26: Compensation receipt

	£
Proceeds	29,000
Less: Cost	(24,500)
Capital gain	4,500
Less: Chargeable now (amount not reinvested)	(1,000)
Gain deferred via no gain/no loss election = rolled into cost of replacement	3,500
Chargeable gain	1,000

(b) Base cost of new painting

	£
Cost	28,000
Less: Gain deferred via no gain/no loss election	(3,500)
Base cost	24,500

Tutorial note

The complete destruction of an asset is a disposal for capital gains purposes.

If compensation is received this becomes the proceeds figure in the calculation of the gain on the disposal.

The date of disposal is the date the insurance monies are received.

If the compensation is used to buy a replacement asset within 12 months an election can be made to treat the disposal as a no gain/no loss disposal.

If all of the compensation is used to replace the asset then no gain is charged now. Instead the gain is deducted from the cost of the replacement asset carried forward.

If some of the compensation is not spent on replacing the asset then part of the gain is charged now. This part is the lower of:

(i) the total gain

(ii) the compensation not spent

The balance of the gain is deducted from the cost of the replacement asset carried forward.

79 POLA

Key answer tips

Note that in answering questions about chargeable and exempt periods for a private residence, you should present the information in a tabular format.

(a) Pola – Private residence relief

Period	Chargeable	Exempt	Let	Reason
1 May 2017 – 30 Apr 2021		X		Working elsewhere in UK – maximum of four years (Note)
1 May 2021 – 30 Nov 2024	X			Did not reoccupy – 3 years for any reason does not apply
1 Dec 2024 – 31 Aug 2025		X		Last 9 months of ownership

Tutorial note

A taxpayer's private residence is exempt for the periods when it is occupied or deemed occupied.

The last 9 months of ownership are always deemed occupation even if the taxpayer has another residence by then.

Other deemed residence periods:

(i) Any period working abroad

(ii) Up to a total of 4 years working elsewhere in the UK – this covers 4 years for Pola

(iii) Up to a total of 3 years for any reason.

These periods must be preceded at some time by actual occupation and followed by actual occupation (except occupation after the absence is not insisted on for (i) and (ii) if the taxpayer cannot return to the residence by reason of employment due to being moved elsewhere to work).

This means that the 3 years for any reason cannot be applied to the time Pola moves to another UK city.

(b) Due dates

Residential property – tax is due 60 days after the disposal, i.e. by 30 October 2025.

Final payment for the tax year 2025/26 – tax is due by 31 January 2027.

Key answer tips

Make sure you learn the due dates for each tax. These are regularly tested and are easy marks to gain in the exam if you know the rules.

80 SANDRA

Key answer tips

This question deals with the commonly examined area of rollover relief.

What is not so commonly tested is the fact that the replacement asset is fixed plant and machinery. This is classed as a depreciating asset for rollover relief purposes and does not affect the amount of the deferred gain, but does affect how the gain is deferred.

(a) Sandra – Chargeable gain 2025/26

	£
Capital gain	80,000
Deferred gain (Balancing figure) (Note)	(70,000)
Chargeable now = Proceeds not reinvested (£220,000 – £210,000)	10,000

The gain remaining chargeable is not eligible for BADR because Sandra has not sold her entire business.

Tutorial note

Rollover relief is available where the proceeds of sale of qualifying business assets are reinvested in other qualifying business assets.

Sandra has not reinvested all her proceeds so cannot rollover all of her gain.

The gain that is chargeable now is the lower of:

(i) the proceeds not reinvested

(ii) the total gain.

Where the replacement asset is a depreciating asset (most common example is fixed plant and machinery as here) the gain is not deducted from the cost of the replacement asset but is deferred until the earliest of three events (see part (b)).

(b) The gain will be deferred until the earliest of three events:

- The sale of the fixed plant and machinery.
- The fixed plant and machinery ceasing to be used in the trade.
- The 10th anniversary of the purchase of the fixed plant and machinery (i.e. 10 June 2035).

81 SUSANNAH

Key answer tips

This question tests the deemed occupation rules for a private residence.

Actual and deemed periods of occupation

Period	**Reason**	**Occupation (exempt) months**	**Non-Occupation (chargeable) months**
1 May 2012 to 31 July 2013	Lived in	15	
1 Aug 2013 to 31 July 2019	Worked abroad	72	
1 Aug 2019 to 31 Dec 2023	Worked elsewhere in UK – maximum of 4 years	48	
	5 months for any reason (reoccupied property)	5	
1 Jan 2024 to 31 Oct 2025	Lived in	22	
Totals		162	0

Gain:

There is no gain on the disposal of the property.

Tutorial note

A taxpayer's private residence is exempt for the periods when it is occupied or deemed occupied. Otherwise the period is not exempt.

The last 9 months of ownership are always deemed occupation (and therefore exempt) even if the taxpayer has another residence during that time.

Other deemed residence (i.e. exempt) periods are:

(i) Any period working abroad – this covers Susannah's time abroad.

(ii) Up to a total of 4 years working elsewhere in the UK

(iii) Up to a total of 3 years for any reason.

However, to be exempt, these periods must be preceded at some time by actual occupation and followed by actual occupation (except occupation after the absence is not insisted on for (i) and (ii) if the taxpayer cannot return to the residence by reason of employment due to being moved elsewhere to work).

Key answer tips

In the June 2014 examination report, the examining team stated that reasons had to be given to earn full marks. In the December 2016 examination report, they stated that only copying the dates given in the question did not score any marks.

Examiner's report

This was a five-mark question on private residence relief (PRR).

Unfortunately, most candidates did not do as requested. This question, as is usual for PRR questions, required candidates to produce a table showing periods which were covered by PRR and those periods which were not.

The table should have shown each event separately and should have given a reason why, or why not, the relevant period is covered by PRR. In this case every period was covered by PRR and therefore there was no gain on the disposal and the disposal was exempt from capital gains tax.

The periods of actual occupation were obviously covered by PRR and this was well known. What caused problems for candidates was the other periods where candidates had to determine if these were treated as deemed occupation and thus exempt from CGT. Firstly, provided there is actual occupation before and after the relevant period then any period, regardless of length, when the individual is working abroad and any period up to four years when the individual is working in UK are deemed periods of occupation. In addition to these periods, any period of absence of up to three years for any reason (again subject to actual occupation before and after) and the last 9 months of ownership are also classed as deemed periods of occupation.

Some marks were given where candidates counted the number of months incorrectly, as long as the reasoning given was correct.

ACCA Marking scheme

	Marks
First lived in period	0.5
Period working abroad	1.0
4 years working elsewhere in UK	1.0
5 months for any reason	1.0
Second lived in period	0.5
No gain on disposal	1.0
Total	**5.0**

82 HALINA

Key answer tips

This question tests gains qualifying for BADR and other gains. It is important to consider how to offset the annual exempt amount and any losses between these types of gains.

Capital gains tax liability – 2025/26

		BADR	Other gains
		£	£
House (W1)			96,200
Ordinary shares in Straight Ltd (W2)			26,400
Warehouse		3,700	
Total chargeable gains		3,700	122,600
Less: Annual exempt amount			(3,000)
			119,600
Less: Brought forward capital loss			(7,200)
Taxable gain		3,700	112,400
	£		£
Gains qualifying for BADR:	3,700 × 14%		518
Other gains: lower rate	10,055 × 18% (W3)		1,810
Other gains: higher rate	102,345 × 24%		24,563
	116,100		
Capital gains tax liability			26,891

Tutorial note

The annual exempt amount and losses should be offset against gains not qualifying for BADR in priority to gains qualifying for BADR in order to save the maximum amount of tax.

Halina has taxable income that uses some of, but not all of, her basic rate band. The remaining basic rate band is £13,755. £3,700 of this is automatically used by the BADR gains first, leaving £10,055 to set against the other gains.

Workings

(W1) House

	£
Disposal proceeds	282,200
Less: Cost	(186,000)
Chargeable gain	96,200

(W2) Shares in Straight Ltd

	£
Disposal proceeds	62,400
Less: Cost (£48,000 × 15,000/20,000)	(36,000)
Chargeable gain	26,400

Tutorial note

It is not clear what percentage interest Halina has in Straight Ltd and whether it is her personal trading company (i.e. she holds 5% interest or more). However, even if she does hold at least 5%, BADR is not available as Halina does not work for the company.

However, the disposal of a business which has been held for over two years does qualify for BADR.

(W3) Remaining basic rate band

	£
Basic rate band	37,700
Less: Taxable income	(23,945)
	13,755
Utilised by BADR gains	(3,700)
Remaining basic rate band	10,055

83 ANDREA

Key answer tips

This question tests the relief for the gift/sale at an undervalue of a business asset. Remember that full gift holdover relief is not available when the actual proceeds received exceed the original cost.

(a) Andrea – Chargeable gain on shares

	£
Market value – November 2025	60,000
Less: Cost	(40,000)
Capital gain	20,000
Less: Gift holdover relief	(5,000)
Chargeable now (£55,000 – £40,000) (Note)	15,000

Note:

Sales proceeds £55,000 less cost £40,000

(b) Claim date

Claim must be made four years from the end of the tax year in which the gift was made i.e. by 5 April 2030.

Tutorial note

If an asset is given away, sold at an undervalue or sold to a connected person, then market value must be used for the disposal proceeds in the gain calculation and this also becomes the deemed 'cost' for the donee.

Gift holdover relief is available for:

- *Assets used in the trade of the:*
  - *donor (i.e. where the individual is a sole trader), or*
  - *donor's personal company*
- *Shares and securities of trading companies provided that the:*
  - *shares or securities are those of the individual's personal company, or*
  - *shares or securities are not quoted on either a recognised stock exchange or the unlisted securities market.*

An individual's ***personal company*** *is one in which the taxpayer holds at least 5% of the voting rights.*

If the asset is gifted then provided both donor and donee elect, the gain is not charged now but is deferred and transferred to the donee by reducing the individual's base cost by the amount of the gain deferred.

If the disposal is a sale at undervalue and the actual proceeds received exceed the original cost, then part of the gain is charged now.

The amount charged now is the lower of:

(i) the gain

(ii) (Proceeds actually received – Original cost)

The balance of the gain is deferred and reduces the base cost for the donee.

Examiner's report

This 5-mark question tested the computation of a chargeable gain on a sale at undervalue and included a claim for relief for gift of business assets. The second part of the question tested knowledge of the due date for the claim to be made.

ACCA Marking scheme	
	Marks
Deemed proceeds – market value	1.0
Cost	1.0
Gift holdover relief – balancing figure	1.0
Chargeable gain – actual proceeds less cost	1.0
Claim date	1.0
Total	**5.0**

84 BRODIE

Key answer tips

This question tests gains qualifying for BADR and other gains. It is important to consider how to offset the annual exempt amount and any losses between these types of gains.

Capital gains tax liability – 2025/26

		BADR gains	Other gains
		£	£
Shares in Xtrema Ltd (W1)		12,000	
Residential property (W2)			58,700
Total chargeable gains		12,000	58,700
Less: Annual exempt amount			(3,000)
			55,700
Less: Brought forward capital loss			(7,100)
Taxable gain		12,000	48,600
	£		£
Gains qualifying for BADR:	12,000 × 14%		1,680
Other gains: lower rate (W4)	10,030 × 18%		1,805
Other gains: higher rate	38,570 × 24%		9,257
	60,600		
Capital gains tax liability			12,742

Tutorial note

The annual exempt amount and losses should be offset against gains not qualifying for BADR in priority to gains qualifying for BADR in order to save the maximum amount of tax.

Brodie has taxable income that uses some of, but not all of, his basic rate band. The remaining basic rate band is £22,030. £12,000 of this is automatically used by the BADR gains first, leaving £10,030 to set against the other gains.

Workings

(W1) Shares in Xtrema Ltd

	£
Disposal proceeds	32,000
Less: Cost (£30,000 × 40,000/60,000)	(20,000)
Chargeable gain	12,000

Tutorial note

BADR results in a tax rate on the first £1 million of qualifying gains of 14%, regardless of the taxpayer's level of income.

Disposals that qualify for BADR include:

- *the whole or part of a business carried on by the individual either alone or in partnership*
- *shares **provided** the:*
  - *shares are in the individual's 'personal trading company', and*
  - *the individual is an employee of the company (part time or full time).*

*Broadly an individual's **personal company** is one in which the individual holds at least 5% of the voting rights.*

Brodie has owned at least 5% of the shares in a trading company and has worked for the company, for at least two years. Hence the gain on the disposal of shares qualifies for BADR.

(W2) Residential property

	£
Disposal proceeds	516,000
Less: Cost	(457,300)
Chargeable gain	58,700

(W3) Car

Disposal of the car is an exempt loss for capital gains purposes.

(W4) Remaining basic rate band

	£
Basic rate band	37,700
Less: Taxable income	(15,670)
	22,030
Utilised by BADR gains	(12,000)
Remaining basic rate band	10,030

Examiner's report (amended for change in rates since the exam was set)

Answers to [this] capital gains tax question were not very good, in large part because candidates struggled with how to deal with the capital gains tax chargeable on the disposals of a business asset and on a residential property.

In the capital gains calculation for the disposal of the shares, some candidates mistakenly used the full cost of all 60,000 shares in their capital gains calculation, instead of pro-rating the cost for the actual number of shares sold. Some candidates calculated a capital gain on the disposal of the car when this was exempt from capital gains tax. Generally, candidates scored well on calculating the gain on the disposal of the residential property.

The shares being disposed of were in an unquoted, trading company where Brodie had been an employee, which meant that the share disposal qualified for business asset disposal relief (BADR). This allows the capital gains tax on the shares to be calculated at 14%.

However, before any gains are taxed, the annual exempt amount (AEA) and capital losses brought forward should be deducted from the gain(s) which are NOT eligible for BADR i.e. the residential property gain. But if there is any basic rate band remaining, the gains which are eligible for BADR, use up the basic rate band first. Many candidates were unaware of these rules and simply grouped all gains together in their computations.

When it came to calculating the capital gains tax on the disposal of the residential property, candidates often assumed that because the taxpayer was a basic rate taxpayer, the whole gain on the property should be charged at 18%. Only the better prepared candidates were able to work out the basic rate band remaining and apply 18% and 24% rates accordingly.

CORPORATION TAX

Key answer tips

The examining team have published a very useful article to help students in answering the 15 mark question on corporation tax.

The examining team states that the main issues candidates seem to have with this question are as follows:

"The first problem is that some candidates confuse a company assessment and that of an individual. This may be due to exam pressure; however, the question will always make it clear that it is a company (plc or Ltd) – there should never be a doubt. When doing a company assessment all income and gains are assessed in one total column, the breakdown of income into the three categories of non-savings, savings and dividend relates to individuals only, never companies. On a similar note, companies do not get personal allowances or the annual exempt amount for capital gains tax."

Other specific comments made by the examining team are quoted below where applicable to a particular aspect of a question.

In the conclusion of the article however it is important to note the closing remarks:

"Candidates must prepare properly for this type of question. Practice of questions taken from the recommended exam kits will give candidates the required experience and practice of dealing with this type of question."

The questions contained in this kit provide the practice necessary to give you the required experience.

85 PACIFIC PLC

Key answer tips

This is an unusual question which requires you to explain how and why you would make certain adjustments to the accounting profit.

Note you are not required to do an adjusted profit computation.

Adjustment of profit before income taxes for tax purposes

1 Add back £2,500.

Entertainment of customers is disallowed by statute, whilst entertaining staff is allowable.

2 Add back £20,000.

The expenditure on the warehouse relates to damage which occurred before the building was acquired, and is spent in order to make the property usable. It is capital expenditure and is treated as part of the cost of the warehouse. The expenditure on the general office repairs is allowable.

3 No adjustment.

The loan was used for trading purposes, so the interest payable is allowed as a trading expense on an accruals basis.

4 Add back £300.

Lease rentals for cars with CO_2 emissions exceeding 50g/km, have 15% of the payments made disallowed. Where the car has emissions of no more than 50g/km, there is no adjustment required.

5 No adjustment.

The net effect is nil. Companies may claim an annual investment allowance of 100%. The initial deduction is added back as a capital cost and then 100% capital allowance is claimed. The net effect is nil.

6 No adjustment.

The proceeds are a trading receipt as they replace lost profits.

7 Deduct £14,000.

The sale proceeds (restricted to cost if necessary) are brought into the capital allowances computation. The proceeds reduce the tax written down value (TWDV) of the main pool and may give rise to a balancing charge if they exceed the TWDV. If the proceeds exceed cost, any excess is taxable as a chargeable gain.

Tutorial note

In a company's accounts prepared under IFRS® Standard *IFRS18, the term 'profit before income taxes' is used to label the net profit. However, companies actually pay corporation tax on taxable profits in the period. The 'profit before income taxes' is adjusted to calculate the trading profits for corporation tax purposes.*

Only brief explanations are required.

If the plant and machinery purchased during the year is new, full expensing (100% FYA) is also available, but the annual investment allowance (AIA) is preferred to avoid an immediate balancing charge when the plant is sold in future.

86 CARGO LTD

Key answer tips

This is a detailed capital allowances computation that includes many of the frequently examined complications.

Capital allowances are an important topic, which must be mastered as they are examined in every examination.

In the June 2012 examination, a 10 mark capital allowances question tested this topic. In their examiner's report in relation to these issues, the examining team said:

"The most common mistakes made by candidates were:

- Candidates apportioned allowances based on periods of ownership. Allowances are only apportioned when the accounting period is less than 12 months.
- Many candidates invented a car pool. There is no such thing. Cars with a CO_2 emission rate of more than 50 g/km are treated as special rate pool items and those with 50 g/km or less go in the main pool. Neither type of car is entitled to AIA.

The examining team also stressed the importance of using the standard presentation for such questions as follows:

"The layout shown in the suggested solutions would have aided candidates to do their calculations but many made up their own layouts and provided their actions were correct marks were still awarded".

Capital allowances – year ending 31 March 2026

	AIA	Main pool	Special rate pool	Allowances
	£	£	£	£
TWDV b/f		248,000	9,000	
Additions (No AIA):				
Car (Aug)			26,000	
Car (Nov) (£3,000 + 11,000)		14,000		
Additions – AIA:				
Plant	37,000			
AIA 100%	(37,000)			37,000
	0			
Disposals		(3,000)	(7,000)	
		259,000	28,000	
WDA @ (18% × £259,000)		(46,620)		46,620
WDA @ (6% × £28,000)			(1,680)	1,680
TWDV c/f		212,380	26,320	
Total capital allowances				85,300

Tutorial note

1 *Private use of assets by an employee is irrelevant in a company's capital allowances computation; the allowances are available in full. The individual is taxed on the private use element in the personal income tax computation as an employment income benefit. Restricting the capital allowance because of the private use by a director was a common error in the December 2015 and December 2017 examinations.*

2 *Capital allowances on car purchases are calculated based on the CO_2 emissions of the car as follows:*

– *CO_2 emissions up to 50g/km:*

put in main pool and eligible for a WDA at 18%

– *CO_2 emissions of > 50g/km:*

put in special rate pool and eligible for a WDA at 6%

3 *On the purchase of the new plant, the annual investment allowance (AIA) of 100% has been claimed in preference to full expensing, although there would be no difference in the percentage allowance available. By claiming the AIA, there will be no immediate balancing charge on a future disposal of this asset.*

4 *Disposals are deducted at the lower of cost and sale proceeds.*

ACCA Marking scheme

		Marks
TWDV b/f		0.5
Additions without AIA	– special rate car, no private use adjustment	2.0
	– part-exchange car	2.0
Addition with AIA		1.0
Disposals	– special rate car	1.0
	– part exchange	1.0
WDA – main pool		1.0
WDA – special rate pool		1.0
Total allowances		0.5
Total		**10.0**

87 STONEY PAVING LTD

Key answer tips

This is a question covering capital allowances for a company. It involves a typical capital allowances computation. It is important to use the appropriate layout when doing a capital allowances computation.

Capital allowances – year ended 31 March 2026

	AIA	FYA	Main pool	Special rate pool	Allowances
	£	£	£	£	£
TWDV b/f			1,276,000		
Addition with no AIA or FYA					
Car ≤ 50g/km			24,000		
Addition with AIA					
Integral features	1,020,000				
AIA (Max)	(1,000,000)				1,000,000
Balance for 50% FYA		20,000			
Disposal: BC					(4,000)
			1,300,000	0	
WDA @ (18% × £1,300,000)			(234,000)		234,000
Additions with FYA:					
50% FYA for SRP		(10,000)			10,000
Balance to SRP				10,000	
Zero-emission car		32,600			
FYA @ 100%		(32,600)			32,600
			0		
TWDV c/f			1,066,000	10,000	
Total allowances					1,272,600

Tutorial note

Capital allowances on car purchases are calculated based on the CO_2 emissions of the car.

If the car has zero emissions, it qualifies for FYA, if the CO_2 emissions are up to 50g/km then the car is put in the main pool and is eligible for a WDA at 18%.

Integral features are classified as a special rate pool asset. The annual investment allowance of 100% is available of up to £1m for a 12m accounting period. Additions over the AIA limit are eligible for FYA 50%.

The sales proceeds of the asset on which the 130% super deduction was claimed are not deducted from the main pool, instead the sales proceeds are treated as a balancing charge.

88 UK FABRICS LTD

Key answer tips

This is a question covering mainstream corporation tax topics – capital allowances and adjustment of profits. In this question the requirement is very clear; however in other questions it is not necessarily so clear.

The examining team's corporation tax article states that:

".. trading income ... comes from the trading activities of the company and may be given as 'adjusted' or 'unadjusted'. It is vital that candidates ensure that they check whether the figure given in the question is before or after adjustments – many candidates adjust the figure given when it does not require adjusting.

When the term 'trading profits after the deduction of...' is used, then this indicates that the profit figure needs adjusting to arrive at the taxable trading income. Whereas when the terms 'trading income' or 'adjusted trading profits' are used, then this indicates that no adjustment to the figure is required. Occasionally, the question will state 'adjusted trading profit before interest and capital allowances' – this term will mean that the profit has been partially adjusted but will need further adjustment for the interest and capital allowances (including any ... structure and buildings allowances) given.

If capital allowances are not already deducted from the trading income figure given, but are given separately, then these must be deducted from the trading profit and not from any other income. If they are deducted elsewhere in the assessment no mark will be awarded for the deduction".

Note that when preparing an adjusted profit computation, you should mention items that do not require adjustment in order to show the marker that you have not just forgotten the items.

Tax adjusted trading profits – year ended 31 March 2026

	£
Profit before income taxes	1,653,000
Deduct:	
Profit on sale of a non-current asset	(141,000)
Rental income	(168,000)
Add back:	
Depreciation	70,000
Wages	0
Power and light	0
Increase in specific allowance	0
Trade debt collection (allowable)	0
Entertainment of customers	2,000
Gifts (food hampers) to customers	3,000
Renewal of short lease (allowable)	0
Parking fines incurred by employees (allowable)	0
Staff training courses (allowable)	0
Office expenses	0
Adjusted profits before capital allowances	1,419,000
Less: Capital allowances	(304,000)
Tax adjusted trading profits	1,115,000

Tutorial note

1 *The profit on sale of the non-current asset is the accounting profit and is deducted from the accounting profit. A chargeable gain or allowable loss is then calculated on the asset using capital gains rules. Any gain is included as part of the taxable total profits (TTP) but this calculation was not required here.*

2 *Rental income is taxable but not as part of tax adjusted trading profits. It is included as a separate item in the calculation of TTP.*

3 *Gifts to customers costing no more than £50 per person and carrying a conspicuous advertisement for the business are tax allowable. However, gifts of food, drink and tobacco are not allowable.*

4 *Legal costs for renewing a short (≤ 50 years) lease are allowable.*

5 *Parking fines incurred by employees in the course of the company's business are allowable, as are trade related training courses.*

89 DANDY PLC

Key answer tips

This is a tricky question which tests your knowledge of non-trade income in particular.

Remember when adjusting the profit for non-trade income and expenses you can only deduct or add the figures actually included in the accounting profit. However, when calculating the taxable total profits (TTP) you should include the amounts actually taxable or allowable.

Note also that the basis of calculating property income for a company is different from that used for an individual taxpayer, where the cash basis usually applies.

(a) Tax adjusted trading profit

		£
Profit before income taxes		115,000
Deduct:	UK dividends: 40% subsidiary	(4,500)
	60% subsidiaries (£6,300 × 2)	(12,600)
	Insurance recovery (trade receipt)	0
	Rent	(8,000)
	Loan note interest	(10,000)
	Interest accrual re 2020 loan: (£180,000 × 5%) – £8,000	(1,000)
		78,900
Add back:	Interest on trading loan	0
	Interest – non-trading loan (let property)	6,000
	Qualifying charitable donation	3,000
Adjusted profit		87,900
Less: Capital allowances		(16,000)
Tax adjusted trading profit		71,900

Tutorial note

1 *Dividends received by a company are not taxable and if they have been included in the accounting profit then they must be deducted. Dividends from non-associated companies are then included in the calculation of augmented profits.*

2 *The rent is not taxable as trading profit so the £8,000 included in the accounting profit is removed from the trading profit by deducting it. When calculating the amount of property income to include in the calculation of TTP, the full amount of rent receivable (£9,000) is included as property income, as property income is always taxed on the accruals basis for a company (not the cash basis as usually applies for an individual taxpayer).*

3 *The loan note interest received is for non-trade purposes. It is removed from the trading profit by deducting it and is then taxed as a separate item in calculating TTP.*

4 *Interest payable on the loan to buy a factory for use by the company is a trade item and would not normally need any adjustment. However, it is allowed on an accruals basis so the unpaid amount of £1,000 (interest due £180,000 × 5% – interest paid of £8,000) is deducted as an additional allowable expense.*

5 *Interest paid on the loan to buy an investment property (the factory being let out) is non-trade related and must be added back to trade profits. It can then be deducted from the non-trade interest receivable in calculating TTP.*

6 *The donation to Oxfam is added back and allowed as a qualifying charitable donation in calculating TTP.*

(b) Corporation tax liability – year ended 31 March 2026

	£	£
Tax adjusted trading profit		71,900
Interest income (£10,000 – £6,000) (Note 1)		4,000
Property income (accruals basis) (Note 2)		9,000
Chargeable gain	9,000	
Less: Capital loss b/f (Note 3)	(3,000)	6,000
Total profits		90,900
Less: Qualifying charitable donations (Note 4)		(3,000)
Taxable total profits		87,900
Corporation tax liability (W)		
FY2025 (£87,900 × 25%)		21,975

Working: Augmented profits

	£
Taxable total profits	87,900
Add: Dividends received from non-group companies	4,500
Augmented profits	92,400

Limits: based on Dandy plc and two associated companies (Note 6)

	£
Upper limit: £250,000/3	83,333
Lower limit: £50,000/3	16,667

Tutorial note

The notes below explain some of the key points to remember when compiling a corporation tax computation. The parts in quotation marks are quotes from the examining team's corporation tax article.

1 *Interest income should be included as one figure in the corporation tax computation. "Non-trade interest payable must be pooled with interest received to give one net figure. This is then included in the corporation tax assessment as 'interest income'. Failure to net the figures together and, thus, show two separate figures in the assessment will result in the loss of marks".*

2 *Property income must be calculated on the accruals basis.*

"Candidates should ensure that they include any rent outstanding for the period – the actual date of payment is irrelevant, it is taxed in the year that it is due".

3 *Interest payable in respect of a rental property (i.e. non-trade interest) is deducted from interest income not from property income.*

4 *Allowable capital losses can only be set against chargeable gains and no other income.*

"If capital losses are given, either for the same period or carried forward from an earlier period, then these losses must be deducted from the aggregate gains to give a net chargeable gains figure. Once again if capital losses are deducted from the wrong income full marks cannot be awarded. Candidates should note that companies are not entitled to the annual exempt amount".

"A common mistake made by candidates is to deduct capital allowances from capital gains – this is wrong as they are totally different areas. Chargeable gains are the profits on the sale of capital assets, whereas capital allowances are 'tax depreciation' on capital assets held by a company – they should not be mixed together."

5 *Companies pay qualifying charitable donations gross so no grossing up is required. They are labelled as qualifying charitable donations in the corporation tax computation. They should be deducted from total profits after current year and brought forward trade and property losses.*

6 *If a company has associated companies, the upper (£250,000) and lower (£50,000) limits must be divided by the total number of associated companies to determine the appropriate rate of corporation tax.*

If marginal relief applies, use the reduced upper limit in the formula. In this question marginal relief does not apply as the augmented profits are above the reduced upper limit.

Remember to calculate the tax on the company's taxable total profits, not augmented profits.

90 THOMPSON BROTHERS LTD

Key answer tips

This question tests a short accounting period of nine months. This affects the calculation of the maximum AIA and the WDA in the capital allowances computation.

In the examiner's report for June 2012, the examining team said that one of the common mistakes made in a similar question was that "candidates apportioned allowances based on periods of ownership. Allowances are only apportioned when the accounting period is less than 12 months".

Be careful when reading the name of a question. This question is called Thompson Brothers Ltd. The danger is that you think that because it is called Thompson Brothers, you mistakenly treat the business as a partnership, not a company.

The examining team have stated in the corporation tax article:

"The first problem is that some candidates confuse a company assessment and that of an individual. This may be due to exam pressure; however, the question will always make it clear that it is a company (plc or Ltd) – there should never be a doubt."

(a) Capital allowances – nine months ended 31 December 2025

	AIA	Full Expense	Main pool	Special rate pool	Allowances
	£	£	£	£	£
TWDV b/f			140,000		
Purchases – no AIA					
Car > 50g/km				22,000	
Purchases with AIA					
Plant	775,000				
AIA (max £1,000,000 × 9/12)	(750,000)				750,000
Balance for 100% FYA		25,000			
FYA 100% (full expensing)		(25,000)			25,000
Disposals			(23,000)		
			117,000	22,000	
WDA @ (18% × 9/12)			(15,795)		15,795
WDA @ (6% × 9/12)				(990)	990
TWDV c/f			101,205	21,010	
Total allowances					791,785

Tutorial note

1 *The period is only nine months long. The maximum AIA and the WDA must be scaled down by multiplying by 9/12.*

2 *The purchase of the plant qualifies for AIA as well as 100% full expensing. It is beneficial to claim AIA to the maximum extent possible first. This will not impact the amount of allowance claimed on purchase, but it reduces the balancing charge on disposal of the asset in future.*

3 *The car has CO_2 emissions >50 g/km so is placed in the special rate pool and written down at 6% p.a.*

4 *Private use of a car by an employee (the director) does not affect the capital allowances computation. Restricting the capital allowance because of the private use by a director was a common error in the December 2015 examination.*

5 *The disposal of plant and machinery was of an asset where no claim for first year allowances had been made. Hence the disposal does not result in a balancing charge. It is treated as normal with a deduction of proceeds from the relevant column (main pool).*

(b) Corporation tax computation – 9 m/e 31 December 2025

	£
Adjusted profits	974,307
Less: Capital allowances (Note 1)	(791,785)
Tax adjusted trading profit	182,522
Property income (9/12 × £10,000) (Note 2)	7,500
Interest income (Note 3) (W1)	2,500
Total profits	192,522
Less: Qualifying charitable donation (Note 4)	(7,000)
Taxable total profits	185,522
Corporation tax (Note 5):	
185,522 × 25% (W2)	46,381

Workings

(W1) Interest income

	£
Loan note interest (£120,000 × 5% × 9/12)	4,500
Less: Interest for late payment of tax	(2,000)
Interest income	2,500

(W2) Augmented profits and upper limit

Augmented profits = £185,522 + £18,000 = £203,522

Upper limit = £250,000 × 9/12 = £187,500

Augmented profits exceed the upper limit so the main rate applies.

Tutorial note

The notes below explain some of the key points to remember when compiling a corporation tax computation. The parts in quotation marks are quotes from the examining team's corporation tax article.

1 *Capital allowances must be deducted in the correct place in the computation.*

"If capital allowances are not already deducted from the trading income figure given, but are given separately, then these must be deducted from the trading profit and not from any other income. If they are deducted elsewhere in the assessment no mark will be awarded for the deduction".

2 *Property income must be calculated on the accruals basis (not the cash basis as for individual taxpayers).*

The accounting period is only nine months long so only 9/12 of a full year's rental income should be included.

"Candidates should ensure that they include any rent outstanding for the period – the actual date of payment is irrelevant, it is taxed in the year that it is due."

3 *Interest income should be included as one figure in the corporation tax computation. The accounting period is only nine months long so only 9/12 of loan note interest receivable should be included.*

Interest on late paid tax is allowed as an expense for companies against the non-trade interest receivable. Note that interest on late paid tax is not allowed as a deduction for individuals.

"Non-trade interest payable must be pooled with interest received to give one net figure. This is then included in the corporation tax assessment as 'interest income'. Failure to net the figures together and, thus, show separate figures in the assessment will result in the loss of marks".

4 *Companies pay qualifying charitable donations gross so no grossing up is required. They are labelled as qualifying charitable donations in the corporation tax computation. They should be deducted from total profits after current year and brought forward trade and property losses.*

5 *Dividends received are not taxable but increase augmented profits for determining the rate of corporation tax payable. The upper and lower limits are reduced due to the short accounting period, and so the augmented profits here exceed the upper limit, meaning corporation tax is payable on the taxable total profits at the main rate.*

91 PARKER PLC

Key answer tips

This is a question dealing with corporation tax administration. Online filing and electronic payments are popular issues.

The normal due date for corporation tax for companies that are not large (i.e. with taxable total profits of not more than £1,500,000) is nine months and one day after the end of the accounting period.

However, a large company must pay corporation tax in instalments if they were also a large company in the previous year. The £1,500,000 threshold is scaled down for periods of less than one year.

It is important to be precise when giving dates.

The examiner's June 2012 report stated that "no marks will be awarded for near misses or dates without the year stated or simply statements such as October 2013".

Remember that a large company must estimate its corporation tax liability for the year and make instalment payments in relation to that tax liability during the accounting period.

The June 2013 examiner's report stated that "many made the mistake of choosing the prior year's figure (as you would for a sole trader) when in fact a company uses its anticipated profit figure for the current year."

(a) Corporation tax – year ended 31 March 2026

Corporation tax liability: (£1,600,000 × 25%)	£400,000

(b) Instalments due

Each instalment = (£400,000 ÷ 4)	£100,000
Payment dates:	
14 October 2025	£100,000
14 January 2026	£100,000
14 April 2026	£100,000
14 July 2026	£100,000

(c) The corporation tax must be paid electronically.

Tutorial note

1 *Remember that the instalments start in the accounting period. They are due on the 14th day of months 7, 10, 13 and 16 after the start of an accounting period. You are only required to know how instalments will work for a 12 month period. The rules for instalments for short accounting periods are not examinable.*

2 *All limited companies must pay their corporation tax electronically.*

92 YELLOW LTD

Key answer tips

This is a short accounting period of eight months. The maximum AIA and WDA must be time apportioned but a first year allowance is not time apportioned.

Be careful with the short life assets. This question included a short life asset brought forward and the purchase of a short life asset, similar to a question in the June 2012 examination.

In the examiner's report, the examining team was disappointed that "the question stated that the asset should be treated as a short life asset but many candidates either ignored this and included it in the main pool or as a special rate pool item and calculated WDA at [6%] instead of [18%]".

(Note that the rates in this quote have been updated to the FY2025 rates, rather than those which were in force at the time the comment was made.)

Be careful with the disposal of the asset on which a 130% super deduction claim was made on purchase. The sales proceeds are not deducted from the main pool. Instead the sale proceeds are treated as a balancing charge.

Capital allowances – period ended 30 November 2025

	AIA	**Full expense**	**Main pool**	**SLA(1)**	**SLA(2)**	**Allowances**
	£	£	£	£	£	£
TWDV b/f			76,000	6,560		
Additions with AIA						
Machine – 1 May	750,000					
AIA (W)	(666,667)					666,667
					83,333	
P&M – 2 August	500,000					
AIA (W)	(0)					
Balance for full expensing		500,000				
FYA 100%		(500,000)				500,000
Disposal						
SLA (1)				(2,400)		
Furniture (BC)						(20,000)
			76,000	4,160	83,333	
Balancing allowance				(4,160)		4,160
WDA @ (18% × 8/12)			(9,120)			9,120
WDA @ (18% × 8/12)					(10,000)	10,000
			0			
TWDV c/f			66,880		73,333	
Total allowances						1,169,947

Working: Maximum AIA

Maximum AIA = £666,667 (£1,000,000 × 8/12).

The AIA is first allocated to the second-hand asset over the other addition of plant and machinery which qualifies for FYA.

Tutorial note

1 *The period is only eight months long. The maximum AIA and the WDA must be scaled down by multiplying by 8/12.*

2 *The treatment of short-life assets is as follows:*

- (i) *Each short-life asset is the subject of a separate computation.*
- (ii) *The AIA and WDAs are given under the normal rules. However, note that the business can choose the expenditure against which the AIA is matched.*
- (iii) *If the SLA expenditure is reduced by deducting the AIA, the WDA of 18% will be claimed on the remaining expenditure.*
- (iv) *If there is expenditure in excess of the maximum AIA, it will usually be advantageous for the AIA to be allocated against the main pool expenditure, rather than a short life asset. However, in this case the other main pool expenditure is new and so qualifies for full expensing, whereas the short life asset does not and so is allocated the AIA.*
- (v) *On disposal within eight years a balancing allowance is given or balancing charge arises. The election therefore will be advantageous if it is anticipated that a balancing allowance will arise.*

3 *The disposal of the furniture was of an asset on which the 130% super deduction was claimed. Therefore, the sales proceeds are automatically treated as a balancing charge.*

93 SCARLET LTD

Key answer tips

This question tests your knowledge of long periods of account. This has always been an examination favourite as it allows the examining team to test two sets of rules at once – normal and short accounting periods. As stated in the examiner's report on the December 2015 exam – "if a period of account exceeds 12 months, then the corporation tax MUST be calculated for two separate accounting periods."

The examining team stated in the corporation tax article that where there is a period exceeding 12 months:

"The calculations should be done with the two periods side by side in columnar format and a calculation for each period shown – the totals should not be added together. Care must be taken to ensure that income and expenditure goes into the correct period, especially when it relates to amounts that are in arrears or advance. Candidates are advised to check the recommended text to ensure they are aware of the correct method of allocating the different types of income and expenditure to the correct period".

Therefore, as advised by the examining team, always use a columnar layout as shown in this answer.

(a) Corporation tax computation – periods ended 30 June 2026

	y/e 31 March 2026	3 m/e 30 June 2026
	£	£
Adjusted profit		
(£1,400,500 × 12/15)	1,120,400	
(£1,400,500 × 3/15)		280,100
Less: Capital allowances (W) (Note 3)	(144,000)	(29,520)
Tax adjusted trading profit	976,400	250,580
Property income (12:3)	84,000	21,000
Chargeable gain (Note 4)	28,000	
(£4,000 – £5,000) = £1,000 capital loss c/f		0
Total profits	1,088,400	271,580
Less: Qualifying charitable donation (Note 5)		(8,000)
Taxable total profits	1,088,400	263,580
Corporation tax liability (Note 6) (25%)	272,100	65,895

(b) Due dates of payment

Year ended 31 March 2026	1 January 2027
3 months ended 30 June 2026	1 April 2027

(c) Corporation tax return filing date

A return should be prepared for each period but both will have the same filing date of 30 June 2027 (i.e. 12 months after the end of the period of account).

Tutorial note

The notes below explain some of the key points to remember when compiling a corporation tax computation. The parts in quotation marks are quotes from the examining team's corporation tax article.

1 *A long period of account must be split into two accounting periods (Aps) as follows:*

AP1: First 12 months

AP2: Balance period

No other split is permitted.

2 *The income and gains for the long period must be allocated as follows:*

Adjusted trading profit is time apportioned.

Separate computations for each accounting period are required for capital allowances. These should be deducted from the adjusted profit AFTER it has been split into two periods.

Interest income is allocated on an accruals basis.

Property income is time apportioned (where accruals information is not available).

Chargeable gains are allocated according to the date of disposal and qualifying charitable donations according to the date of payment.

3 *Capital allowances must be deducted in the correct place in the computation.*

"If capital allowances are not already deducted from the trading income figure given, but are given separately, then these must be deducted from the trading profit and not from any other income. If they are deducted elsewhere in the assessment no mark will be awarded for the deduction".

4 *Allowable capital losses can only be set against chargeable gains and no other income.*

"If capital losses are given, either for the same period or carried forward from an earlier period, then these losses must be deducted from the aggregate gains to give a net chargeable gains figure. Once again if capital losses are deducted from the wrong income full marks cannot be awarded. Candidates should note that companies are not entitled to the annual exempt amount".

"A common mistake made by candidates is to deduct capital allowances from capital gains – this is wrong as they are totally different areas. Chargeable gains are the profits on the sale of capital assets, whereas capital allowances are 'tax depreciation' on capital assets held by a company – they should not be mixed together."

5 *Companies pay qualifying charitable donations gross so no grossing up is required. They are labelled as qualifying charitable donations in the corporation tax computation. They should be deducted from total profits after current year and brought forward trade and property losses.*

6 *For the year ended 31 March 2026, the augmented profits (here, equal to taxable total profits) are above £250,000, therefore the rate applicable is 25%. For the three-month period ended 30 June 2026, the augmented profits (taxable total profits) are above the reduced upper limit of £62,500 (£250,000 × 3/12). Therefore the rate applicable is also 25%.*

Working: Capital allowances

	Main pool
12 months to 31 March 2026	£
TWDV b/f	800,000
WDA @ 18%	(144,000)
	656,000
3 months to 30 June 2026	
WDA @ (18% × 3/12)	(29,520)
	626,480

Tutorial note

The WDA for the three-month period must be time apportioned by multiplying by 3/12.

94 FGV LTD

Key answer tips

This question covers an adjustment to profits and calculation of taxable total profits. There are brought forward capital and trading losses to deal with, and these must be deducted at the correct stage in the computation.

This is a time pressured question so do not spend too long thinking about each item.

Corporation tax payable for the year ended 31 March 2026

	£	£
Tax adjusted trading profit (W)		248,800
Non-trading interest – receivable	15,000	
– payable	(4,000)	
	———	11,000
Chargeable gain	82,000	
Capital loss brought forward	(17,000)	
	———	65,000
		———
Total profits		324,800
Trading loss brought forward		(39,000)
		———
Total profits after loss relief		285,800
Qualifying charitable donation		(1,500)
		———
Taxable total profits		284,300
		———
Corporation tax payable		
£284,300 × 25% (Note 5)		71,075
		———

Dividends received are not taxable.

Tutorial note

The notes below explain some of the key points to remember when compiling a corporation tax computation. The parts in quotation marks are quotes from the examining team's corporation tax article.

1 *Interest income should be included as one figure in the corporation tax computation. "Non-trade interest payable must be pooled with interest received to give one net figure. This is then included in the corporation tax assessment as 'interest income'. Failure to net the figures together and, thus, show two separate figures in the assessment will result in the loss of marks".*

2 *Allowable capital losses can only be set against chargeable gains and no other income.*

"If capital losses are given, either for the same period or carried forward from an earlier period, then these losses must be deducted from the aggregate gains to give a net chargeable gains figure. Once again if capital losses are deducted from the wrong income full marks cannot be awarded. Candidates should note that companies are not entitled to the annual exempt amount".

3 *Trading losses brought forward are offset against total profits (before QCDs). The claim can specify the amount of the loss to offset. Property losses brought forward are offset at the same point, and again the amount to offset can be specified. Note that where you show the loss set off in the corporation tax computation is very important and although the answer would not change, it would be incorrect to show the loss relief anywhere else other than directly below total profits (before QCDs).*

4 *Companies pay qualifying charitable donations gross so no grossing up is required. They are labelled as qualifying charitable donations in the corporation tax computation. They should be deducted from total profits after current year and brought forward trade and property losses.*

5 *Dividends received are not taxable but non-group dividends do increase augmented profits.*

Working: Tax adjusted trading profit

	£
Profit before income taxes	290,000
Deduct:	
Dividends	(18,000)
Non-trading interest	(15,000)
Add back:	
Depreciation	42,000
Salaries	0
Director's remuneration	0
Interest on loans – to buy a machine	0
– to buy an investment property	4,000
Donation to a national charity	1,500
Gifts to customers – mouse mats	0
– wine	5,000
Entertainment of customers	2,000
Adjusted profits before capital allowances	311,500
Less: Capital allowances	(62,700)
Tax adjusted trading profits	248,800

Tutorial note

1 *Dividends are not taxable income so if they have been credited in arriving at the accounting profit they should be removed by deducting them.*

2 *Bank interest received is a non-trade item. It should be removed from the accounting profits by deducting it. The interest receivable will then be included as income in the calculation of TTP.*

3 *The salaries, director's remuneration and loan interest to buy a machine are all for trade purposes so need no adjustment. However, it is good practice to note them as it shows the marker you have not just forgotten these items. The instruction in this question requires this, so marks would be lost if not noted like this.*

4 *Interest paid on the loan to buy an investment property is non-trade related and must be added back to trade profits. It can then be deducted from the non-trade interest receivable in calculating TTP.*

5 *The donation to a national charity is added back and allowed as a qualifying charitable donation in calculating TTP.*

6 *Gifts to customers costing no more than £50 per person and carrying a conspicuous advertisement for the business are tax allowable. However, gifts of food, drink and tobacco are not allowable.*

Examiner's report

This was a now familiar 15-mark question on corporation tax examining many common items, all of which have been examined on several occasions and, on this occasion, it examined the adjustment of trading profits for tax purposes.

The main problem here was that several candidates did not do as requested in the question requirements. The question clearly stated that the profit was to be adjusted by starting with the [profit before income taxes] figure of £290,000 and be adjusted accordingly, indicating with a zero any items that were not to be adjusted.

On a positive note many candidates knew which items had to be adjusted. The two items causing most problems were the interest payments and the gifts to customers.

Interest payments for loans where the capital has been used to purchase items used in the business can be deducted from trading profits whereas payments of interest where the capital is used to purchase items used for investment must be deducted from non-trading income and shown in the main corporation tax calculation. Therefore, in this case, £5,000 should have remained unadjusted and £4,000 added back to the profit figure.

Gifts of alcohol, food and tobacco to customers are never allowed as deductions from profit and £5,000 should have been added back. Other gifts are allowed if they are less than £50 per recipient and have a conspicuous advertisement for the donor and therefore £2,000 should have been left unadjusted.

The calculation of the corporation tax needed to show the calculation of the non-trading interest (including the amount added back to the trading profit) and the correct use of the two losses. Capital losses must be deducted from capital gains only and trading losses brought forward must be deducted from total income before the deduction of qualifying charitable donations (again, on this occasion, the donation that was added back to the trading profit).

Finally, many candidates did not state, as was required by the question, that the dividend received was not taxable.

ACCA Marking scheme	
	Marks
Tax adjusted trading profit	0.5
Non-trading interest received	1.0
Non-trading interest paid	1.0
Chargeable gain	1.0
Capital loss brought forward	1.0
Trading loss brought forward	1.0
Qualifying charitable deduction	1.0
Corporation tax payable	1.0
Dividends received not taxable	1.0
Adjustment of profits:	
Dividends	0.5
Non-trading interest	0.5
Depreciation	0.5
Salaries	0.5
Director's remuneration	0.5
Interest on loan – machine	0.5
Interest on loan – investment property	0.5
Donation to national charity	0.5
Gifts to customers – mouse mats	0.5
Gifts to customers – wine	0.5
Entertaining customers	0.5
Capital allowances	1.0
Total	**15.0**

95 ZVC LTD (ADAPTED)

Key answer tips

This is a good revision question covering a number of mainstream corporation tax areas, including the calculation of a chargeable gain for a company and the use of various losses brought forward.

It is important to calculate each type of income included in the corporation tax computation separately, either in a working or on the face of the computation.

Losses must be offset at the correct stage and against the correct income or gains.

Corporation tax computation – year ended 31 March 2026

	£	£
Tax adjusted trading profit		80,000
Non-trade interest (Note 1)	11,000	
Amount receivable for March 2026	1,000	
	———	12,000
Property income	14,000	
Amount for March 2025	(2,000)	
Amount receivable for March 2026	3,000	
	———	15,000
Chargeable gain (working)	126,440	
Capital loss brought forward (Note 2)	(22,000)	
	———	104,440
		———
Total profits		211,440
Less: Property loss b/f (Note 3)		(5,000)
Less: Trading loss b/f (Note 3)		(42,000)
		———
Total profits after loss relief		164,440
Less: Qualifying charitable donation (Note 4)		(3,500)
		———
Taxable total profits		160,940
		———

Corporation tax (Note 5)

	£
(£160,940 × 25%)	40,235
Less: Marginal relief	
(250,000 – 160,940) × 3/200	(1,336)
	———
	38,899
	———
Due date of payment	1 January 2027

Tutorial note

The notes below explain some of the key points to remember when compiling a corporation tax computation. The parts in quotation marks are quotes from the examining team's corporation tax article.

1 *Non-trade interest income must be shown in the computation as one figure. It is calculated as non-trade interest receivable less non-trade interest payable. The figures must be calculated using the accruals basis including amounts due or owed at the year end.*

"Non-trade interest payable must be pooled with interest received to give one net figure. This is then included in the corporation tax assessment as 'interest income'. Failure to net the figures together and, thus, show separate figures in the assessment will result in the loss of marks".

2 *Allowable capital losses can only be set against chargeable gains and no other income.*

"If capital losses are given, either for the same period or carried forward from an earlier period, then these losses must be deducted from the aggregate gains to give a net chargeable gains figure. Once again if capital losses are deducted from the wrong income full marks cannot be awarded. Candidates should note that companies are not entitled to the annual exempt amount".

3 *Trading losses brought forward are offset against total profits (before QCDs). The claim can specify the amount of the loss to offset. Property losses brought forward are offset at the same point, and again the amount to offset can be specified. Note that where you show the loss set off in the corporation tax computation is very important and although the answer would not change, it would be incorrect to show the loss relief anywhere else other than directly below total profits (before QCDs).*

4 *Companies pay qualifying charitable donations gross so no grossing up is required. They are labelled as qualifying charitable donations in the corporation tax computation and are deducted in the period when paid, not on an accruals basis. They should be deducted from total profits after current year and brought forward trade and property losses.*

5 *Marginal relief applies as augmented profits (here, equal to taxable total profits) are between the lower and upper limits of £50,000 and £250,000.*

Working: Chargeable gain

	£
Proceeds	400,000
Less: Cost	(100,000)
Costs of acquisition	(20,000)
Extension	(51,920)
Unindexed gain	228,080
Less: Indexation allowance	
(0.847 × £120,000 (£100,000 + £20,000))	(101,640)
Chargeable gain	126,440

Tutorial note

In the corporation tax article the examining team stated that in relation to chargeable gains for a company:

"The figures for chargeable gains and losses will usually be given in the question. On occasion, however, the question may require the candidate to calculate the gain. In a typical question this calculation will be a basic gain – technical calculations will be examined in a separate question. Candidates are reminded that for assets purchased prior to December 2017 companies get a deduction for inflation, called indexation allowance.

In order to enable the gain to be calculated indexation factors will always be given – not retail price indexes".

Examiner's report

This was the 15-mark question on corporation tax examining many common items, all of which have been examined on several occasions.

Candidates should be aware of the accruals basis on which both the interest and business property income are assessed. This means that the full amount due for the current period should be included in the tax assessment, therefore, any receipts in the current period that relate to a different period must be deducted and any amounts not received that relate to the current period must be added.

Knowledge of the [new] loss relief rules was limited. The [new] rules allow both trade losses and business property losses brought forward to be deducted from total income, before qualifying charitable donations. Capital losses must still be deducted from capital gains only. Full marks cannot be awarded if the losses are deducted from the wrong income.

Most candidates calculated the capital gain correctly. *[The other comments regarding the gain are not relevant due to changes in the way gains for companies are now examined.]*

It was disappointing that many candidates also missed out on an easy mark for the date of payment by not stating the date even though it was required by the question.

ACCA Marking scheme

	Marks
Tax adjusted trading profit	0.5
Non-trading interest	0.5
Amount receivable for March 2026	1.0
Business property income	0.5
Amount for March 2025	1.0
Amount receivable for March 2026	1.0
Capital loss brought forward	1.0
Trading loss brought forward	1.0
Property loss brought forward	1.0
Qualifying charitable deduction	0.5
Corporation tax at main rate	1.0
Marginal relief	1.5
Due date of payment	1.0
Chargeable gain:	
Proceeds	0.5
Cost	0.5
Costs of acquisition	0.5
Extension	0.5
Indexation allowance (on cost and costs of acquisition)	1.5
Total	**15.0**

96 POPPY LTD

Key answer tips

This question covers an examination favourite topic of a long period of account. This must be split into two accounting periods of 12 months and then the balance. As stated in the examiner's report on the December 2016 exam – "if a period of account exceeds 12 months, then the corporation tax MUST be calculated for two separate accounting periods."

The examining team have stated in the corporation tax article that where there is a period exceeding 12 months:

"The calculations should be done with the two periods side by side in columnar format and a calculation for each period shown – the totals should not be added together. Care must be taken to ensure that income and expenditure goes into the correct period, especially when it relates to amounts that are in arrears or advance. Candidates are advised to check the recommended text to ensure they are aware of the correct method of allocating the different types of income and expenditure to the correct period".

Therefore, as advised by the examining team, always use a columnar layout as shown in this answer.

Part (b) covers the rule for the offset of allowable capital losses and its application and impact in a long period of account question.

(a) Corporation tax – periods ended 31 May 2026

	y/e 31 March 2026	**2 m/e 31 May 2026**
	£	£
Adjusted profit: £1,316,000 (12:2)	1,128,000	188,000
Less: Capital allowances (W1) (Note 3)	(192,900)	(108,683)
Tax adjusted trading profit	935,100	79,317
Interest income (W2)	11,000	3,000
Chargeable gain	219,900	0
Taxable total profits	1,166,000	82,317
Corporation tax liability:		
£1,166,000/£82,317 × 25%	291,500	20,579

Tutorial note

The notes below explain some of the key points to remember when compiling a corporation tax computation. The parts in quotation marks are quotes from the examining team's corporation tax article.

1 *A long period of account must be split into two accounting periods (APs) as follows:*

AP1: First 12 months

AP2: Balance period

No other split is permitted.

2 *The income and gains for the long period must be allocated as follows:*

Adjusted profit is time apportioned.

Separate computations for each accounting period are required for capital allowances. These should be deducted from the adjusted profit AFTER it has been split into two periods.

Interest income is allocated on an accruals basis.

Property income is time apportioned (where accruals information is not available).

Chargeable gains are allocated according to date of disposal, and qualifying charitable donations (there are none of those in this scenario) according to the date of payment.

3 *Capital allowances have to be calculated in this answer, and then must be deducted in the correct place in the computation.*

"If capital allowances are not already deducted from the trading income figure given, but are given separately, then these must be deducted from the trading profit and not from any other income. If they are deducted elsewhere in the assessment no mark will be awarded for the deduction".

The short AP affects the capital allowances computation. The maximum AIA and the WDA are time apportioned by multiplying by 2/12.

4 *The main rate of 25% applies to both periods. The augmented profits (here, taxable total profits) of the first 12- month period exceed the upper limit of £250,000. The upper limit is time apportioned for the short two-month period to £41,667 (£250,000 × 2/12) and so again augmented profits exceed this.*

Workings

(W1) Capital allowances

	AIA	Main pool	Allowances
	£	£	£
12 m/e ended 31 March 2026			
TWDV b/f		205,000	
Additions with AIA:			
Machine	156,000		
Less: AIA	(156,000)		156,000
	0		
WDA @ 18%		(36,900)	36,900
TWDV c/f		168,100	
Total allowances			192,900
Period ended 31 May 2026			
Additions with AIA:			
Machine	104,000		
Less: AIA (< limit £1m × 2/12)	(104,000)		104,000
	0		
Disposal (lower of cost/proceeds)		(12,000)	
		156,100	
WDA @ (18% × 2/12)		(4,683)	4,683
TWDV c/f		151,417	
Total allowances			108,683

(W2) Interest income

	y/e 31 March 2026	2 m/e 31 May 2026
	£	£
Bank interest receivable		
(£20,000 – £8,000 + £9,000)	21,000	
(£14,000 – £9,000)		5,000
Less: Interest payable		
(£1,000 × 10)	(10,000)	
(£1,000 × 2)		(2,000)
Interest income	11,000	3,000

Tutorial note

Non-trade interest income must be shown in the computation as one figure. It is calculated as non-trade interest receivable less non-trade interest payable. The figures must be calculated using the accruals basis including amounts due or owed at the year end.

The December 2017 examiner's report noted that in a question involving a 15-month period of account for a company "Most candidates were aware that two calculations were needed, one for the first 12 months and another for the remaining 3 months. Unfortunately, several candidates had problems with the allocation of interest payments and the calculation of capital allowances.

Interest receipts and payments relating to non-trade issues must be allocated on an accruals basis, i.e. to the period they apply to, (not the period they are necessarily paid or received) and must be netted together".

(b) Amount carried forward as at 31 May 2026:

Capital loss c/f: £10,000

Tutorial note

Despite there being a chargeable gain and an allowable capital loss in the same financial accounting period, the gain and the loss fall into different accounting periods for corporation tax purposes.

The gain arises in the first accounting period and the loss in the second accounting period.

Capital losses cannot be carried back and set against previous chargeable gains.

Therefore, the capital loss can only be carried forward and set against future chargeable gains.

97 FIRES LTD

Key answer tips

This question just covers the capital allowances computation as applicable to a company.

The capital allowances computation has a twist in that the costs and proceeds were given including VAT. Capital allowances are available on the cost of plant and machinery to the company.

For all items, except cars (where VAT is irrecoverable), the cost on which capital allowances can be claimed is the VAT-exclusive price.

Therefore, the VAT must be deducted from the VAT-inclusive cost of the additions, except the car, and from the proceeds of sale of the machine.

Capital allowances – year ended 31 March 2026

	AIA	Main pool	Special rate pool	Allowances
		£	£	£
TWDV b/f		124,000		
Addition with no AIA/FYA:				
Car > 50g/km			16,000	
Additions with AIA:				
Machine (£35,880 × 5/6)	29,900			
Computer (£9,360 × 5/6)	7,800			
	37,700			
Less: AIA	(37,700)			37,700
	0			
Disposal (lower of cost/proceeds):				
Machine (£24,000 × 5/6)		(20,000)		
		104,000	16,000	
WDA @ 18%		(18,720)		18,720
WDA @ 6%			(960)	960
TWDV c/f		85,280	15,040	
Total allowances				57,380

Tutorial note

1 *VAT can be reclaimed on the machine and the computer. Therefore, the VAT must be excluded from the cost for capital allowances. VAT cannot be reclaimed on a car unless it is used 100% for business purposes. In the December 2017 examiner's report, it was noted that "Candidates should have known that VAT in relation to the purchase of cars, can never be reclaimed if there is any private use at all. Therefore, the starting point for calculating WDA is the VAT-inclusive cost....".*

2 *Disposals are deducted at the lower of cost and proceeds. In this question the cost figure is lower than the proceeds. Both the cost and the proceeds figures include VAT so this must be removed from whichever figure is used.*

3 *In the June 2017 examiner's report it was noted that "The distinction between inclusive and exclusive is a point that many students have trouble understanding". To find the net of VAT figure you multiply the VAT-inclusive figure by 100/120. This fraction is usually simplified to 5/6.*

4 *When dealing with a company capital allowances computation, remember that private use of a car by an employee is irrelevant. The employee is taxed using the employment income benefit rules. The company is using the car 100% in its business.*

5 *The car has CO_2 emissions which exceed 50g/km so it must be placed in the special rate pool and only given WDA at 6%.*

98 RADIATORS LTD

Key answer tips

This is a reasonably straightforward question as none of the figures require adjustment; they just need to be slotted into the correct place in the corporation tax computation.

Remember that the examining team are particularly keen on figures being presented in the correct place to obtain maximum marks.

Don't miss the easy marks for administration in parts (b) and (c).

(a) Corporation tax computation – year ended 31 March 2026

	£	£
Tax adjusted trading profit		1,540,000
Interest received	8,000	
Less: Interest paid on a non-trading loan	(3,000)	
Interest income (Note)		5,000
Chargeable gain		23,000
Total profits		1,568,000
Less: Qualifying charitable donation		(4,000)
Taxable total profits		1,564,000

Corporation tax liability:

	£
(£1,564,000 × 25%)	391,000

Tutorial note

The interest paid is for non-trade purposes and is deducted from the interest received in calculating the TTP.

(b) Due dates of payment

Radiators Ltd has taxable total profits of £1,564,000. As this exceeds £1,500,000 and the company had profits exceeding this threshold in the previous year, then it must pay tax by quarterly instalments.

Quarterly instalments of £97,750 each (£391,000/4), are due on 14 October 2025, 14 January 2026, 14 April 2026 and 14 July 2026.

(c) Due date for return

31 March 2027, i.e. 12 months from the end of the accounting period.

99 STEM LTD

Key answer tips

This question tests the often-examined topic of a capital allowances computation as it applies to companies.

Capital allowances computation

	AIA	Full expense	Main pool	Special rate pool	Allowances
	£	£	£	£	£
TWDV b/f			310,000	90,000	
Additions not qualifying for AIA:					
Car > 50g/km				20,000	
Additions qualifying for AIA:					
Special rate pool – Lift	521,750				
Less: AIA (W1)	(521,750)				521,750
				0	
Additions qualifying for AIA (main pool):					
Machine	300,000				
Less: AIA (W1)	(228,250)				228,250
Balance for full expensing		71,750			
FYA 100% full expensing		(71,750)			71,750
Disposals:					
Lift – balancing charge (W2)					(18,750)
Lift – remaining proceeds (W2)				(81,250)	
Plant (lower of cost and proceeds)			(4,000)		
			306,000	28,750	
WDA @ (18% × 9/12)			(41,310)		41,310
WDA @ (6% × 9/12)				(1,294)	1,294
TWDV c/f			264,690	27,456	
Capital allowances					845,604

Workings

(W1) Maximum AIA and amount claimed

Maximum AIA: £1,000,000 × 9/12 = £750,000. This is allocated first to the special rate pool expenditure.

(W2) Disposal of lift on which 50% FYA claimed

Balancing charge = £100,000 × 150,000/400,000 × 50% = £18,750.

Remaining proceeds = £100,000 – £18,750 = £81,250.

Tutorial note

1 *The period is only nine months long so the maximum AIA and the WDA must be time apportioned by multiplying by 9/12.*

2 *AIA should be allocated to any special rate pool items (but not cars which do not qualify for AIA) before allocating to main pool items. This is because otherwise the new SRP items get an FYA of 50% whereas new main pool items get an FYA of 100% (full expensing).*

3 *Cars with CO_2 emissions exceeding 50g/km must be put into the special rate pool column and will only receive WDA at 6%.*

4 *The machine purchased on 7 October is bought on hire purchase. This does not affect the availability of capital allowances. These are available based on the cash cost of the machine, as for any normal purchase. The interest cost (£10,000) is not a capital cost, so does not qualify for capital allowances, but gets relief as a trade expense.*

5 *Where plant is sold for more than cost, the proceeds deducted are restricted to the original cost.*

6 *There is a special treatment for disposal of an item on which the 50% FYA has been claimed. The FYA was claimed on only a proportion of the original cost of the old lift. A balancing charge arises of 50% of that proportion of the proceeds. The remaining proceeds (proceeds less balancing charge) are deducted from the special rate pool.*

100 BROOKSIDE LTD

Corporation tax computation – 10-month period ended 31 March 2026

	£	£
Tax adjusted trading profit		65,000
Property income		8,000
Non-trade interest receivable		2,000
Chargeable gain		7,000
Total profits		82,000
Less: Qualifying charitable donation (Note 1)		(2,000)
Taxable total profits		80,000

Corporation tax liability:

	£
£80,000 × 25%	20,000
Less: Marginal relief (Note 3)	
(£104,167 – £95,000) × 3/200 × (£80,000/£95,000)	(116)
	19,884

Working: Augmented profits and limits	£
Taxable total profits	80,000
Add: Dividends received (Note 3)	15,000
Augmented profits	95,000
Lower limit: (£50,000/2) × 10/12 (Note 2)	20,833
Upper limit: (£250,000/2) × 10/12 (Note 2)	104,167
Marginal relief is applicable (Note 3)	

Tutorial note

1 *Companies pay qualifying charitable donations gross so no grossing up is required. They are labelled as qualifying charitable donations in the corporation tax computation. They should be deducted on a paid basis from total profits.*

2 *The upper and lower limits for determining corporation tax rates are reduced for a short accounting period. They are also divided by the number of associated companies – here two, including Brookside Ltd itself. Companies are associated with each other if one company controls the other or they are both under common control, which is established by the shareholding being over 50%.*

3 *Dividends are not taxable but they are included in the calculation of augmented profits used to determine the rate of corporation tax payable. As augmented profits here are between the upper and lower limits, marginal relief applies.*

CORPORATION TAX LOSSES

101 LOSSMAKER LTD

Key answer tips

This question is a straightforward test of knowledge.

The loss relief rules are important and need to be learnt. Make sure you give sufficient detail and state exactly which type of income can be relieved and in which periods.

Company trading loss relief

The trading loss can be relieved as follows:

(i) **Current period claim**

An election can be made to set the trading loss against total profits i.e. all other sources of income and gains before qualifying charitable donations (QCDs) in the same accounting period, i.e. the year ended 31 December 2025. This is an all or nothing claim, therefore any QCDs may be wasted.

The claim must be made within two years of the end of the loss-making period, i.e. by 31 December 2027.

(ii) **Carry forward**

Alternatively, an election can be made to carry forward the trade loss.

The losses carried forward will be relieved against future total profits before QCDs. The claim must specify the amount of loss offset and the period in which it is relieved and must be made within two years of the end of the accounting period in which the loss is relieved.

Tutorial note

When losses are carried forward it is not necessary to claim the maximum possible relief. So an amount of loss relief may be specified that preserves relief for the QCDs.

Contrast this with a current period and prior period claims which are all or nothing claims against total profits before QCDs and therefore potentially waste relief for QCDs.

102 LGT LTD

Key answer tips

This question is testing your knowledge of the reliefs available to a company which suffers a trading loss. Note that as the company has ceased trading the trading loss can be carried back 36 months instead of the usual 12 months.

Always use a columnar layout when dealing with losses.

Loss relief for four years ended 31 December 2025

	Year ended 31 December			
	2022	**2023**	**2024**	**2025**
	£	£	£	£
Trading profit	40,000	20,000	17,000	
Chargeable gain			7,000	
Capital loss carried forward			(7,000)	
Total profits	40,000	20,000	17,000	0
Less: Trading loss relief carried back	(25,000)	(20,000)	(17,000)	
	15,000	0	0	0
Less: Qualifying charitable donation	(3,000)		Unused	
Taxable total profits	12,000	0	0	0
Capital loss unused			1,000	

Loss memorandum

	£
Trading loss for year ended 31 December 2025	62,000
Less: Carry back relief (terminal loss)	
y/e 31 December 2024	(17,000)
y/e 31 December 2023	(20,000)
y/e 31 December 2022 (balance)	(25,000)
Loss unused	0

Tutorial note

When a company ceases to trade, the normal 12 month carry back period is extended to 36 months.

The trading loss is carried back on a LIFO basis (i.e. the total profits of the most recent year are relieved first, and then the previous year and so on) until either the loss is used up, or the total profits of the previous 36 months are covered.

The trading loss is deducted from total profits before qualifying charitable donations.

Examiner's report

This was a five-mark question on the claiming of loss relief by a company.

Unfortunately, this question was poorly answered with most candidates not knowing what income losses could be set against.

Firstly, a common error made in several past examinations, capital losses can only be set off against capital gains and therefore the capital loss in the year to 31 December 2023 should have been carried forward to offset against the gain in the year ended 31 December 2024 reducing it to nil. The remaining loss of £1,000 remained unused and should have been noted as per the question requirement.

On cessation of business, a company can carry back the trading loss of the last 12 months against total profits, before qualifying charitable payments (QCDs), of the three previous years on a LIFO basis. Hence £17,000 should have been used in the year ended 31 December 2024, £20,000 in the year ended 31 December 2023 and the remaining £25,000 in the year ended 31 December 2022. No trading loss remained.

The QCD in the year ended 31 December 2022 reduced the remaining profits to £12,000 but the QCD in the year ended 31 December 2024 was wasted (unused).

ACCA Marking scheme	
	Marks
Trading profit	0.5
Capital loss offset against gain	1.0
Trading loss carried back	1.5
Qualifying charitable donation	1.0
Taxable total profits	0.5
Capital loss unused	0.5
Total	**5.0**

103 BLUE LTD

Key answer tips

This question asks you to relieve the trading loss at the earliest opportunity. This means you should make a current year claim followed by a claim to carry the loss back 12 months.

The loss can then be carried forward against future total profits.

The fact that the period following the loss-making year is less than 12 months has no effect.

(a) Trading loss relief

	Y/e 31 Mar 2025	**Y/e 31 Mar 2026**	**P/e 31 Dec 2026**
	£	£	£
Tax adjusted trading profit	20,000	0	40,000
Property income	9,000	12,000	12,000
Chargeable gain	10,000		
Total profits	39,000	12,000	52,000
Less: Trading loss			
– Current year		(12,000)	
– Carried back	(39,000)		
– Brought forward			(50,000)
Less: Qualifying charitable donations	wasted	wasted	(2,000)
Taxable total profits	0	0	0

Trading Loss memo		£
Year ended 31 March 2026		180,000
Year ended 31 March 2026	– current year	(12,000)
Year ended 31 March 2025	– carry back	(39,000)
Period ended 31 December 2026	– carry forward	(50,000)
Loss c/f		79,000

(b) Corporation tax refund

Before the loss carry back, the taxable total profits for the year ended 31 March 2025 would have been £37,000 (total profits of £39,000 less qualifying charitable donations of £2,000).

The small profits rate applies as these profits are below the lower limit. The corporation tax saving is therefore £7,030 (£37,000 × 19%).

Tutorial note

When a company wishes to claim trading losses against total profits of the previous 12 months, they must first make a claim against total profits of the loss-making accounting period.

The loss of the year ending 31 March 2026 can be carried back 12 months against the profits before qualifying charitable donations of the year ended 31 March 2025.

For a current and prior year loss relief claim the amount of the loss relieved cannot be restricted for example to preserve relief for QCDs. In comparison, a loss carry forward claim can specify the amount of the loss to be offset. In this case it has been restricted to £50,000 to ensure that relief for the QCDs is not wasted.

104 BULB LTD

Key answer tips

This question covers all the usual points about corporation tax computations.

It also contains the treatment of both trading and non-trading losses (i.e. capital losses and property losses) brought forward. Interest income, involving both interest receivable and payable, is also tested.

Make sure you deduct the losses in the appropriate place in the computation to obtain maximum marks.

Corporation tax computation – year ended 31 March 2026

	£	£
Tax adjusted trading profit		600,000
Rental income (£18,000 + £2,000 accrued) (Note 1)		20,000
Non-trade interest receivable	20,000	
Less: Non-trade interest payable	(4,000)	
Interest income (Note 2)		16,000
Chargeable gain	10,000	
Less: Capital loss b/f (Note 3)	(3,000)	
		7,000
Total profits		643,000
Less: Property loss brought forward (Note 4)		(5,000)
Less: Trading loss b/f (Note 4)		(220,000)
		418,000
Less: Qualifying charitable donations (Note 5)		(6,000)
Taxable total profits		412,000
		£
Corporation tax liability:		
(£412,000 × 25%)		103,000

Tutorial note

The notes below explain some of the key points to remember when compiling a corporation tax computation. The parts in quotation marks are quotes from the examining team's corporation tax article.

1 *For a company property income is calculated using the accruals basis. The rent not paid until April, must be added to the rent already received.*

2 *Non-trade interest income must be shown in the computation as one figure. It is calculated as non-trade interest receivable less non-trade interest payable. The figures must be calculated using the accruals basis including amounts due or owed at the year end.*

"Non-trade interest payable must be pooled with interest received to give one net figure. This is then included in the corporation tax assessment as 'interest income'. Failure to net the figures together and, thus, show two separate figures in the assessment will result in the loss of marks".

3 *Allowable capital losses can only be set against chargeable gains and no other income.*

"If capital losses are given, either for the same period or carried forward from an earlier period, then these losses must be deducted from the aggregate gains to give a net chargeable gains figure. Once again if capital losses are deducted from the wrong income full marks cannot be awarded. Candidates should note that companies are not entitled to the annual exempt amount".

4 *Property losses and trading losses brought forward may be offset against future total profits. The amount of the loss offset can be restricted, but in this case you are told to offset the losses as soon as possible. Note that where you show the loss set off in the corporation tax computation is very important and although the answer would not change, it would be incorrect to show the loss relief anywhere else other than directly below total profits (before QCDs).*

5 *Companies pay qualifying charitable donations gross so no grossing up is required. They are labelled as qualifying charitable donations in the corporation tax computation. They should be deducted from total profits after current year and brought forward trade and property losses.*

CAPITAL GAINS: COMPANIES

Key answer tips

In the corporation tax article the examining team stated that in relation to chargeable gains for a company:

"the figures for chargeable gains and losses will usually be given in the question. On occasion, however, the question may require the candidate to calculate the gain. In a typical question this calculation will be a basic gain – technical calculations will be examined in a separate question. Candidates are reminded that for assets purchased prior to December 2017 companies get a deduction for inflation, called indexation allowance.

In order to enable the gain to be calculated indexation factors will always be given – not retail price indexes".

Remember that the indexation allowance has been frozen as at December 2017. In relation to reliefs available, the examining team have said that in the 15 mark corporation tax question in the examination "No reliefs such as rollover relief will be examined in the question – rollover relief and any other reliefs will be examined in a separate question".

105 ST LTD

Key answer tips

This question tests replacement of business assets relief (rollover relief). However, remember that the relief is modified when the reinvestment is in depreciating assets.

It is often useful to draw a timeline in your workings in chargeable gains questions so that you can see exactly when each event occurs.

Sale of factory – August 2015

	£
Chargeable gain before reliefs	50,000
Less: Rollover relief – gain deferred	(20,000)
Chargeable gain in August 2015 – proceeds not reinvested	30,000

Sale of fixed plant – year ended 31 March 2026

No gain can arise on the scrapping of the plant as there are no proceeds. In addition no capital loss is allowable as any fall in value will already have been claimed in a capital allowances computation.

As the fixed plant is a depreciating asset the £20,000 deferred gain becomes chargeable in July 2025 when the plant ceases to be used for the purposes of the trade.

The total gain chargeable in the chargeable accounting period ended 31 March 2026 is therefore £20,000.

Tutorial note

1 *Rollover relief is available where an individual or a company:*

- *disposes of a qualifying business asset, and*
- *replaces it with another qualifying business asset*
- *within 12 months before, and 36 months after the date of disposal.*

The qualifying assets do not have to be of the same type.

2 *If all of the sale proceeds are reinvested, the whole of the chargeable gain can be deferred. If not all of the sale proceeds are reinvested, the chargeable gain now is the*

- *lower of the chargeable gain, and*
- *sale proceeds not reinvested.*

The remaining gain can be deferred with a rollover relief claim.

3 *In this question the replacement asset is a depreciating asset which is one that has an expected useful life of 60 years or less.*

This means that the deferred gain of £20,000 is not deducted from the cost of the new asset but is deferred until the earliest of three events:

- *the new asset is sold or*
- *the new asset ceases to be used for business or*
- *ten years after the purchase of the new asset*

The first of these events that occurs is that the plant ceases to be used for the trade. This causes the deferred gain of £20,000 to be charged.

106 DOVE PLC

Key answer tips

This question tests the calculation of two chargeable gains for a company and the deferral of gains under rollover relief (relief for replacement of business assets).

Remember that rollover relief is the only chargeable gains relief that applies to companies and therefore more likely to be examined in this context.

(a) Chargeable gains – year to 31 December 2025

14 April 2025 – Factory

	£
Proceeds	230,000
Less: Cost	(140,000)
Unindexed gain	90,000
Less: Indexation allowance	
1.083 × £140,000 = 151,620 (restricted to £90,000)	(90,000)
Chargeable gain	0

Tutorial note

Indexation allowance cannot convert a gain into a loss. Where the indexation allowance is greater than the gain, the allowance is restricted to the value of the gain.

Indexation allowance is frozen as at December 2017.

17 September 2025 – Second factory

	£
Proceeds	280,000
Less: Cost	(80,000)
	200,000
Less: Indexation allowance	
0.489 × £80,000	(39,120)
Chargeable gain	160,880

(b) Deferring gains

The gain on the second factory can be rolled over. The factory which the company intends to buy is a qualifying asset for rollover relief purposes provided it is purchased within three years (i.e. by 17 September 2028).

The whole gain of £160,880 will be rolled over on a claim being made as all the proceeds from the sale of the factory are being reinvested.

The gain will be deducted from the base cost of the newly acquired factory. This will increase the gain on a future disposal of the replacement factory.

Tutorial note

1 *Rollover relief is available where an individual or a company:*

- *disposes of a qualifying business asset, and*
- *replaces it with another qualifying business asset*
- *within 12 months before, and 36 months after the date of disposal.*

The qualifying assets do not have to be of the same type.

2 *If all of the sale proceeds are reinvested, the whole of the chargeable gain can be deferred. If not all of the sale proceeds are reinvested, the chargeable gain now is the lower of:*

- *the chargeable gain, and*
- *sale proceeds not reinvested.*

The remaining gain can be deferred with a rollover relief claim.

107 BOX PLC

Key answer tips

In any question involving shares you should first apply the matching rules, then calculate the appropriate gains.

Matching rules

			Number of shares	
1	**Same day acquisitions**		0	
2	**Previous 9 days**			
	22 May 2025	Purchase		2,000
3	**Share pool**			
	26 May 2007	Purchase	6,000	
	24 October 2011	Purchase	5,000	
			———	11,000
				———
	26 May 2025	Disposal of all shares		13,000
				———

Chargeable gains – year to 31 March 2026

2,000 shares acquired within previous 9 days

	£	£
Proceeds (2,000/13,000 × £110,000)	16,923	
Less: Cost	(12,000)	
	———	
Chargeable gain		4,923
11,000 shares from share pool		
Proceeds (11,000/13,000 × £110,000)	93,077	
Less: Cost (W)	(51,500)	
	———	
Unindexed gain	41,577	
Less: Indexation allowance (£64,469 – £51,500) (W)	(12,969)	
	———	
Chargeable gain		28,608
		———
Total chargeable gains		33,531
		———

Working: Share pool

		Number	Cost	Indexed Cost
			£	£
26 May 2007	Acquisition	6,000	24,000	24,000
Indexed to October 2011 (£24,000 × 0.154)				3,696
24 October 2011	Acquisition	5,000	27,500	27,500
		11,000	51,500	55,196
Indexed to Dec 2017 (£55,196 × 0.168)				9,273
				64,469
26 May 2025	Disposal	(11,000)	(51,500)	(64,469)
		0	0	0

Tutorial note

Shares sold by a company are matched with shares:

1. *bought on the same day then*
2. *purchased in the previous 9 days then*
3. *from the share pool.*

In this example 2,000 of the shares sold on 26 May 2025 are matched with the shares bought within the previous 9 days on 22 May 2025.

The remaining shares come out of the share pool. In the pool you must apply indexation before adding or removing shares.

108 CRATE PLC

Key answer tips

Many chargeable gains questions involve a mix of assets. Chattels and part disposals are always popular assets in examination questions.

Chargeable gains – year to 31 March 2026

21 August 2025 – Painting	£	£
Proceeds (deemed)	6,000	
Less: Cost	(8,000)	
Allowable loss (Note 1)	———	(2,000)
12 January 2026 – Land		
Proceeds	380,000	
Less: Allowable cost (Note 2)		
£380,000/(£380,000 + £950,000) × £450,000	(128,571)	
	———	
Unindexed gain	251,429	
Less: Indexation allowance (£128,571 × 0.651) (Note 3)	(83,700)	
	———	167,729
14 February 2026 – Factory		
Proceeds	250,000	
Less: Selling costs	(25,000)	
	———	
	225,000	
Less: Cost (£80,000 + £5,000)	(85,000)	
Less: Improvements	(20,000)	
	———	
Unindexed gain	120,000	
Less: Indexation allowance		
Cost: (£85,000 × 0.489)	(41,565)	
Extension (Note 4)	0	
	———	78,435
		———
Total net chargeable gains		244,164
		———

Tutorial note

1 *Special loss rules apply for chattels when proceeds ≤ £6,000 and the cost > £6,000.*

The allowable capital loss is calculated assuming gross sale proceeds of £6,000.

Indexation allowance cannot increase a loss.

2 *Part disposals are popular in examination questions. The cost of the land sold must be found by applying the part disposal formula to the cost:*

Cost × A/A + B

Where A = gross sales proceeds, and

B = market value of the part of the asset kept.

The examining team have put in the number of hectares sold out of the total number of hectares purchased to tempt you into using those to split the cost instead!

3 *The indexation allowance is frozen at December 2017.*

4 *The extension must be indexed separately from the original expenditure as the expenditure was incurred on different dates. Expenditure on the extension was incurred after December 2017 and therefore does not qualify for the indexation allowance.*

109 PETAL LTD

Key answer tips

This question involves a share pool calculation for a company. Be careful as the disposal is only of part of the shares in the pool.

Share pool

		Shares	Cost	Indexed cost
			£	£
14 June 2007		1,000	3,000	3,000
Indexed to December 2017 (0.342 × £3,000)				1,026
		1,000	3,000	4,026
17 January 2021		3,000	10,000	10,000
		4,000	13,000	14,026
19 October 2025				
Disposal	(3,000/4,000 × £13,000)	(3,000)	(9,750)	
	(3,000/4,000 × £14,026)			(10,520)
Balance c/f after 19 October disposal		1,000	3,250	3,506

Tutorial note

In the pool you must remember to apply indexation (up to December 2017 at the latest) before adding or removing shares.

Not all the pool shares are sold so the cost and indexed cost of the shares sold is found as:

Cost = Number of shares sold/Number of shares in pool × Pool cost

Indexed cost = Number of shares sold/Number of shares in pool × Pool indexed cost.

110 NICHOLS PLC

Key answer tips

This question deals with a share disposal by a company.

There is a bonus issue. Simply add this to the number of shares in the pool and do not index to the date of the bonus issue.

Sale of shares from share pool

	£
Sale proceeds	37,000
Less: Cost (W1)	(9,000)
Unindexed gain	28,000
Less: Indexation allowance (W1)	
(£22,284 – £9,000)	(13,284)
Chargeable gain	14,716

Working: Share pool

Date	**Event**	**No**	**Cost**	**Indexed cost**
			£	£
25 March 1989	Acquisition	6,000	9,000	9,000
3 June 1993	Bonus (1 for 3)	2,000		
		8,000	9,000	9,000
	Indexation to December 2017 (£9,000 × 1.476)			13,284
		8,000	9,000	22,284
30 June 2025	Disposal	(8,000)	(9,000)	(22,284)

Tutorial note

No indexation is calculated up to the date of a bonus issue.

111 KJP LTD

Key answer tips

This question involves calculating gains on two factories and the consideration of rollover relief. Be careful to identify when rollover relief is available and whether it is available in full. There is no indexation available in this question as both factories were purchased after December 2017.

Chargeable gains

	Factory 1	Factory 2
	£	£
Proceeds	260,000	325,000
Cost	(210,000)	(280,000)
	50,000	45,000
Rollover relief (balancing amount)	(40,000)	
Gain (amount not reinvested	10,000	
Gain		45,000
Total chargeable gains (£10,000 + £45,000)		55,000

Tutorial note

The chargeable gain on factory 1 is the amount of proceeds not reinvested in the new factory, i.e. £260,000 – £250,000 = £10,000.

No rollover relief is available on Factory 2 because it is an investment property.

Examiner's report

This was a five-mark question on rollover relief with both business and non-business assets being sold. This question was well attempted with several candidates knowing that rollover relief was not available on non-business assets.

Two easy marks were available for basic calculations on the disposal of two factories, with the remaining marks being awarded for claiming the restricted rollover relief on the sale of the business asset. Candidates are reminded that the rollover relief is restricted by the amount of any proceeds not reinvested in another business asset, £10,000 in this case.

ACCA Marking scheme	
	Marks
Gains before relief	2.0
Rollover relief (balancing amount)	1.0
Chargeable gain on factory 1	1.0
Chargeable gain on factory 2	0.5
Total chargeable gains	0.5
	——
Total	**5.0**
	——

VALUE ADDED TAX

112 EMMA

Key answer tips

This is a typical VAT question, asking the student to prepare a calculation of VAT payable. The main area of concern may have been the irrecoverable debt relief. It is important to read the question carefully to determine whether the figures provided are inclusive or exclusive of VAT, in order to calculate the correct VAT figures.

In the June 2012 examiner's report in relation to a similar VAT return question, the examining team stated that the common mistakes were:

- Using the wrong rate of tax or using the fraction of 1/6 instead of 20%.
- Applying VAT at 20% to zero-rated supplies.
- Adding up all the VAT calculated instead of deducting the VAT on the expenses and inventory purchases (input tax) from the VAT (output tax) on the sales.

VAT payable for the period ended 31 March 2026

	£	£
Output VAT		
Standard-rated sales (£450,000 × 20%)		90,000
Discounts taken (£25,000 × 4% × 20%)		(200)
Zero-rated sales		0
		————
		89,800
Input VAT		
Inventory (£180,000 × 20%)	36,000	
Electricity (£40,000 × 1/6)	6,667	
Car expenses (£15,000 × 1/6)	2,500	
Irrecoverable debts (£1,200 × 20%)	240	
	————	(45,407)
		————
VAT payable		44,393
		————

Tutorial note

Where a prompt payment discount is offered output VAT is charged on the actual amount received, i.e. for the invoices which were settled within 30 days output VAT is due on the value of the sale less the 4% discount. However, the supplier will not know, when the invoice is raised, whether the customer will qualify for the discount by paying promptly. The supplier must therefore charge VAT on the invoice on the full price. If the discount is taken the supplier must then make an adjustment so that output tax is only accounted for on the amount received.

Irrecoverable debt relief is only available on debts over six months old, so relief cannot yet be claimed on the debt due on 13 October 2025.

To find the amount of VAT on a VAT-inclusive figure you multiply by 20/120. This fraction is usually simplified to 1/6.

113 MONTY

Key answer tips

Part (a) is a written question on VAT which includes the important late notification penalty. Part (b) requires examples of 'blocked' (also known as irrecoverable) VAT.

(a) VAT penalties

Late notification penalties are a percentage of the net VAT due from the date Monty should have been registered until the date when notification is made:

- The percentage is based on the standard penalty regime for late notification and incorrect returns which applies across all taxes.
- The penalty can range from 0% to 100% of the unpaid tax depending on the taxpayer's behaviour and whether disclosure is prompted or unprompted.

Tutorial note

You cannot calculate the amount of penalty as it is a % of the VAT due.

(b) Blocked VAT

VAT is blocked and therefore cannot be recovered on the following items:

- Cars not used 100% for business purposes
- Business entertainment except for staff and overseas customers.

> ***Tutorial note***
>
> *Input VAT can be recovered on entertainment of employees and overseas customers.*

114 OMAR

> **Key answer tips**
>
> This is a tricky written question on tax points. Tax points are also referred to as the time of supply.

(a) Tax points

The basic tax point is usually the earliest of the following dates:

The date of delivery	16 July 2025
The date of the invoice	20 July 2025
The date of payment	14 May 2025 (deposit) and 31 August 2025 (balance).

Therefore, the tax point for the deposit is 14 May 2025.

However, as regards the balance, the invoice date of 20 July 2025 applies as the invoice was issued within 14 days of the delivery date (the basic tax point).

> ***Tutorial note***
>
> *The basic tax point is the date of delivery of goods or the date of performance of services.*
>
> *However, if goods or services are paid for or a tax invoice is issued before the basic tax point, then the date of payment or the invoice date becomes the actual tax point date.*
>
> *If a part payment such as a deposit is paid in advance then there will be two tax points, one for the deposit and one for the balance of the supply.*
>
> *Where goods are not paid for or invoiced before the basic tax point, a later actual tax point can arise if a tax invoice is raised within 14 days after the basic tax point. This is referred to as the '14 day rule'.*

(b) If goods are supplied on a sale or return basis, the tax point is the earlier of the date of adoption by the customer or 12 months after the dispatch of the goods to the customer.

(c) For continuous supplies of services, the tax point is the earlier of the receipt of payment or the date of the VAT invoice.

115 YEE-LING

Key answer tips

Tax points are an important topic in VAT and the rules need to be learnt.

Part (c) of this question specifically asks you why they are important.

(a) Tax point (time of supply) for VAT

The basic tax point is the date the goods are dispatched or otherwise made available to the customer.

However, the basic tax point is overridden in the following circumstances:

(i) If an invoice is issued or payment is received before the goods are dispatched. In this case the earliest of these dates replaces the dispatch date.

(ii) If a tax point has not already arisen under (i) above and an invoice is issued within 14 days after the goods have been dispatched. The invoice date will then replace the dispatch date.

(b) Tax point for the transaction

The tax points for the transaction are therefore:

For the deposit of £400:	28 May 2025 (cash receipt)
For the balance of £2,600:	2 July 2025 (14 day rule)

(c) Importance of determining the correct tax point

Any one of the following is acceptable:

- To calculate the turnover for initial registration.
- To include the sale in the correct VAT return.
- To identify the correct rate of VAT (if there is a change).
- To identify the correct category of VAT (zero rate, reduced rate, standard rate or exempt – if there is a change).

Tutorial note

The basic tax point is the date of delivery of goods or the date of performance of services.

However, if goods or services are paid for or a tax invoice is issued before the basic tax point, then the date of payment or the invoice date becomes the actual tax point date.

If a part payment such as a deposit is paid in advance then there will be two tax points, one for the deposit and one for the balance of the supply.

Where goods are not paid for or invoiced before the basic tax point, a later actual tax point can arise if a tax invoice is raised within 14 days after the basic tax point. This is referred to as the '14 day rule'.

116 MARTHA

Key answer tips

This question covers VAT registration and recovery of pre-registration VAT.

It is important to make sure a business registers for VAT on time as otherwise a late notification penalty can be charged.

(a) Martha – Value added tax (VAT) registration

The VAT registration threshold is £90,000. Martha's taxable turnover will exceed this at the end of March 2026 (£15,100 × 6 months = £90,600). Martha must therefore notify HMRC within 30 days (i.e. 30 April 2026).

Martha will be registered from the first day of the second month following the month in which the £90,000 was exceeded (i.e. 1 May 2026) (or an earlier date, if requested).

Tutorial note

The historic registration test is based on achieving £90,000 of taxable turnover in the last 12 months or since starting in business if this is less than 12 months. Taxable turnover excludes exempt supplies but includes zero-rated supplies.

In the June 2012 examiner's report, the examining team advised candidates to be careful when quoting dates and working out 30 days. You need to remember which months do not have 31 days (i.e. there is no such date as 31 April!).

(b) Recovery of pre-registration VAT

Input VAT can be recovered on goods purchased prior to registration provided the goods were acquired for business purposes and were not sold or consumed prior to registration. The goods must also have been acquired in the four years prior to registration.

Input VAT can be recovered on services supplied prior to registration provided the services were supplied for business purposes within the six months prior to registration.

Tutorial note

Goods can be non-current assets or inventory. For example, if a trader buys a computer for business use but registers for VAT four months later, the trader can reclaim the input VAT on the computer on the first VAT return provided the trader still uses it for business at the time of registration.

117 MARJORIE

Key answer tips

This is a typical VAT question, asking the student to prepare a calculation of VAT payable. The only areas of concern may have been the irrecoverable debt relief.

It is important to read the question carefully to determine whether the figures provided are inclusive or exclusive of VAT, in order to calculate the correct VAT figures.

VAT – quarter ended 31 March 2026

		£
Output VAT:		
Standard-rated sales	£260,000 × 20%	52,000
Exempt sales	£40,000	0
		52,000
Input VAT:		
Purchases	£108,000 × 1/6	(18,000)
Van	£27,000 × 1/6	(4,500)
Impairment relief:		
May 2025	£3,000 × 20%	(600)
November 2025	Not 6 months old	0
VAT payable		28,900

Tutorial note

Irrecoverable debt relief is only available on debts over six months old so relief cannot yet be claimed on the debt due in November 2025.

To find the amount of VAT in a VAT-inclusive figure you multiply by 20/120. This fraction is usually simplified to 1/6.

In the June 2012 examiner's report in relation to a similar VAT return question, the examining team stated that the common mistakes were:

- *Using the wrong rate of tax or using the fraction of 1/6 instead of 20%. This was also commented on in the June 2014 report.*
- *Applying VAT at 20% to zero-rated supplies.*
- *Adding up all the VAT calculated instead of deducting the VAT on the expenses and inventory purchases (input tax) from the VAT (output tax) on the sales.*

Examiner's report

This was a five-mark question on the calculation of value added tax (VAT).

This question was well answered, which was pleasing to see. Most candidates knew when to use 20% or 1/6th. If figures are quoted exclusive of VAT then 20% should be used to calculate the VAT but if they are quoted as inclusive then 1/6th should be used.

VAT on vans can only be reclaimed if used 100% for business purposes (as in this question). Relief for bad debts can only be claimed if the debts are written off in the accounts and are over six months old – hence VAT relief could be claimed on the debt in May 2025 but not the one in November 2025. Unfortunately, it would appear that a few candidates misread the question and claimed relief on the wrong debt.

ACCA Marking scheme	
	Marks
Standard rated sales	1.0
Exempt sales	0.5
Purchases	1.0
Van	1.0
May 2025 debt	0.5
November 2025 debt	0.5
VAT due	0.5
Total	**5.0**

118 ATHLETIC LTD

Key answer tips

This question deals with a range of registration issues, all of which are important.

(a) Athletic Ltd – Notification of VAT registration

		£
1 December 2025 – 28 February 2026		23,000
1 March 2026 – 31 May 2026		30,000
June 2026	(£60,000 × 1/3)	20,000
July 2026	(£60,000 × 1/3)	20,000
		93,000

The £90,000 threshold is exceeded at the end of July 2026.

Athletic Ltd must notify HMRC by 30 August 2026 (i.e. within 30 days of the end of July 2026).

(b) Compulsory registration date

Athletic Ltd will be registered on 1 September 2026 (i.e. the first day of the second month following the month the threshold is exceeded).

(c) VAT periods

The normal length of a VAT return is three calendar months.

The VAT return must be submitted online using MTD (Making Tax Digital) compatible software together with any VAT due within one month and 7 days of the end of the VAT period.

(d) Advantages and disadvantages of voluntary registration

Advantages	Registration creates an impression of substantial business activity.
	Input tax may be reclaimed.
Disadvantages	VAT records will have to be kept and compliance requirements met.
	Customers will have 20% added to their bills. VAT registered customers will be able to reclaim the VAT suffered, however, non-VAT registered customers will not.

Tutorial note

The historic registration test is based on achieving £90,000 of taxable turnover in the last 12 months or since starting in business if this is less than 12 months. Taxable turnover excludes exempt supplies but includes zero-rated supplies.

Voluntary registration is possible if a business is making or intending to make taxable supplies.

119 EMAIL

Key answer tips

There are several ways you could set out your answer but a simple memo style layout should be sufficient.

Email to Financial Accountant

To: Financial Accountant

From: Junior accountant

Date: 16 July 2026

Subject: VAT return

Please be advised that I have just completed the VAT return for the quarter ended 30 June 2026. The amount of VAT payable is £11,657.42.

This should be paid electronically with the submission of the VAT return by 7 August 2026.

The amount of VAT due will need to be included in the company cash flow forecasts to ensure that there will be sufficient funds available in the company bank account on the due date.

Kind regards

Junior accountant

120 VECTOR LTD

Key answer tips

Relief for irrecoverable debts cannot be claimed until six months from the time that payment is due. Therefore, relief can only be claimed in respect of the invoices due for payment on 15 August and 15 September 2025.

Input VAT cannot be recovered in respect of the car as it is not exclusively used for business purposes. However, VAT on the plant can be recovered. In their December 2014 report, the examining team commented that "Some students did not include the VAT on the machine. VAT is calculated on both revenue and capital expenditure".

In the June 2013 examiner's report in relation to a similar VAT return question, the examining team stated that the common mistakes were:

- Using the wrong rate of tax or using the fraction of 1/6 instead of 20%.
- Applying VAT at 20% to zero-rated supplies.
- Adding up all the VAT calculated instead of deducting the VAT on the expenses and inventory purchases (input tax) from the VAT (output tax) on the sales.

VAT return – Quarter ended 31 March 2026

	£	£
Output VAT		
Sales – standard-rated (£128,000 × 20%)		25,600
Sales – zero-rated		0
Deposit (£4,500 × 1/6)		750
		26,350
Input VAT		
Expenses (£74,800 – £4,200) × 20%	14,120	
Irrecoverable debts (£800 + £800)	1,600	
Plant (£16,500 × 1/6)	2,750	
		(18,470)
VAT payable		7,880

No VAT input tax reclaimable on the car.

Tutorial note

1 *Irrecoverable debt relief is only available on debts which were due for payment six months prior to 31 March 2026 (the end of the VAT period) so relief cannot yet be claimed on the debt due in October 2025.*

2 *The basic tax point is the date of delivery of goods or the date of performance of services. However, if goods or services are paid for or a tax invoice is issued before the basic tax point, then the date of payment or the invoice date becomes the actual tax point date. If a part payment such as a deposit is paid in advance then there will be two tax points, one for the deposit and one for the balance of the supply.*

3 *To find the amount of VAT in a VAT-inclusive figure you multiply by 20/120. This fraction is usually simplified to 1/6.*

121 DOUGLAS

Key answer tips

For parts (i) and (ii), make sure your answer relates specifically to the facts stated in the question by:

(i) showing your calculation of taxable turnover,

(ii) specifying the date by which HM Revenue and Customs must be notified, and

(iii) stating from when registration takes effect.

For parts (iii) and (iv) a simple knowledge of the penalty regime is required. These are facts that must be learned in order not to miss out on easy marks.

(i) The VAT registration limit was exceeded on 30 November 2025.

(7 months × £14,000 = £98,000)

Douglas should have notified HM Revenue and Customs (HMRC) by: 30 December 2025.

(ii) Douglas should have been registered for VAT on: 1 January 2026.

(iii) The maximum penalty for late registration (i.e. the failure to notify penalty) is 100% of the lost revenue.

(iv) The penalty may be reduced to zero if the taxpayer makes a full and unprompted voluntary disclosure to HMRC within 12 months of the date the VAT would have been due.

Tutorial note

The historic registration test is based on achieving £90,000 of taxable turnover in the last 12 months or since starting in business if this is less than 12 months. Taxable turnover excludes exempt supplies but includes zero-rated supplies.

Examiner's report

This was a five-mark theory question on value added tax (VAT) registration. This question was poorly answered with many candidates stating dates which did not seem to have any relevance to the dates given in the question.

As a reminder, registration is required when the VAT threshold is exceeded. In this case it was exceeded on 30 November 2025 and therefore the taxpayer should have notified HMRC within 30 days i.e. 30 December 2025 (note – not the end of the following month as a few candidates suggested). Registration would then have been from the first of the next month i.e. 1 January 2026.

The maximum penalty for late registration is 100% of the lost revenue but this could be reduced to zero if the taxpayer makes a full unprompted disclosure within 12 months.

ACCA Marking scheme	
	Marks
Date registration limit was exceeded	1.0
Notification date	1.0
Effective registration date	1.0
Maximum penalty for late registration	1.0
Reduction in penalty for disclosure	1.0
Total	**5.0**

122 BATTERY LTD

Key answer tips

A short question covering the contents of VAT invoices and the future turnover test.

(a) VAT invoice

The following additional information is required:

1 Battery Ltd's VAT registration number.

2 The tax point.

3 The rate of VAT for each supply.

4 The VAT-exclusive amount for each supply.

(b) Future turnover test for registration

If taxable supplies in the next 30 days in isolation are expected to exceed the annual registration threshold, HMRC should be notified within 30 days of that date. Registration is effective from the beginning of the 30-day period.

123 CONFUSED LTD

Key answer tips

Part (a) of the question tests that you understand the very important difference between making wholly standard-rated, zero-rated and exempt supplies.

Part (b) deals with errors – a very examinable topic.

(a) Registration and VAT due

Standard-rated supplies

Confused Ltd will be required to register for VAT as it is making taxable supplies in excess of the registration threshold of £90,000.

Output VAT of £18,200 (£91,000 × 20%) per month will be due, and input VAT of £1,667 (£10,000 × 1/6) per month will be recoverable.

Tutorial note

To find the amount of VAT in a VAT-inclusive figure you multiply by 20/120. This fraction is usually simplified to 1/6.

Zero-rated supplies

Zero-rated supplies are taxable supplies and therefore Confused Ltd is permitted to register for VAT. However, the company can apply for exemption from registration, as it is only making zero-rated supplies.

If the company does register for VAT output VAT will not be due, but input VAT of £1,667 per month will be recoverable.

Exempt supplies

Confused Ltd will not be required or permitted to register for VAT as it will not be making taxable supplies.

Output VAT will not be due and no input VAT will be recoverable.

(b) Voluntary disclosure of errors

If the net errors total less than the higher of £10,000 or 1% turnover (capped at £50,000), they can be voluntarily disclosed by entering them on the next VAT return.

If the net errors exceed this figure, they cannot be entered on the next return. Instead, disclosure must be made separately to HM Revenue and Customs.

Tutorial note

When a trader discovers a VAT error they must inform HMRC. If the net error is less than a certain limit and is not deliberate, it can be included on the next VAT return.

If not, it must be disclosed separately on a form or in a letter.

The limit operates as follows:

- *Net errors up to £10,000 can always be included on the next VAT return.*
- *Net errors above £50,000 must always be separately disclosed.*
- *Errors between these limits can be included on the next VAT return if they are no more than 1% of turnover.*

124 VAT ERRORS

Key answer tips

This question requires you to apply your knowledge of VAT errors to decide how a series of errors must be corrected.

	Net error	Turnover	Treatment
	£	£	
1	24,567	2,000,000	The error is between £10,000 and £50,000 so it can be included on the next VAT return if it is ≤ 1% of turnover. 1% of £2,000,000 is only £20,000 so the error must be separately disclosed.
2	4,568	85,400	This error can automatically be corrected on the next VAT return as it is less than £10,000.
3	35,980	4,567,090	The error is between £10,000 and £50,000 so it can be included on the next VAT return if it is ≤ 1% of turnover. 1% of £4,567,090 is £45,671 so this error can be included on the next VAT return.
4	51,600	10,000,000	This error must be separately disclosed as it exceeds £50,000.

Tutorial note

When a trader discovers a VAT error, they must inform HMRC. If the net error is less than a certain limit and is not deliberate, it can be included on the next VAT return. If not, it must be disclosed separately on a form or in a letter.

The limit operates as follows:

- *Net errors up to £10,000 can always be included on the next VAT return.*
- *Net errors above £50,000 must always be separately disclosed.*
- *Errors between these limits can be included on the next VAT return if they are no more than 1% of turnover.*

125 ASTUTE LTD

Key answer tips

There are three special schemes for VAT accounting all of which are important to learn for the examination. When answering a question on one of these schemes it is important to observe the requirement and focus the answer on the scheme the question relates to, and not to write about other schemes or VAT in general.

This question concerns the annual accounting scheme.

Annual accounting scheme

Astute Ltd can apply to use the annual accounting scheme if its expected taxable turnover for the next 12 months does not exceed £1,350,000 exclusive of VAT. The company must also be up to date with its VAT returns.

The advantages of using the scheme:

- The company will only have to submit one VAT return each year.
- Budgeting and possibly cash flow may be improved if the business is expanding as the company will be required to make payments on account based on the previous year's VAT liability.

Tutorial note

The annual accounting scheme allows businesses to submit one VAT return each year. This is due two months after the year end.

VAT payments on account have to be made throughout the year. VAT is not just paid once a year with the return. These payments on account are based on last year's VAT liability.

126 BRIGHT LTD

Key answer tips

There are three special schemes for VAT accounting all of which are important to learn for the examination. When answering a question on one of these schemes it is important to observe the requirement and focus the answer on the scheme the question relates to, and not to write about other schemes or VAT in general.

This question concerns the flat rate scheme which was examined in December 2012 and June 2017.

The examiner's report for both these sittings commented that the flat rate scheme question was not well answered.

It is therefore very important to make sure that these schemes are learnt and understood.

Flat rate scheme

(a) Conditions and advantages

Bright Ltd can use the flat rate scheme if its expected taxable turnover for the next 12 months does not exceed £150,000.

The main advantage of the scheme is the simplified VAT administration as there is no need to keep detailed records of input VAT suffered.

In addition, in this question, as Bright Ltd's customers are not VAT registered there will be no need to issue VAT invoices which gives an added administrative advantage.

Tax savings can also be made, although this is not usually the primary reason for joining the scheme.

Bright Ltd must leave the scheme if total turnover (including VAT) exceeds £230,000.

(b) Potential annual tax saving

Using the normal basis of calculating the VAT liability, Bright Ltd will have to pay annual VAT of £10,167 (£75,000 – £13,000 – £1,000 = £61,000 × 1/6).

Whereas if Bright Ltd uses the flat rate scheme, it will pay VAT of £9,000 (£75,000 × 12%), which is the flat rate percentage applied to the VAT-inclusive total turnover of the business.

An annual saving of £1,167 (£10,167 – £9,000) will be achieved under the flat rate scheme.

Note that under the flat rate scheme Bright Ltd does not recover any input tax on specific purchases and details of VAT on each purchase and expense does not need to be calculated.

Tutorial note

The flat rate percentage used by a business is fixed by reference to the average outputs less inputs for a typical business in that particular trade sector.

A business can join the flat rate scheme provided their taxable turnover (excluding VAT) is less than £150,000. They have to leave the scheme when their total turnover exceeds £230,000 (including VAT and exempt supplies).

The VAT calculation is based on VAT-inclusive TOTAL turnover, not just taxable turnover.

It is possible for a business to pay less VAT under the flat rate scheme than under the normal accounting scheme.

127 CLEVER LTD

Key answer tips

There are three special schemes for VAT accounting, all of which are important to learn for the examination. When answering a question on one of these schemes it is important to observe the requirement and focus the answer on the scheme the question relates to, and not to write about other schemes or VAT in general.

This question concerns the cash accounting scheme.

Cash accounting scheme

Clever Ltd can use the cash accounting scheme if its expected taxable turnover for the next 12 months does not exceed £1,350,000 exclusive of VAT. The company must also be up to date with its VAT returns and VAT payments. There should have been no VAT offences in the previous 12 months.

The scheme is advantageous as output VAT will be accounted for three months later than at present as the tax point will be the date that payment is received from customers. The recovery of input VAT on expenses will not be affected as these are paid in cash.

The scheme will also provide automatic irrecoverable debt relief should a customer default on the payment of a debt as output tax is not payable until the customer pays the debt.

Tutorial note

The cash accounting scheme allows businesses to pay over output tax when customers pay and reclaim input tax when suppliers are paid. Output and input VAT totals are taken from the cash book.

With the cash accounting scheme, the tax point date is the date the payment is received/paid.

128 CITY MERCHANDISE LTD

Key answer tips

This is a typical VAT question, requiring a calculation of VAT payable. The only area of concern may have been the discount on the standard-rated sales. It is important to read the question carefully to determine whether the figures provided are inclusive or exclusive of VAT, in order to calculate the correct VAT figures.

In the June 2012 examiner's report in relation to a similar VAT return question, the examining team stated that the common mistakes were:

- Using the wrong rate of tax or using the fraction of 1/6 instead of 20%.
- Adding up all the VAT calculated instead of deducting the VAT on the expenses and inventory purchases (input tax) from the VAT (output tax) on the sales.

Input VAT can be recovered in respect of the car as it is used exclusively for business purposes.

VAT – quarter ended 31 March 2026

	£	£
Standard-rated sales (£110,000 × 20%) (Note 1)		22,000
Discount adjustment (£55,000 × 5% × 20%) (Note 1)		(550)
Standard-rated purchases (£60,000 × 20%)	12,000	
Electricity (£4,000 × 1/6) (Note 2)	667	
Repairs (£2,500 × 1/6)	417	
Entertaining UK customers (blocked) (Note 3)	0	
Entertaining overseas customers (£900 × 1/6)	150	
Car (£12,600 × 1/6)	2,100	
	———	(15,334)
VAT payable		6,116

Wages are outside the scope of VAT and no output VAT is due on zero-rated supplies.

The VAT must be paid electronically by 7 May 2026 (i.e. one month and seven days after the quarter end).

Tutorial note

1 *Where a prompt payment discount is offered output VAT is charged on the actual amount received, i.e. for the invoices which were settled within 10 days output VAT is due on the value of the sale less the 5% discount. However, the supplier will not know, when the invoice is raised, whether the customer will qualify for the discount by paying promptly. The supplier must therefore charge VAT on the invoice on the full price. If the discount is taken the supplier must then make an adjustment so that output tax is only accounted for on the amount received.*

2 *To find the amount of VAT in a VAT-inclusive figure you multiply by 20/120. This fraction is usually simplified to 1/6.*

3 *VAT is recoverable on entertaining overseas customers but not UK customers.*

129 DEFINITIONS

Key answer tips

You should learn definitions like these as they can be tested in MCQs or long form questions.

(a) A taxable person is someone who is or is required to be registered for VAT.

(b) In order for a supply to be a taxable supply it must be made:

(i) by a taxable person

(ii) for a consideration

(iii) in the UK

(iv) in the course or furtherance of a business.

Tutorial note

A taxable person can be a company, partnership or individual.

130 BADRU

Key answer tips

There are many administration rules for VAT which you must learn. This question concerns VAT invoices and records.

Part (c) of this question concerns the recovery of input VAT on pre-registration expenditure.

(a) Items that must be included on a VAT invoice

Any four of the following are acceptable:

- an identifying number
- the date of supply
- the supplier's name and address
- the supplier's VAT registration number
- the customer's name and address
- the type of supply made
- a description that identifies the goods or services supplied
- the value and rate of VAT for each supply
- the total VAT-exclusive amount
- the rate of any cash discount offered
- the amount of VAT payable

(b) VAT record keeping

Badru must keep her VAT records for six years.

(c) Rules to recover pre-registration input VAT

Pre-registration input VAT may be recovered on goods acquired in the four years pre-registration, that were bought for the purpose of business and that are still held.

Examiner's report

This question required knowledge of VAT administrative rules which were generally not well known. Candidates are reminded that the rules relating to tax administration are an important part of the syllabus at this level and, since they are regularly tested, they should not be overlooked.

ACCA Marking scheme	
	Marks
Four invoice items, 0.5 per item	2.0
Time limit for VAT records	1.0
Pre-registration – four years	1.0
Pre-registration – still held	1.0
Total	**5.0**

TAX RETURNS

131 ABRAHAM

Tax return entries:

Box 34	£18,000
Box 35	£2,690
Box 36	£3,000
Box 42	£268
Box 44	£6,455
Box 45	£280
Box 46	£30,693

Tutorial note

In the examiner's report on the December 2015 exam, it was highlighted that many students completing this return failed to read the question properly. It is important to read the detail for the boxes on the form. The examining team stated that "boxes 17 – 31 require the FULL amount of expenses (simply copying the question) and boxes 32 – 45 require the amount that should be disallowed for tax purposes. Unfortunately, many candidates put the allowable amounts in boxes 17 – 31 and nothing in the other boxes."

In this question boxes 17 – 31 were already completed for you, but that will not always be the case.

132 JACK

Tax return entries:

Box 49	£22,560
Box 50	£12,400
Box 51	£2,560
Box 57	£37,520

133 LYNNE

Tax return entries:

Box 16	£138,240 (£230,400 × 3/5)
Box 17	£20,000
Box 18	£118,240
Box 20	£118,240
Box 28	£3,726 (£6,210 × 3/5)

134 BROADHURST

Box 1	£35,112 (W1)
Box 4	(£22,348) (W2)
Box 5	£12,764 (£35,112 – £22,348)
Box 6	£175,560
Box 7	£123,981 (W3)

Tutorial note

In their report on the December 2013 examination, the examining team commented that "many candidates simply made an attempt to calculate VAT without stating which figure would be entered in which box. It would appear that those candidates who did make an attempt to enter figures into boxes did not read the box descriptions carefully because often the wrong figures were entered despite candidates doing the workings correctly.

Tax returns of one tax or another will continue to be examined and candidates must learn to read the detail of each box carefully before entering figures."

Workings

(W1) Output VAT

	£
Sales (£175,560 × 20%)	35,112

(W2) Input VAT

	£
Purchases (£113,670 × 20%)	22,734
Purchase returns (£5,249 × 20%)	(1,050)
Entertaining overseas customers (£1,560 × 20%)	312
Impaired debt relief (£1,760 × 20%)	352
	22,348

Tutorial note

VAT can be recovered on entertaining overseas customers but not UK customers.

VAT cannot be recovered on cars unless they are used 100% for business.

(W3) Purchases and other inputs

	£
Purchases	113,670
Purchase returns	(5,249)
Car	14,000
Entertaining overseas customers	1,560
	123,981

135 RACHAEL

Tax return entries:

	Rachael
Box 1	
Box 23	3
Box 24	£37,200
Box 25	£31,000
Box 26	£8,200
Box 27	£2,000
Box 45	£3,200
Box 47	£1,800

Tutorial note

In the examiner's report on the June 2013 examination, the examining team commented that in completing the capital gains summary sheet "candidates simply had to read the requirement of each box and enter the amount from the detail given."

"Tax returns of one tax or another will continue to be examined and candidates must learn to read the detail of each box carefully before entering figures."

Working: Capital losses b/f

	£
May 2025 (£20,200 – £14,000)	6,200
November 2025 (£10,000 – £8,000)	2,000
Less : CY capital loss (£7,000 – £9,000)	(2,000)
	6,200
Less: AEA	(3,000)
Less: Capital losses b/f	(3,200)
Taxable gains	0
Capital losses b/f	5,000
Less: Used in 2025/26	(3,200)
Capital losses c/f	1,800

136 PANDORA

Tax return entries:

Box 1	**Pandora**
Box 3	1
Box 4	£110,000
Box 5	£45,000
Box 6	£65,000
Box 9	£65,000
Box 10	£14,880
Box 31	2
Box 32	£50,000
Box 33	£32,000
Box 34	£18,000

137 HUMMEL LTD

Tax return entries:

Box 145	£1,000,000
Box 155	£585,000
Box 165	£585,000
Box 170	£20,000
Box 190	£200,000
Box 210	£110,000
Box 220	£110,000
Box 235	£915,000
Box 300	£915,000
Box 305	£20,000
Box 315	£895,000

138 JO LTD

Tax return entries:

Box 330	2025
Box 335	£375,000
Box 340	25%
Box 345	£93,750
Box 430	£93,750
Box 440	£93,750

139 LEAFY LTD

Tax return entries:

Box 326	1
Box 329	X
Box 330	2025
Box 335	£113,000
Box 340	25%
Box 345	£28,250
Box 430	£28,250
Box 435	£180
Box 440	£28,070

Working: Corporation tax liability

	£
£113,000 × 25%	28,250
Less: Marginal relief	
(£125,000 – £113,000) × 3/200	(180)
	28,070

The upper limit, as used in the marginal relief calculation, is £125,000 as there are two associated companies (£250,000/2 = £125,000)

Section 5

CBE SPECIMEN EXAM QUESTIONS

SECTION A

This section of the exam contains **15 objective test (OT) questions**

Each question is worth **2 marks** and is compulsory

This exam section is worth **30 marks** in total

1 **Which form shows an employee's end of year pay summary, and by which date should the individual receive it?**

A P11D by 6 July following the relevant tax year

B P11D by 31 May following the relevant tax year

C P60 by 6 July following the relevant tax year

D P60 by 31 May following the relevant tax year **(2 marks)**

2 James is a sole trader preparing accounts annually to 31 March. James uses his car for both business and private purposes throughout the whole of the year ended 31 March 2026. The car has a CO_2 emission rate of 60 grams per kilometre and cost £18,000. The private mileage for James' accounting period ended 31 March 2026 represented 20% of the total mileage for that year.

What is the maximum amount of capital allowances that James can claim in respect of the car for the accounting year ended 31 March 2026?

A £864

B £3,240

C £1,080

D £2,592 **(2 marks)**

3 Bernie is an employee. His employer provided him with the use of free accommodation for the whole of the tax year 2025/26. It was not deemed to be job-related.

The accommodation cost Bernie's employer £100,000 in February 2022 and has an annual value of £8,000. The market value of the property on 6 April 2025 was £190,000.

In addition to the basic charge of £8,000, what is Bernie's taxable benefit in respect of the accommodation provided in the tax year 2025/26?

A £4,313

B £7,125

C £938

D £3,750 **(2 marks)**

4 Rosie is a sole trader and has £40,000 trading profits for her accounting year ended 31 March 2026.

What is Rosie's class 4 national insurance contributions (NIC) liability for the tax year 2025/26?

A £2,194

B £1,646

C £2,400

D £3,200 **(2 marks)**

5 **(AMENDED)**

Ted, Pearl and Aide are in partnership sharing profits and losses equally. In their accounting year ended 31 March 2026 they made a trading loss of £39,000.

Which of the following statements is true?

A The partners must make the same loss relief claims

B The partners can each carry their own share of the trading loss back to the tax year 2024/25 against total income

C Ted can give Pearl his share of the trading loss

D The partners can each carry their own share of the trading loss forward against total income **(2 marks)**

6 Nigel has the use of an asset provided by his employer from 6 November 2025. The asset had cost the employer £4,000 but the market value of the asset in November 2025 was £3,000. Nigel pays £20 a month for the use of the asset. The asset has not been used by any other employee.

What is Nigel's taxable benefit in respect of the asset provided for his use in the tax year 2025/26?

A £233

B £700

C £150

D £500 **(2 marks)**

7 A company prepared financial statements for the 15-month period of account ended 31 December 2025. The company is regarded as small for corporation tax purposes.

By which date(s) should the company pay its corporation tax liability for the period of account ended 31 December 2025 to avoid incurring interest and penalties?

A One payment by 1 October 2026

B Two separate payments by 1 July 2026 and 1 October 2026

C Two separate payments by 1 October 2025 and 1 October 2026

D One payment by 31 January 2026 **(2 marks)**

8 **With regards to a company, which of the following statements is true?**

A Property business losses can only be used against property business income

B Allowable capital losses can be used against chargeable gains of the previous year

C Trading losses can be carried forward and used against total profits (before QCDs) in future years

D Trading losses can be carried forward against future trade income only **(2 marks)**

9 A company has the following expenses in its accounting period ended 31 March 2026:

Legal expenses in respect of trade debt collecting	£800
Depreciation of plant and machinery	£1,200
Staff entertainment	£900
Gifts of food to clients	£600

How much should the company add back to its accounting profit to arrive at its tax adjusted trading profit?

A £2,700

B £2,600

C £1,800

D £2,100 **(2 marks)**

10 **(AMENDED)**

A UK taxpayer sold two assets in the tax year 2025/26. One resulted in a chargeable gain and the other in an allowable loss.

In which circumstances is there no need to report full details of these disposals to HM Revenue and Customs (HMRC)?

A Where the net gains (after losses) are not more than £3,000

B Where the proceeds of sale are not more than £50,000

C Where the net gains (after losses) are not more than £3,000 and the proceeds of sale are not more than £50,000

D Where the total gains (before losses) are not more than £3,000 and the proceeds of sale are not more than £50,000 **(2 marks)**

11 Mary has two taxable gains (after deduction of the annual exempt amount) in the tax year 2025/26:

£10,000 – qualifying for business asset disposal relief

£12,000 – not qualifying for business asset disposal relief

Mary has taxable income of £33,000 in the tax year 2025/26.

What is Mary's capital gains tax liability for the tax year 2025/26?

A £3,960

B £3,998

C £4,280

D £4,998 **(2 marks)**

12 Chi gives his daughter some shares in the family business. The shares had cost Chi £80,000 and have a current market value of £120,000. The company's total assets are worth £800,000 of which 10% are held for investment and 20% is in cash.

What is the maximum gift holdover relief which Chi and his daughter may claim in respect of the gift of shares?

A £40,000

B £32,000

C £28,000

D £35,000 **(2 marks)**

13 In the tax year 2025/26 Silvia pays £8,000 to her employer's HM Revenue and Customs (HMRC) approved occupational pension scheme. Silvia's employer contributes £4,000.

Which of the following statements is true?

A Silvia's taxable employment income is reduced by £12,000

B The basic rate band is extended by the gross contribution of £10,000

C Silvia has a taxable benefit of £4,000 and her taxable employment income is reduced by £8,000

D Silvia has a tax exempt benefit of £4,000 and her taxable employment income is reduced by £8,000 **(2 marks)**

14 A sole trader, who is registered for value added tax (VAT), sells standard rated inventory valued at £1,000 (exclusive of VAT) in March 2026. A trade discount of 10% is applied to the value of £1,000.

How much VAT must the sole trader charge on the sale?

A £200

B £167

C £180

D £150 **(2 marks)**

15 In regard to value added tax (VAT) which of the following is true?

A When traders cease to make taxable supplies they must notify HM Revenue and Customs (HMRC) within 30 days and the company will be deregistered from the day of notification

B Traders making taxable supplies, with a turnover below the VAT registration threshold, can voluntarily register for VAT at any time

C Traders can voluntarily deregister if at any time their turnover was below the VAT deregistration threshold in the last 12 months

D Traders do not pay VAT on purchases if they are not registered for VAT **(2 marks)**

(Total: 30 marks)

SECTION B

This section of the exam contains 8 constructed response questions

Some questions may contain a scenario which relates to one or more requirement(s) which may be split over multiple question screens.

The total marks for each constructed response question range from **5 to 15 marks**.

This exam section is worth **70 marks** in total.

All questions are compulsory.

16 STELLA

Stella is an employee of a large company. Stella received a salary of £188,369 for the tax year 2025/26.

In May 2025 Stella received a bonus of £12,000 based on the company profits for the year ended 31 December 2024.

Stella's company provided Stella with the use of a company van on 6 October 2025. Stella uses the van 40% for private purposes and 60% for business purposes. The company pays for all of the petrol for both the private and business mileage.

Stella's employer has deducted £75,223 income tax (under PAYE) from Stella's income for the tax year 2025/26.

During the tax year 2025/26 Stella also received the following amounts of other income:

Dividend income	£4,000
NS&I Investment account interest	£600
Bank deposit interest	£2,000

During the tax year 2025/26 Stella contributed £8,000 net contributions to her personal pension fund.

Required:

Calculate the income tax payable by Stella for the tax year 2025/26. (15 marks)

17 LACE LTD

Lace Ltd is registered for value added tax (VAT). Lace Ltd prepared financial statements annually to 31 March. During October 2025, the company decided to change its accounting reference date to 31 December.

As a consequence, Lace Ltd prepared its most recent set of financial statements for the nine months ended 31 December 2025.

Lace Ltd had the following results for the nine-month period of account ended 31 December 2025:

	£
Adjusted trading profit (before capital allowances)	1,820,050
Non-trade investment income	45,000
Chargeable gains	195,000
Dividend received (from non-group companies)	9,000
Qualifying charitable donation	14,000

The investment income was the full amount receivable for the nine-month period ended 31 December 2025.

The chargeable gains include any chargeable gain arising from the disposal of the machine described below.

Lace Ltd brought forward capital losses of £10,000 and trading losses of £28,000 on 1 April 2025 both of which arose in the year ended 31 March 2025.

For capital allowances purposes Lace Ltd brought forward the following tax written down values as at 1 April 2025:

Main pool	£210,000
Special rate pool	£40,000

Lace Ltd purchased assets which qualified as integral features for £960,000 on 14 June 2025 and sold an old machine, which had cost £24,000, for £28,800 on 4 December 2025. A claim for the 130% super deduction had been made on the purchase of this machine. All figures relating to additions and disposals are inclusive of VAT.

Required:

Calculate the corporation tax payable by Lace Ltd for the nine-month period of account ended 31 December 2025. Your answer should identify any item which is not taxable and state why it is not included in your calculation. (15 marks)

18 REBECCA

Rebecca made the following disposals of capital assets in the tax year 2025/26:

15 August 2025	Part of a field was sold for £24,000. This was part of a ten-hectare field, which Rebecca had purchased in 2011 for £80,000. The remaining part of the field had a market value of £126,000 in August 2025. Expenses of sale amounted to £1,500.
14 November 2025	A military medal was sold for £8,000. Rebecca had inherited the medal from her father (who had been awarded the medal in 1946) in 2007 when it had a market value of £1,400.
2 January 2026	A building was sold for £295,000. Expenses of sale amounted to £15,000. The building had cost £190,000 in August 2010 and was extended at a cost of £19,700 in May 2015. Structures and buildings allowances were not available on the building.

None of the assets were business assets.

Rebecca earns a salary of £120,000 per year.

Required:

Calculate the capital gains tax payable by Rebecca for the tax year 2025/26. (10 marks)

19 BUD PLC

Bud plc is registered for value added tax (VAT). During the three-month VAT period ended 31 March 2026, Bud plc made the following transactions:

	£
Sales:	
Standard-rated sales	240,000
Zero-rated sales	80,000
Purchases:	
Inventory (all standard-rated)	110,000
A machine for use in the business	40,000
A car for both private and business use	25,000

Two debts were written off during the three-month period ended 31 March 2026:

– A debt which was due on 31 August 2025	3,000
– A debt which was due on 30 November 2025	5,000

Both debts relate to standard-rated sales.

All figures are exclusive of VAT.

Required:

Calculate the value added tax (VAT) payable to HM Revenue and Customs (HMRC) by Bud plc for the three-month period ended 31 March 2026.

Note: Your answer should clearly state why VAT is not calculated on any of the figures listed in the scenario. **(10 marks)**

20 BETTY

Betty is a basic rate tax payer. Included in her total income for the tax year 2025/26 were the following amounts of investment income:

	£
NS&I Investment account interest	400
Interest from an individual savings account (ISA) held in a UK bank	1,000
Interest from a UK bank deposit account	6,000
Interest from a UK bank current account	500
Proceeds from NS&I certificates	3,000
Dividend from UK companies	7,000
Dividends from a UK ISA account	900
Premium bond winnings	250

Required:

An extract from the self-assessment tax return is shown in the spreadsheet below. Using the information provided, complete the entries for boxes 1, 2, 4 and 5 only. **(5 marks)**

Interest and dividends from UK banks and building societies

1	Taxed UK interest	**5**	Other dividends
	£		**£**
2	Untaxed UK interest	**6**	Foreign dividends (up to £500)
	£		**£**
3	Untaxed foreign interest (up to £2,000)	**7**	Tax taken off foreign dividends
	£		**£**
4	Dividends from UK companies		
	£		

21 JENNIFER

In the tax year 2025/26 Jennifer rented out a furnished residential property for an annual rent of £12,000. The full amount was received during the tax year, with the exception of £1,000 due for March 2026, which was received in May 2026.

Jennifer paid the following expenses in connection with the property:

	£
Water rates	400
Insurance	300
Kitchen extension	3,000
Redecoration	500
New bed	750

The old bed was sold for £50.

Required:

Calculate Jennifer's property income for the tax year 2025/26. Your answer should clearly state why any item is not included in your calculation. **(5 marks)**

22 PLANT PLC

Plant plc prepares financial statements annually to 31 March. On 31 January 2026, Plant plc sold a factory, which it had used in its business, for £840,000. The factory had originally cost Plant plc £410,000 in May 2003. No structures and buildings allowances had been claimed in respect of the factory.

In August 2026, Plant plc intends to purchase a plot of land, which will be used in its business, for £780,000.

Plant plc always claims any reliefs that it is entitled to.

Required:

Calculate Plant plc's chargeable gain for the year ended 31 March 2026.

Note: The indexation factor for May 2003 to December 2017 is 0.532. **(5 marks)**

23 DAVID

Note that this is a new question, as the question in the current ACCA CBE specimen exam tests an area that is no longer examinable.

David started to trade on 6 April 2025 and prepared accounts for the year ended 5 April 2026.

David supplied the following information for his first period of account:

	£
Cash from customers (£13,000 relates to work done in June 2026)	98,000
Payment for a new machine	7,000
Expenses incurred (£1,500 paid in May 2026)	33,000
Payment for new car (48g/km, 60% business use by David)	25,000
Car expenses (6,000 business miles)	5,200

David will claim HMRC approved mileage allowances.

Required:

Calculate David's trading income for the tax year 2025/26. Any item that is not deductible should be shown as zero (i.e. 0).

Ignore VAT. **(5 marks)**

Section 6

ANSWERS TO CBE SPECIMEN EXAM QUESTIONS

SECTION A

1 D

Form P60 must be given to an employee by 31 May following the relevant tax year. A P11D is the form used to report the benefits given to an employee.

2 A

Cars are not entitled to the annual investment allowance. The car is treated as a special rate item (as the CO_2 emissions exceed 50g/km) and is therefore entitled to writing down allowance at 6%. The allowance is restricted because of the private use. The total amount due is:

(£18,000 × 6% × 80%) = £864

3 C

Accommodation provided for private use by an employer is taxed on the annual value plus an additional amount if the accommodation cost the company more than £75,000. The correct calculation of the additional benefit is:

Additional charge:	£
(£100,000 – £75,000) × 3.75%	938

Tutorial note

The calculation of the additional charge is as follows:

(Cost – £75,000) × Official rate of interest at 6 April.

The market value of the property is only used if the employee moved in more than six years after the employer purchased the property. That is not the case here.

4 B

	£
Class 4	
(£40,000 – £12,570) × 6%	1,646

5 B

The partners can choose their own separate loss relief claims. They can choose to carry back their share of the trading loss to the tax year 2024/25 against total income. They can carry forward their own share of trading loss, however, carried forward losses are offset against the first available trading profits of the same trade (not against total income) for individuals.

6 C

The benefit is calculated by multiplying the market value of the asset at the time when it is first used by an employee, by 20%. The benefit is time apportioned for the period it is available for use in the tax year. Any employee contribution towards the use of the asset is deducted from the benefit value. Therefore, the benefit for the tax year 2025/26 is (£3,000 × 20% × 5/12) – £100 i.e. £150.

7 B

A 15-month period of account is split into two chargeable periods, the first being the first 12 months and the second being the remaining three months. Each period has a separate tax calculation resulting in different payment dates of 9 months and 1 day after each relevant period.

8 C

Property business losses can be used against total income of the same period before qualifying charitable donations.

Capital losses cannot be carried back to previous years.

Trade losses can be carried forward against total profits before QCDs.

Therefore, statements A, B and D are all untrue and C is correct.

9 C

Legal fees for debt collecting are trade expenses, staff entertainment is specifically allowed by statute (entertainment of customers would not be allowed), depreciation is disallowed and is replaced by capital allowances and gifts of food are never allowable expenses.

Therefore, the amount to be added back to trading profits is £1,800 (£1,200 + £600).

10 D

There is no need to report details of capital disposals where the total chargeable gains BEFORE allowable losses are not more than the annual exempt amount (3,000) and proceeds are not more than £50,000.

11 C

Chargeable gains subject to business asset disposal relief (BADR) are taxed at 14% regardless of the taxpayer's level of income. These chargeable gains will use up, before non-qualifying gains, any remaining basic rate band not used by total income for income tax purposes (£37,700 – £33,000 = £4,700). Therefore, the chargeable gains not entitled to BADR will be taxed at 24%.

The correct answer is therefore (£10,000 × 14%) + (£12,000 × 24%) = £4,280.

12 D

The gain before gift holdover relief is £40,000 (£120,000 – £80,000).

The amount of the gift holdover relief claim is restricted to the total gain multiplied by the ratio of chargeable business assets to total chargeable assets.

Cash is not chargeable to capital gains tax and investments are not business assets. Therefore, the chargeable business assets are £560,000 (£800,000 × 70%) and the chargeable assets are £640,000 (£800,000 × 80%).

Therefore, the claim is £40,000 × £560,000/£640,000 = £35,000.

13 D

Employee contributions to an occupational pension scheme reduce the employee's employment income. Employer contributions are an exempt benefit.

14 C

Value added tax (VAT) is calculated on the discounted price. The amount is exclusive of VAT therefore the rate of 20% is used to calculate the amount of VAT.

Therefore, VAT due is £1,000 × 90% × 20% = £180

15 B

Cessation would take effect on the day taxable supplies cease.

Voluntary deregistration is allowed if the turnover in the next 12 months is expected to be below the VAT deregistration threshold.

A non-value added tax (VAT) registered trader would still have to pay VAT on its purchases.

Therefore, the correct answer is that voluntary registration is allowed at any time providing the trader is making taxable supplies.

SECTION B

16 STELLA

Key answer tips

One of the 15 mark questions will always be on income tax. It will usually include an income tax liability calculation and it is important to use a layout like the one given here.

Note the effect of the personal pension contribution. It is paid net but the grossed up amount reduces net income for the purposes of calculating the personal allowance and it also increases the basic rate and higher rate thresholds. The examining team have commented that personal pension contributions are often dealt with incorrectly.

Income tax computation – 2025/26

	Non-savings income	**Savings income**	**Dividend income**	**Total**
	£	£	£	£
Salary	188,369			188,369
Bonus	12,000			12,000
Van benefit (W1)	2,395			2,395
	———			———
Employment income	202,764			202,764
Bank deposit interest		2,000		2,000
NS&I investment account interest		600		600
Dividend income			4,000	4,000
	———	———	———	———
Total income = Net income	202,764	2,600	4,000	209,364
Less: Personal allowance (W2)	(0)			(0)
	———	———	———	———
Taxable income	202,764	2,600	4,000	209,364
	———	———	———	———

Income tax:

Non-savings income – Basic rate (W3)	47,700 × 20%	9,540
Non-savings income – Higher rate	87,440 × 40%	34,976
	135,140	
Non-savings income – Additional rate	67,624 × 45%	30,431
	202,764	
Savings income – Additional rate	2,600 × 45%	1,170
Dividend income – Nil rate	500 × 0%	0
Dividend income – Additional rate	3,500 × 39.35%	1,377
	209,364	
Income tax liability		77,494
Less: PAYE		(75,223)
Income tax payable		2,271

Workings

(W1) Van benefit

	£
Use of van (£4,020 × 6/12)	2,010
Van fuel benefit (£769 × 6/12)	385
	2,395

(W2) Personal allowance

As ANI exceeds £125,140, no personal allowance is available (see tutorial note 1).

(W3) Extension of bands

	Basic rate band	Higher rate band
	£	£
Band threshold	37,700	125,140
Plus: Gross PPC (£8,000 × 100/80)	10,000	10,000
Revised band threshold	47,700	135,140

Tutorial note

1 *The personal allowance (PA) is reduced if adjusted net income (including non-savings income, savings and dividends) exceeds £100,000.*

The restriction is:

50% × (Adjusted net income – £100,000)

Adjusted net income (ANI) is reduced by gross gift aid payments and gross personal pension contributions.

Where adjusted net income is greater than £125,140 (£100,000 + 2 × PA £12,570), then no PA is given.

Here, ANI is £199,364 (£209,364 – £10,000 gross PPC) so no PA is available.

However, it is important to state this fact in the answer to obtain full marks – just putting '£0' against the personal allowance line in the computation will not gain full marks.

2 *A savings income nil rate band is not available as Stella is an additional rate taxpayer.*

3 *The dividend nil rate band is available to all taxpayers.*

ACCA Marking scheme

	Marks
Salary	0.5
Bonus	0.5
Van benefit	1.5
Van fuel benefit	1.5
Bank deposit interest	1.0
NS&I investment account interest	1.0
Dividend income	1.0
Personal allowance – Nil deducted and reason	1.0
Extension of basic rate band	1.5
Extension of higher rate band	1.5
Income tax payable:	
Non-savings – Basic rate	0.5
Non-savings – Higher rate	0.5
Non-savings – Additional rate	0.5
Savings – Additional rate	0.5
Dividends – Nil rate	0.5
Dividends – Additional rate	0.5
PAYE	0.5
Tax payable	0.5
Total	**15.0**

17 LACE LTD

Key answer tips

One of the 15 mark questions will always be on corporation tax. It will always include a corporation tax liability calculation.

In this question you have a short accounting period of nine months. In the capital allowances computation the maximum annual investment allowance and the writing down allowances must be time apportioned by multiplying them by 9/12. However, the first year allowance is not reduced for a short accounting period.

Corporation tax – 9 m/e 31 December 2025

	£	£
Adjusted trading profit		1,820,050
Less: Capital allowances (W1) (Note 1)		(785,150)
Trading income		1,034,900
Interest income		45,000
Chargeable gain	195,000	
Less: Capital loss brought forward (Note 2)	(10,000)	
		185,000
Total profits		1,264,900
Less: Trading loss brought forward		(28,000)
Less: Qualifying charitable donation (Note 3)		(14,000)
Taxable total profits		1,222,900
Corporation tax liability (£1,222,900 × 25%) (W2)		305,725

Dividend income is exempt.

Tutorial note

1 *Capital allowances are deducted from the tax adjusted trading profits to give the taxable trading profits for the period. The examining team's recent article 'Corporation tax' states that "if capital allowances are not already deducted from the trading income figure given, but are given separately, then these must be deducted from the trading profit and* ***not*** *from any other income. If they are deducted elsewhere in the assessment no mark will be awarded for the deduction".*

2 *Capital losses can only be set against chargeable gains and no other income. The examining team's recent article 'Corporation tax' states that "If capital losses are given, either for the same period or carried forward from an earlier period, then these losses must be deducted from the aggregated gains to give a net chargeable gains figure. Once again if capital losses are deducted from the wrong income full marks cannot be awarded. Candidates should note that companies are not entitled to the annual exempt amount".*

3 *Companies pay qualifying charitable donations gross so no grossing up is required. They are labelled as qualifying charitable donations in the corporation tax computation. The examining team's recent article 'Corporation tax' states that "Donations [by companies] are always made gross and, therefore, candidates must not gross the payment up as they would for an individual... The payment must be deducted from total profits after any other relief; it should not be deducted elsewhere in the assessment otherwise full marks cannot be awarded".*

4 *Dividends received are not included in taxable total profits but they are included in augmented profits, when determining the corporation tax rate applicable.*

Here, the augmented profits for the company are greater than the upper limit. Hence the rate applicable is 25%.

Augmented profits = £1,222,900 + £9,000 = £1,231,900

Upper limit = £250,000 × 9/12 = £187,500

The upper limit is reduced for the short accounting period.

Remember that augmented profits are used to determine corporation tax rate, but the rate is then applied to the taxable total profits figure.

Workings

(W1) Capital allowances

	AIA	**FYA**	**Main pool**	**Special rate pool**	**Allowances**
	£	£	£	£	£
TWDV b/f			210,000	40,000	
Purchases (special rate pool) (£960,000 × 100/120)	800,000				
AIA (Max £1,000,000 × 9/12)	(750,000)				750,000
Balance for 50% FYA		50,000			
Disposal: Balancing charge (£24,000 × 100/120)					(20,000)
			210,000	40,000	
WDA @ (18% × 9/12)			(28,350)		28,350
WDA @ (6% × 9/12)				(1,800)	1,800
FYA @ 50%		(25,000)			25,000
Transfer to SRP				25,000	
TWDV c/f			181,650	63,200	
Total allowances					785,150

Tutorial note

Where a business is VAT registered it must include additions to capital allowances at the net cost to the business. Where the business is able to recover the input VAT on a purchase it must be included at the VAT-exclusive price in the capital allowances computation. Disposals should be dealt with in the same manner.

As this is a nine month accounting period, the maximum AIA is £750,000 (£1,000,000 × 9/12). The balance of the integral features cost is £50,000 (£800,000 – £750,000) and this is eligible for FYA at 50%.

(W2) Augmented profits and limits

	£
TTP	1,222,900
Dividends received	9,000
Augmented profits	1,231,900

Lower Limit: £50,000 × 9/12 = £37,500

Upper limit: £250,000 × 9/12 = £187,500

ACCA Marking scheme	
	Marks
Corporation tax for the nine-month accounting period:	
Investment income	1.0
Chargeable gain	1.0
Capital loss brought forward	1.0
Trading loss brought forward	1.0
Qualifying charitable donation	1.0
Dividend income not taxed	1.0
Corporation tax liability	1.0
Capital allowances:	
Purchase	1.0
Annual investment allowance	2.0
Disposal – 4 December 2025	1.0
Writing down allowance (18% × 9/12)	1.5
Writing down allowance (6% × 9/12)	1.5
Augmented profits	0.5
Limits	0.5
Total	**15.0**

18 REBECCA

Key answer tips

The examining team have not specified which topics will be covered in the 10 and 5 mark questions in the examination.

This question is a typical capital gains computation for an individual with several disposals to consider. It includes a part disposal, which is always an examination favourite.

Capital gains tax – 2025/26

		£	£
15 August 2025	Proceeds	24,000	
	Less: Expenses of sale	(1,500)	
		22,500	
	Less: Allowable cost:		
	$£80,000 \times \frac{£24,000}{£24,000 + £126,000}$	(12,800)	
	Chargeable gain		9,700
14 November 2025	Medal – exempt		0
2 January 2026	Proceeds	295,000	
	Less: Expenses of sale	(15,000)	
		280,000	
	Less: Cost	(190,000)	
	Extension	(19,700)	
	Chargeable gain		70,300
Total chargeable gains			80,000
Less: Annual exempt amount			(3,000)
Total taxable gains			77,000
Capital gains tax payable (£77,000 × 24%)			18,480

Tutorial note

1 *With part disposals remember that you must apportion the cost of the part sold by using the A/A+B rule where A = Gross proceeds of the part sold and B = the market value of the part remaining.*

2 *The medal is exempt because Rebecca had inherited it. If she had purchased the medal it would be a chargeable asset, although the 5/3 rule for chattels bought for less than £6,000 would apply.*

3 *Rebecca has a salary of £120,000 and therefore is a higher rate taxpayer. She has no balance of basic rate band remaining and all her taxable gains are taxed at 24%.*

ACCA Marking scheme

	Marks
15 August 2025	
Proceeds	0.5
Expenses of sale	0.5
Cost	2.5
14 November 2025	
Medal – exempt	1.0
2 January 2026	
Proceeds	0.5
Expenses of sale	0.5
Cost	1.0
Extension	1.0
Total gains	0.5
Annual exempt amount	1.0
CGT payable	1.0
Total	**10.0**

19 BUD PLC

Key answer tips

This question can be on any topic.

This question covers the popular topic of calculating the VAT due for the quarter.

Value added tax (VAT) payable for the three months ended 31 March 2026

			£	£
Output tax:				
Sales	– Standard-rated	(£240,000 × 20%)		48,000
	– Zero-rated			0
				48,000
Input tax:				
Purchases	– Inventory	(£110,000 × 20%)	22,000	
	– Machine	(£40,000 × 20%)	8,000	
	– Car	(VAT not recoverable)		
Irrecoverable debts	– 31 Aug 2025	(£3,000 × 20%)	600	
	– 30 Nov 2025	(< 6 month old)	0	
				(30,600)
VAT payable				17,400

Tutorial note

1 *VAT on cars is not recoverable unless the car is used 100% for business.*

2 *VAT on irrecoverable debts can be recovered if the following conditions are met:*

- *(i) The debt has been written off in the accounting records.*
- *(ii) At least 6 months have passed since the debt was due for payment (or the date of supply if later).*

ACCA Marking scheme	
	Marks
Output tax:	
Standard-rated sales	1.5
Zero-rated sales	1.0
Input tax:	
Purchases– Inventory	1.5
– Machine	1.5
– Car	1.0
Irrecoverable debts – 31 August 2025	1.5
– 30 November 2025	1.5
VAT payable	0.5
Total	**10.0**

20 BETTY

Key answer tips

This question can be on any topic.

In this question, you have to complete the investment income section of the tax return.

Interest and dividends from UK banks and building societies

1	Taxed UK interest	5	Other dividends
	£0		**£0**
2	Untaxed UK interest	6	Foreign dividends (up to £500)
	£6,900		£
3	Untaxed foreign interest (up to £2,000)	7	Tax taken off foreign dividends
	£		£
4	Dividends from UK companies		
	£7,000		

Working – Box 2

£400 + £6,000 + £500 = £6,900

Tutorial note

ISA account interest, proceeds from NS&I certificates and dividends from an ISA are all exempt income and are not included in any boxes on the tax return.

There are no receipts within the FTX syllabus that would be included in boxes 1 or 5, therefore the answer in respect of these boxes would always be £0.

ACCA Marking scheme	
	Marks
½ mark for each correct action (each of 8 sources of interest)	4.0
Stating all amounts in full	1.0
(i.e. not deducting savings and dividend nil rate bands)	
Total	**5.0**

21 JENNIFER

Key answer tips

This question can be on any topic.

This question covers the popular topic of property income.

Property income – 2025/26

		£
Rent – amount received (cash basis)		11,000
Less: Expenses		
–	water rates	(400)
–	insurance	(300)
–	redecoration	(500)
		9,800
Replacement of domestic items relief (£750 – £50)		(700)
Property income		9,100

No deduction is taken in respect of the kitchen extension as this is capital expenditure.

Tutorial note

For an individual taxpayer, property income is usually calculated using the cash basis (not the accruals basis, as for companies).

Under the cash basis a deduction is normally allowed for capital expenditure except for certain items such as cars, assets provided for use in a residential property and non-depreciating assets with a useful life of 20 years or more, such as a building. A deduction is therefore not allowed for the kitchen extension.

However, replacement of domestic items relief is available for the replacement bed.

The cost of the extension will be added to the cost of the property and given relief in the capital gains tax computation when the property is sold.

ACCA Marking scheme	
	Marks
Rent – amount received	1.0
Expenses – water rates	0.5
– insurance	0.5
– redecoration	0.5
Replacement of domestic items relief	1.5
No deduction for the extension	1.0
Total	**5.0**

22 PLANT PLC

Key answer tips

This question can be on any topic.

In this question you need to calculate a company chargeable gain and then apply rollover relief. Remember that companies get indexation allowance to reduce their gains, but only until December 2017.

Rollover relief is the only capital gains relief that companies can claim so it is a very examinable topic, particularly in a corporate scenario.

Chargeable gain – year ended 31 March 2026

	£
Proceeds	840,000
Less: Cost	(410,000)
Gain before indexation allowance	430,000
Less: Indexation allowance (0.532 × £410,000)	(218,120)
	211,880
Less: Rollover relief	(151,880)
Chargeable gain now (W)	60,000

Working: Chargeable gain now

Sale proceeds	840,000
Less: Amount reinvested	(780,000)
	60,000

Tutorial note

Rollover relief applies when a qualifying asset is sold and a new qualifying asset is purchased within the period of 12 months before and up to 36 months after the disposal. Land and buildings used in a trade are the most common rollover assets.

Full rollover relief allows the gain on the first asset to be deducted from the cost of the second. This only applies when all the proceeds of sale of the first asset are reinvested in the second.

In this question, the first asset is sold for £840,000 and the new asset is bought for £780,000. £60,000 of the proceeds are not reinvested.

The gain chargeable now, which cannot be rolled over, is the lower of:

(i) The total gain £211,880

(ii) The proceeds not reinvested £60,000

Therefore £60,000 of the gain cannot be rolled over and will be charged immediately.

The balance of the gain of £151,880 can be rolled over and is deducted from the base cost of the new asset. The base cost of the replacement asset is £628,120 (£780,000 – £151,880).

ACCA Marking scheme	
	Marks
Gain	1.0
Indexation allowance	1.0
Amount rolled over	1.0
Gain chargeable	2.0
Total	**5.0**

23 DAVID

	£
Cash received from customers	98,000
Less:	
Payment for machine	(7,000)
Expenses paid (£33,000 – £1,500)	(31,500)
Flat rate expenses (£0.45 × 6,000)	(2,700)
Payment for car	(0)
Car expenses	(0)
Trading income	56,800

Tutorial note

The cash basis is the default basis for unincorporated businesses. You will be told if the taxpayer elects to use the accruals basis.

The full amount of cash received from customers is included in the calculation as the period it is earned is irrelevant under the cash basis.

Under the cash basis a deduction is normally allowed for capital expenditure, except cars.

Capital allowances and motor expenses are not an allowable deduction for the car when the taxpayer claims HMRC approved mileage allowances.

Marking scheme

	Marks
Cash from customers	1.0
Machine	1.0
Expenses	1.0
Flat rate expenses	1.0
Payment for car	0.5
Motor expenses	0.5
Total	**5.0**